The Palgrave Macmillan Series in International Political Communication

Series Editor
Alister Miskimmon
History, Anthropology, Philosophy & Politics
Queen's University Belfast
Belfast, UK

From democratization to terrorism, economic development to conflict resolution, global political dynamics are affected by the increasing pervasiveness and influence of communication media. This series examines the participants and their tools, their strategies and their impact.

More information about this series at
http://www.palgrave.com/gp/series/14418

Berta García-Orosa
Editor

Digital Political Communication Strategies

Multidisciplinary Reflections

palgrave
macmillan

Editor
Berta García-Orosa
University of Santiago de Compostela
Santiago de Compostela, Spain

The Palgrave Macmillan Series in International Political Communication
ISBN 978-3-030-81567-7   ISBN 978-3-030-81568-4 (eBook)
https://doi.org/10.1007/978-3-030-81568-4

This Palgrave Macmillan imprint is published by the registered company Springer Nature Switzerland AG.
The registered company address is: Gewerbestrasse 11, 6330 Cham, Switzerland

Foreword

Digital Politics: A Paradigm Shift

Political power relationships are played out in the realm of communication. This has been so throughout history, and this is why pulpits and mosques were sites of power and counterpower: pamphlets were essential, books were either restricted or burned by the dominant elites, and the majority of people, and particularly women, were carefully kept out of literacy. The advent of what I have conceptualized as mass self-communication, based on the Internet (an old technology, first deployed in 1969), and digital networks distributed by ubiquitous wireless communication, has radically transformed the landscape of power formation. Because power is rooted in our minds, be it through persuasion or intimidation. And so is counterpower, the capacity of humans to revolt against what they consider an unjust condition. Revolts that always require communication with other humans feeling alike. Digital communication networks connect our neural networks to other neural networks, and to the biological networks that structure life, both material and social. Over 2/3 of humankind are now connected via the Internet (albeit with different quality of their communication technology), and over seven million mobile phone users (60% of them being smartphones) are the backbone on which our capacity to communicate and organize (or disorganize) is based. The recent explosion of 5G wireless networks increases exponentially the volume, speed, and latency of our communication system. I called it mass self-communication because it potentially reaches more people than traditional mass media. But it is self because the sender is also the receiver, and we select the direction of the flows while connecting permanently to the digital hypertext where all information is stocked in the cloud, this mysterious entity, permeating all what we do and intend to do. For the great joy of the surveillance apparatus, what I have defined as the globally networked surveillance bureaucracy. But no, this is not the triumph of Big Brother, because we the people can intervene in this ocean of communication flows and bypass the monopoly of mass communication that was exercised until recently by corporations and governments. Networked social movements rose powerfully in the last two decades, challenging the powers that be, from Tahrir Square to Puerta del Sol and to Liberty Park. However, no, this is not either the kingdom of freedom. Because after an initial moment of confusion that took institutions and companies by surprise, their counterattack was ferocious. They quickly learned to shift their machinery to social networks and did not hesitate in engaging in mass disinformation, fake news, use of deep fake in political campaigns, blurring forever the lines of the democratic debate that has now long foregone in just a few years. The immediate outcome of these new political communication strategies is the rise of monsters such as Bolsonaro or Trump, that are here to stay, as well as the institutional crises, exemplified by Brexit, that challenge the European dream of unity, peace, and a borderless continent. The crisis of political legitimacy that has shaken liberal democracy on a global scale is amplified by this new communication system. At the roots of the crisis, of course, it is not technological change. But if power is constructed in communication and communication networks radically change, the political game (that is not just online but digital in its variety of dimensions) is altered forever. The old forms of democracy are superseded. Democracy is not. But it will have to be re-imagined in the new communication paradigm. This fundamental crisis, that disables societies to debate and manage their conflicts in a democratic mode, has been exacerbated by the pandemics we are in. In fact, at this point, disinformation kills by the thousands. Tyrants and demagogues manipulate a terrified populace, and apocalyptic prophecies enter the world or real virtuality literally threatening our very survival as a species. We must not indulge in this darkness, letting ourselves go into the dark aesthetics of end of the worldism. More than ever, we must fight, reconstruct, re-imagine our lives, and overcome these multiple crises by opening up to new avenues of experimentation and solidarity. For this, we do have the powerful tool of the social networks, reconfigured around democratic and egalitarian values. Technology does not determine us. But we cannot either ignore technology, we have to fight the battles of each time with the instruments adequate to the historic time we live. Thus, it is essential to recover the dream of the Internet as freedom. While not forgetting any longer that freedom allows humans, all humans, in their thorny diversity, to engage in the political battles being fought in the networks. We have to win democratic elections by asserting values of democracy, equality, and love. Yet, to win these elections, we, those who believe in a better world, must conquer cultural hegemony for these values, where it matters nowadays: in the digital communication networks.

The research presented in this volume is a critical instrument for understanding political communication in our century, thus lighting the path for the revival of democracy.

Madrid, year II of the Pandemics.

Wallis Annenberg Chair in Communication Technology and Society,
University of Southern California,
Los Angeles, CA, USA

Manuel Castells

Acknowledgments

This research has been developed within the research project "Digital Native Media in Spain: Storytelling Formats and Mobile Strategy" (RTI2018–093346-B-C33), funded by the Ministry of Science, Innovation and Universities (Government of Spain) in Novos Medios Group Research and the ERDF structural fund.

Contents

Notes on Contributors

Magomed-Emin Aliev holds a Master's in Media and Creative Industries (MCI) and an International Bachelor in Economics and Business Economics (IBEB) from the Erasmus University Rotterdam (EUR, the Netherlands). After graduating, he started working as a junior consultant and researcher at EMMA which is communication, research, and participation bureau. He works there on wide-ranging projects including the energy transition and governance issues. Aliev's main research interests, however, lie in the fields of representation, meaning-making, and sociocultural change.

Ana Almansa-Martínez is a professor at the Department of Audiovisual Communication and Advertising, Faculty of Communication Sciences, University of Málaga. She is teacher and researcher in political communication, communication management, and public relations. She holds a degree in Communication from the Autonomous University of Barcelona and PhD from the University of Malaga. She is a visiting professor at European and American universities, where she has participated in postgraduate courses and given conferences. She is the editor of the *International Journal of Public Relations*, coordinator of the Official Master's Degree in Strategic Management and Innovation in Communication, University of Malaga, and Secretary of the Academic Commission in Malaga of the Interuniversity Doctorate in Communication (universities of Seville, Malaga, Cadiz, and Huelva).

Daniel Barredo Ibáñez is a senior lecturer at the Universidad del Rosario (Colombia). He serves as Coordinator of the Working Group on Digital

Communication, Networks, and Processes, of the Latin American Association of Communication Researchers. He is also an invited researcher at Fudan University (China).

María José Benítez de Gracia holds a bachelor's degree in Journalism (*Universidad Europea de Madrid*, 2000), a master's degree in Applied Media Research from Carlos III University of Madrid (2016), and a PhD in Media Research from the latter as well. She has received the Outstanding Doctorate Award, and the focus of her work has been on new narratives and the study of new technologies. Since April 2020, she has been working at the Universidad Isabel I de Castilla, where she is Professor of Journalism.

Eva Campos-Domínguez holds a PhD in Communication. She is Associate Professor of Journalism at the University of Valladolid in Spain. Her research focuses on the analysis of political and parliamentary communication. For more than 15 years, she has been researching the development of parliaments' digital communication. Her publications address the contemporary transformations of parliament on the Internet, including the communication between legislative representatives and citizens. She is investigating the potential effects of bots and disinformation strategies in connection with parliaments' social media practices.

João Canavilhas holds a PhD and DEA in Communication, Culture and Education (USAL, Spain) and Bachelor in Social Communication (UBI, Portugal). He is an associate professor at the Universidade da Beira Interior (Covilhã, Portugal) and researcher at Labcom–Communication and Arts. He is the author or co-author of 10 books, 38 chapter books, and 50 papers in national and international scientific journals. His research interest focuses on various aspects of journalism and new technologies.

Antonio Castillo-Esparcia is a professor at the School of Communication Sciences of the University of Málaga. He teaches theory and history of public relations, political communication (lobbies and think tanks), and communication in NGOs and social movements. He holds a bachelor's and doctoral degrees from the Autonomous University of Barcelona (UAB). He is a coordinator of the master's degree program in "Strategic management and innovation in communication", of the University of Malaga. He is a visiting professor at European and American universities, where he has participated in conferences, postgraduate courses, and professional study programs. He is Director of the Department of Audiovisual

Communication and Advertising of the University of Malaga and President of the Association of Public Relations Researchers.

Deborah Castro is a Marie Skłodowska-Curie Research Fellow in the Department of Arts and Culture Studies at Erasmus University Rotterdam. Her main research interests lie in the fields of audience and television studies. She was a visiting scholar at the Department of Radio-Television-Film, The University of Texas, Austin. She moved to Portugal in 2016 as a postdoctoral researcher at Madeira Interactive Technologies Institute. There, she designed and coordinated a project at the junction of human-computer interaction and media studies, focusing on the exploration of the binge-watching experience. She was also a visiting assistant professor at the University of Madeira (2017–2018) and a lecturer in the Department of Media and Communication at Erasmus University Rotterdam (2018–2020). Her work has been presented at several international venues.

Sandra Flores-Guevara is Researcher Professor of the Academic Area of Communication of the Institute of Social Sciences and Humanities at the Autonomous University of the State of Hidalgo since 2000. He holds a degree in Social Communication, Master's in Communication and Politics, PhD in Social Sciences from the Autonomous Metropolitan University, Xochimilco Unit. He has PRODEP profile and is member of the Academic Body Communication Scenarios where he develops the line of generation and application of knowledge about cyberculture processes and social processes, politics, gender, and analysis of socio-media discourse.

Santiago Gallur Santorum is a full professor of the Technological Institute of Santo Domingo (INTEC) in the Bachelor of Social Communication and Digital Media, and in the Bachelor of Education, Doctor in Contemporary and Latin American History (2011, USC, Spain), Doctor in Communication and Information (2017, USC, Spain), Master in Contemporary and Latin American History (2009, USC, Spain), Postgraduate in Education (2008, CAP, USC, Spain), Master in Journalism (2017, Spain), Qualified Teacher Status (2011, Wales), Qualified Teacher Status (2011, England), Bachelor of Journalism (2008, USC, Spain), member of the National System of Researchers of Mexico with the SNI 1 category, recognized with the categories of Contracted Professor Doctor, University Professor Private, and Assistant Professor of the ANECA (2017, Spain).

Berta García-Orosa holds a BA in Communication Sciences, a BA in Political and Administration Sciences, and a PhD in Communication Sciences from the University of Santiago de Compostela, Madrid, Spain.

She is a full professor at the University of Santiago de Compostela and has studied communication and politics for more than 20 years. She has collaborated in more than 50 research projects and international research networks, the results of which have been published over 100 times in databases such as Scopus and JCR and publishing houses such as Springer, McGraw Hill, and Thomson. She has completed visiting research and training stays at Universidade do Minho (Portugal), Mexico, Costa Rica, Brazil, Cuba, and Uruguay.

Spain's Ministry of Education awarded her three 6-year research terms. In addition to her research, she has overseen doctoral and MA theses, as well as undergraduate capstone projects, and she has taught undergraduate courses in journalism and audiovisual communication, as well as courses at the master's level in political science, communication sciences, and Hispanic studies. Since 2009, she has coordinated teaching innovation in IACODI (Innovation in Digital Communication Learning).

In terms of managerial experience, she has served as a department secretary, vice-dean, undergraduate and master's coordinator, and coordinator of the SICUE mobility program.

Gisela Gonçalves holds a PhD in Communication Sciences. She is a professor at the University of Beira Interior (UBI) and an integrated member of Labcom–Communication and Arts Research Unit. Since 2011, she coordinates the Master in Strategic Communication at UBI. She has published two books and edited ten collective volumes. She is also a former chairperson of the ECREA Strategic and Organizational Communication Section and is a board member of SOPCOM—the Portuguese Association of Communication Sciences. Her research interests concern communication ethics, public relations theories, political communication, and strategic communication.

Erika Jaráiz Gulías is Associate Professor of Political Science at the University of Santiago de Compostela (USC). She holds a PhD in Contemporary Political Processes, and her main lines of research are the study of electoral analysis, electoral behavior, and political communication, areas in which she has published several papers.

Nieves Lagares Diez is Associate Professor of Political Science at the University of Santiago de Compostela (USC). A PhD in Political Science, her main lines of research are political communication and electoral behavior, areas in which she has published several papers. She has been Dean of the Faculty of Political and Social Science in the USC.

Ainara Larrondo-Ureta holds a PhD in Journalism and Master's in Contemporary History. Larrondo-Ureta is a senior lecturer at the University of the Basque Country (Spain), main researcher of "Gureiker" Research Group (A) (Basque University System) and KZBerri, Research Group on Innovation in Online Journalism Education (University of the Basque Country). Larrondo-Ureta's teaching and research subjects include newswriting and reporting, online journalism, innovation in communication, organizational communication, political communication, women, genre, and media.

Xosé López-García is Full Professor of Journalism in the Department of Communication Sciences at the University of Santiago de Compostela (USC). He holds a PhD in History and is a journalist. He coordinates the Novos Medios research group (USC), whose lines focus on the study of digital and printed media, the analysis of the impact of technology in mediated communication, and the performance and funding of cultural industries. In recent years, he has participated as a researcher in publicly funded projects and has also directed several R&D projects about digital journalism.

Paulo Carlos López-López is a lecturer in the Department of Political Science and Sociology at the University of Santiago de Compostela, holds a PhD in Communication, and is a journalist and political scientist. He has published more than 60 scientific papers on topics such as communication, social media, and political science. He was awarded the Drago 2019 research award for his study on transparency.

Koldobika Meso-Ayerdi holds a PhD in Journalism. He is a senior lecturer and head of the Department of Journalism at the University of the Basque Country (Spain). He is member of a several research groups, such as Gureiker and a Spanish Group on the role of the audiences in the hybrid media system, funded by the Ministry of Science, Innovation, and Universities. Co-author of the first book on online journalism in Spain, his main research lines are online journalism and media innovation, including active audiences, news reporting, and social media.

María-Cruz Negreira-Rey holds a PhD in Communication. She is Lecturer in Journalism at the Department of Communication Sciences, University of Santiago de Compostela (USC), and member of Novos Medios research group (USC). Her research focuses on local journalism and the development of local and hyperlocal media in Spain, digital journalism, and social media.

Laura Georgina Ortega-Luna holds a PhD and is Professor of Social Sciences, and BA in Communication Sciences from the Autonomous University of the State of Hidalgo. She works in the research lines of Cyberpolitics, Discourse Analysis and Gender Studies.

María Pereira López is Lecturer in Political Science at USC. He holds a degree in Political Science and Administration and a PhD in Political Science from USC. His publications include: Jaráiz, E., Lagares, N. and M. Pereira (2020). "Emotions and Voting Decisions: Components of the Vote in the General Elections of 2016 in Spain", REIS, 170:115–136.

Sara Pérez-Seijo is PhD student in Communication and Contemporary Information at University of Santiago de Compostela (USC) and member of the Novos Medios research group at the same university. She is beneficiary of the Training University Lecturers' (FPU) Program funded by the Spanish Ministry of Science, Innovation, and Universities (Spanish government). Her research is linked to non-fiction digital storytelling, focusing on VR and 360-degree video storytelling and immersive narratives.

Irene Ramos-Vielba holds a PhD in Political Science and Sociology. She is a senior researcher at the Danish Centre for Studies in Research and Research Policy, in the Department of Political Science at Aarhus University, Denmark. In her doctoral and postdoctoral research, she addressed the topics of parliaments' digital communication and the opening of the parliament to society. In the field of research and innovation policy, she has focused on the study of different forms of science-society interconnections, including university-industry cooperation, knowledge transfer processes, and/or research funding-related issues. Legislative science advice is also part of her research interests.

Ana-Isabel Rodríguez-Vázquez holds a degree in Information Sciences from the Complutense University of Madrid (UCM) and a PhD in Journalism from the University of Santiago de Compostela (USC). He is a member of the audiovisual studies group (GEA) where he researches and publishes in topics related to programming and audiences, news genres on television, and the creation and production of formats for TV. He collaborates in research projects of the Novos Medios (USC) and Fonta (UCM) groups.

Gina Sibaja Quesada holds a PhD in Social Sciences from FLACSO (2010), Master in Political Science from Sorbonne Nouvelle University (1995), and Bachelor of Political Science from the University of Costa Rica (1989); is a teacher and researcher at the University of Costa Rica; author of publications on political communication, electoral participation, and political imaginary; and takes part in (ALICE).

Pavel Sidorenko Bautista hails from the Faculty of Communication of the University of Castilla-La Mancha. He is professor in the Faculty of Communication at the Francisco de Vitoria University and in the Master in Communication and Corporate Identity at the International University of La Rioja. He researches on narrative and technological innovation in communication.

Alba Silva-Rodríguez is Professor of Journalism in the University of Santiago de Compostela and member of the research group "Novos Medios" (GI- 1641) which research lines are focused on the analysis of strategies, rhetoric and technological formats for emergent markets in mobile journalism. She is secretary of the *RAEIC* journal (Spanish Journal of Research in Communication).

José Sixto-García is Professor of Journalism at the University of Santiago de Compostela and member of the research group "Novos Medios" (GI-1641) whose research lines are focused on the analysis of strategies, rhetoric, and technological formats for emergent markets in communication.

Jorge Vázquez-Herrero holds a PhD in Communication. He is an assistant professor at the Department of Communication Sciences, University of Santiago de Compostela (USC). He was a visiting scholar at Universidad Nacional de Rosario, Universidade do Minho, University of Leeds, and Tampere University. His research focuses on the impact of technology and platforms in digital journalism, narratives, and social media.

List of Figures

List of Graphs

List of Tables

PART I

CHAPTER 1

Digital Political Communication: Hybrid Intelligence, Algorithms, Automation and Disinformation in the Fourth Wave

Berta García-Orosa

1 25 Years and a Pandemic

Most of the key players in this book were unimaginable 25 years ago. This work arises from the need to reflect on the first quarter-century of digital political communication. It has been marked by changes in technology, given the quasi-immediate and often uncritical uptake of technological innovations. The influence of technological advances on communication and, therefore, on power dynamics has been uneven. The first wave of digital political communication, in the 1990s, featured websites that acted as repositories of one-way, asymmetrical information, with e-mail as a fundamental form of interaction.

B. García-Orosa (✉)
University of Santiago de Compostela, Santiago de Compostela, Spain
e-mail: berta.garcia@usc.es

B. García-Orosa (ed.), *Digital Political Communication Strategies*, The Palgrave Macmillan Series in International Political Communication, https://doi.org/10.1007/978-3-030-81568-4_1

We might term the period from 2004 (the birth of Facebook) to 2008 as the second wave. In it, social networks such as Twitter, YouTube and Facebook begin to flourish. The circulation of messages on different platforms takes centre stage, though without adapting messages to the peculiarities of each platform. The audience also becomes a foundational pillar under the umbrella of engagement and democratic debate. Such debate, however, is often reduced to making messages go viral and to generating page views. Though some initially believed that social media presence in and of itself would create dialogue and engagement, it was quickly understood that this was, in fact, a strategic decision (Smith, 2018) influenced by the social environment, resources, and prioritised modalities of engagement and relating with audiences (Campbell & Lambright, 2020). In this second wave, there emerge distinct online public spaces which could serve as alternatives to traditional ones, as the former facilitate participation, allow citizens to cooperate and express their opinions, and act as society's watchdog in an egalitarian production model (Salikov, 2019).

Scientific literature often refers to the 2008 US election as a milestone, especially with former US President Barack Obama's campaign (Bimber, 2014; Lilleker et al., 2015; Stromer-Galley, 2019) signalling the start of the third wave. The intensive use of social networks and micro-segmentation, as well as the prominence of big data, defines this wave. In it, advances in languages and storytelling, artificial intelligence and gamification stand out, alongside the mise-en-scène of new actors which will cement their place in the fourth wave. Bossetta (2019) notes the strategy of gamification, that is, the application of game design elements in non-gaming contexts which, in this case, promotes a certain political position. Still, the question of whether the power of the game's design is coercive and to what extent it can affect players' political preferences or their confidence in democracy remains unanswered.

Although time constraints are only an analytical reference, we could place the beginning of the fourth wave—the current one—in 2016, with the pronounced emergence of artificial intelligence and astroturfing in the pro-Brexit campaign. The current wave of digital political communication is characterised by: (a) digital platforms as political actors involved in all phases of communication; (b) the intensive use of artificial intelligence and big data in all phases but specially in election campaigns; (c) the validation of lies as a political strategy (among other fake news and post-truth phenomena); (d) the combination of hyperlocal and supranational elements; (e) uncritical technological determinism; (f) the search for engagement with audiences and co-production processes and (g) the three trends that threaten democracy: polarisation, echo chambers and bubble filters.

This technology-intensive path reconfigures the public sphere, the concept of citizenship and the role of citizens in politics (Marsh & Stoker, 1998; McNair, 2017; Clarke et al., 2006). Citizens, as actors in politics, have at their disposal new resources to contribute to building the public sphere, but at the same time find that the powers that be use increasingly sophisticated and concealed strategies to impose their messages, actions and, above all, frames upon the citizenry. Bots, fake news, new political actors, the influence of digital platforms, the use of data mining and AI, therefore, have reshaped the public sphere, and citizens must be prepared for intensive intervention by these new actors.

Occasionally, when a hegemonic frame is fractured or counter-frames arise, the status quo structure quickly institutionalises the new strategy. For example, digital activism on behalf of a campaign will simulate public support of a party's ideas by recruiting digital activists (García-Orosa et al., 2017) or cybertroopers.

In the fourth wave, the SARS-CoV-2 pandemic has changed the rules of the game, as was the case with the 1918 pandemic and the American election campaigns that marked a turning point in political communication. Though we still do not know if COVID-19 may entail permanent transformations for digital political communication, the initial changes have been particularly salient during election cycles, when the hunt for votes intensifies (Landman & Splendore, 2020). Early studies on COVID-19 and political communication highlight the importance of personalisation, trust in leaders and the influence of their messages on social media (Grossman et al., 2020). For the time being, such loyalty and traditional left-right political attitudes seem to be intact (Bol et al., 2021). Nonetheless, politicians have struggled to form coalitions and governments in recent elections (Field, 2020; Pilet, 2020).

During the pandemic, politicians on the campaign trail have faced two challenges: (1) the citizenry's heightened need to trust in leaders in the face of social and economic uncertainty and (2) restrictions on public gatherings.

Political actors vie for the citizenry's presence and engagement. The engagement they seek during election campaigns responds more to the search for communicative interaction, manifesting as clicks, likes, comments, tweets and recommendations, than to online collaboration based on participatory modes of communication (dialogue, co-creation of content, etc.).

Political parties have used novel digital strategies for organising and disseminating their messages to make up for the lack of in-person events.

The pandemic campaigns have been personalist, too, revolving around leaders who require the electorate's confidence more than ever, due to the looming social and economic crisis and the health measures that prevent leaders and voters from interacting in person. Presence is achieved through the sensation of "being there" in the other's reality (Ijsselsteijn & Riva, 2003; Slater & Sanchez-Vives, 2016), in the virtual environment, despite the viewer's physical presence in another reality, and co-presence is attained through video calls or online encounters. Political parties aim for presence but often reject the technologies which heighten the sense of presence, such as virtual reality, due to issues regarding the production and reception of such content.

2 The Fourth Wave: Cognitive Frames, Echo Chambers, Bubble Filters and Disinformation

The fourth wave of digital political communication blurs the defining characteristics of traditional political actors by incorporating new ones, thereby creating a haze of hybrid actions and discourses that mark power relations and reimagine democracy. In this tumultuous mediascape, which researchers, politicians and the citizenry must interpret with innovative hermeneutic perspectives in the coming years, political actors aim not only to mould public opinion and citizen ideology but also to create cognitive frames, that is, the mental structures through which one views the world, much like a window which, in addition to filtering visual information through a pane of glass, allows one to see only what its frame makes visible. It is not about the topics that are routinely discussed but, above all, the cognitive frameworks through which the world is observed, understood and, therefore, acted upon, participated in (or not), and through which public life is built by consolidating the values and interests which define actions.

The frames are often the same, regardless of political positions or ideologies, and it is only within said frames that dialectical debate—far too often polarised, at that—takes place. The homogenisation of cognitive frameworks and topics of debate leads to extremism in messages, such that one can clearly perceive a difference which would not otherwise stand out.

For the construction of frameworks, political actors use different strategies and communication tools which allow them to establish power relations. In recent years, they have combined traditional tactics with strategies which elevate the limited number of frameworks which both benefit the institutions and people who promote them and threaten democracy: subversive political communication and the strategy of lies, and the power of digital platforms and algorithms, which cease to be mere intermediaries and become increasingly powerful political actors, as well as that of political bots and their influence on election campaigns and referenda.

First, rather than pursuing the traditional campaign objectives of mobilising and informing voters, subversive political communication aims to demobilise the electorate and spread disinformation (Römmele & Gibson, 2020). As evidenced by the Oxford Dictionary's designation of *post-truth* as word of the year, as well as *fake news* and *fake news media* receiving the same distinction from Collins Dictionary (Carballo et al., 2018), the use of falsehoods has become mainstream. Political parties have also legitimised the use of lies, and strategic falsehoods have become a valid campaign tactic used to set the public agenda (Gaber & Fisher, 2021). In the same study, Gaber and Fisher point out how recent electoral successes such as the 2016 Brexit referendum, the 2019 UK general election, Trump's victory in 2016 and his growing electoral support in 2020 could solidify the trend whereby politicians caught in a lie do not suffer any consequences at the ballot box.

Second, digital platforms and algorithms are no longer mere intermediaries; rather they have become increasingly powerful political forces. Technology companies in recent years have transitioned from service providers and content distribution channels to political and media actors with great influence on public opinion. The risks presented by the reshaping and erosion of information plurality are (Cardenal et al., 2019; Tamir & Davidson, 2020) difficult to detect (Salge & Karahanna, 2018; Lewis et al., 2019; Vasilkova & Legostaeva, 2019).

Speech content is increasingly programmed, mediated, augmented, supported and produced by social media algorithms (Dillet, 2020), with platforms moderating content and taking on new roles. In addition to their political roles, they create frames for understanding reality by concealing or highlighting different aspects (Popa et al., 2020). Besides contributing to the creation of collective imaginaries, social media platforms often act directly advising governments and political parties or participating directly in political action.

In this sense, Kreiss and McGregor point to a turning point in 2018 with the use of digital platforms in American election campaigns. Facebook, Twitter, Microsoft and Google served as advisors to political parties and shaped the campaigns' digital strategies and content through the development of organisational structures and staffing patterns tailored to the dynamics of American politics.

As such, digital platforms participate in the reimagination of democracy, the public agenda and political action on and off the campaign trail. Nonetheless, they also act as gatekeepers by giving voice to or silencing democratically elected representatives or by proclaiming themselves an international political authority. Sablosky (2021) describes how on 5 February 2019 Facebook labelled four Ethnic Armed Organisations (EAOs) in Myanmar as dangerous organisations, thus formally prohibiting them from using the platform. These four groups are in open conflict with the country's military who, in turn, were being prosecuted for genocide in the International Court of Justice. Sablosky (2021) concludes that "Facebook's content moderation practices have transformed the company into a new governmental apparatus freely adjudicating political speech claims around the globe with virtual impunity".

Third, the political influence of automation and algorithms continues to grow (Montal & Reich, 2017) due to their ability to create artificial public opinion and turn non-existent or minority opinions into majority or dominant ones (Schuchard et al., 2019). The recipients of these messages are helpless since they are not yet able to distinguish real speeches from fake ones, which use deception to conceal their nature (van der Kaa & Krahmer, 2014; Waddell, 2018; Wölker & Powell, 2018; Kušen & Strembeck, 2020). Bots use real-time big data to identify the interests, attitudes and emotions of millions of people and then craft in real time messages that match with their profiles.

Since 2010, political parties and governments have spent more than $500 million on research and development in this field (Bradshaw & Howard, 2018). The impact of automation and algorithms on election and referenda results grows year after year, with formally organised social media manipulation campaigns in 48 countries, compared to 28 the previous year (Bradshaw & Howard, 2018), although their development and influence vary based on the context.

The literature indicates that anywhere from 5% to 25% of Twitter accounts are bots (Keller & Klinger, 2019). Bessi and Ferrara (2016) determined that 20% of their sample consisted of bots; for Forelle et al. (2015) it was less than 10%; and Schuchard et al. (2019) concluded that bots constituted less than 0.3% of their sample. However, despite their limited number, bot accounts are more active than human ones and have a strategic weight in society (Howard & Kollanyi, 2017), as they stand out for being hypersocial in their relational behaviour (Schuchard et al., 2019). In Spain's April 2019 election campaign, less than 1% of users were bot accounts. The figure may seem insignificant, but these accounts sent on average 132 tweets per day, whereas human accounts send only four (García-Orosa et al., 2021).

In addition, previous studies confirm political bots' influence on electoral processes in different political systems and contexts, for example Mexico (Glowacki et al., 2018); Venezuela (Forelle et al., 2015); Chile (Santana & Huerta Cánepa, 2019); Colombia (López Urrea et al., 2016); the United Kingdom (Murthy et al., 2016); the United States (Howard & Kollanyi, 2017; Frey et al., 2018; Luceri et al., 2019); Ecuador (Puyosa, 2017); France (Ferrara, 2017); Argentina (Filer & Fredheim, 2017); and Spain (Campos-Domínguez & García-Orosa, 2018).

This automation of the production of social information has created an international black market, or propaganda soldiers (Ferrara, 2017; Santana & Huerta Cánepa, 2019), who aim to distort public opinion often by generating fake popularity or communities (Hagen et al., 2020).

The combination of these strategies could make it easier to set agendas and build cognitive frames. However, there is no clear actor in the application of tactics or a key player in the phenomena mentioned; rather, as indicated at the beginning of this section, these figures are undergoing hybridisation.

Moreover, their co-creation and blending stands out in the network society, where power is multidimensional and organised around networks programmed based on the interests and values of the empowered actors in every field of human action (Castells, 2009). Among other examples of fluidity, political parties which sprang from social movements have acquired considerable political power (Siddarth et al., 2021). Take, for example, "Teruel exists", a local social movement in Spain which has managed to lodge its frame "empty Spain" in the public agenda and in political discourse. After humble beginnings, this social movement (a *grouping of electors* in Spanish electoral law parlance) now has representation in the

Spanish Parliament. Also noteworthy are social movements such as the Arab Spring and others in Brazil, Turkey, Mexico and Chile (Castells, 2020).

Platforms, audiences and political parties work together in election campaigns by turning user-generated content into party strategy with the collusion of platforms (Kreiss & Mcgregor, 2018; Falasca et al., 2019). As such, audiences become digital volunteers (García-Orosa, 2018) or are reduced to some extent to goods, or robots, which are mainly managed by political parties as tools for generating likes, positive comments and other forms of approval (Falasca et al., 2019).

3 Platformisation of Research

Research on digital political communication, carried out mostly over the past five years (76.2% of articles published in Web Of Science (WOS)), has also designed its own cognitive frameworks and been influenced by the innovations and guidelines of technology companies. Thus, at the beginning, especially with the emergence of social networks, case studies have focused on single countries and platforms, and mostly on election campaigns (Casero-Ripollés, 2018). As such, numerous studies have addressed how political parties and citizens use different platforms, especially Twitter, but few have been interpretive or based on reception studies. The functions, actions and, to a lesser extent, effects of each tool applied were studied separately.

Platforms have been the predominant subject of study in the twenty-first century, but they have also become a research tool, as data mining requires software which is often created by the platforms themselves.

In recent years, political communication experts have continued to analyse the evolution of messages, narratives and languages termed hybrid, heterogeneous and multimodal and the emergence of stylemes and sociolects that seek to foster community (García-Orosa & López-García, 2019); and to create subversive new elements such as memes (Hernández et al., 2019) and GIFs (Dean, 2019; Seiffert-Brockmann et al., 2018; Shomova, 2021; Baishya, 2021). Researchers have also begun to perform cross-platform comparative studies, describing their distinct ecosystems and their involvement in political communication.

Nonetheless, they have also analysed the trends and consequences arising from the at times uncritical use of these platforms in political communication. Among them, researchers highlight polarisation, which they consider a threat to democracy which leads people to such extremely different positions on the same political reality that it becomes nearly impossible for them to find common ground (Kligler-Vilenchik et al., 2020). Yarchi et al. (2020) describes three types of polarisation (interactional, positional and affective), but the literature has mostly focused on the possible origins of this phenomenon. Among the most salient is that it is caused by echo chambers, which homogenise the opinions of people who engage in online communities and can lead such people to dismiss other points of view but accept those of their leaders without question (Salikov, 2019). Though several studies on the subject have been published (Post, 2019; Fletcher et al., 2020), not even social networks can be singled out as the cause of polarisation (Boulianne, 2020; Haw, 2020).

Finally, in the last five years the scientific literature has called for a new model and paradigm to study this fluid and increasingly complex field. The models designed 15 years ago are no longer useful. Mancini's 2004 model was one of the last decade's most utilised, but the researcher (2020) has since updated it to apply it not only to institutions such as the State, political parties and media organisations, but to a broader field of research and more volatile actors, where there is a lack of clear boundaries, procedures and routines. This is the field in which individual citizens can take an active role as communication producers and political actors.

Researchers call for a systemic conceptual framework to determine and evaluate the role of information society tools in solving problems in democracies (Anastasiadou et al., 2021).

Academia is looking for new tools that enable transactional and comparative research. In this sense, Tianru (2020) explores the concurrence of global influence and national resistance in the digital spheres, integrating the homogeneity promoted by increasing levels of internet connectivity and globalisation alongside the heterogeneity seen in different political communication landscapes, which are strongly influenced by lasting social contexts. Tianru identifies three types of transnational political communication spheres—*symmetrical and full-world*, *vigorous but censored*, and *infertile and unanswered*—and identifies their characteristics, internal logics and links with other communication spaces.

Political communication also faces new challenges such as Eurocentrism or Western centrism, which face criticism from people in other countries. Mare et al. (2020) indicate that the dominant narratives about the contemporary problem of "fake news" and online propaganda have focused on how their evolution and manifestation have been closely related to the rise of populist politics, digital capitalism, the transformation of the public sphere, and the structural weaknesses of the liberal and conventional media, while failing to pay attention to the peculiarities of African countries.

From our perspective it would be interesting to apply hybrid intelligence, which allows for combining human and machine intelligence to overcome the deficiencies of existing AI systems (Dellermann et al., 2019; Kamar, 2016). This concept proposes a multidisciplinary approach through AI, NLP and the social sciences, overcoming the above-mentioned heuristic limitations, for example, on automatic bot detection (Morstatter et al., 2016; Perdana et al., 2015; Ramalingam & Chinnaiah, 2018). Previous studies which examined automated bot detection techniques based on message behaviour in the Twitter ecosystem have also suffered from platformisation (Badawy et al., 2019; Lai et al., 2019; Schuchard et al., 2019; Wang et al., 2020; Zheng et al., 2019).

Finally, in addition to new hermeneutic and methodological perspectives, this situation requires new regulations and governance (Yurievich et al., 2019). In some jurisdictions, regulation lags a few steps behind technology companies, which have become important global political actors. In this cat-and-mouse game of sorts, States must show more skill, determination and collaboration, and tech companies should be more socially responsible (Smokvina & Pavleska, 2019).

4 Kaleidoscope Approaches

Be our guest on a behind-the-scenes tour, at times disturbing and at others heartening, of political communication. We invite the reader to go beyond the boundaries drawn by the viralisation of content, bots, eco chambers and bubble filters, within which citizens the world over are far too often trapped.

We aim to trace a longitudinal path through politics, describing the mechanisms, structures, dynamics and effects which political actions seek to bring about. As these phenomena flow over space and time, the mediascape becomes increasingly limited, and issues and approaches more homogeneous.

Serving as your guides will be 30 renowned researchers, who will provide you with a multidisciplinary analysis of the subject at hand.

Reading their work should help to understand which communication strategies have led to the political polarisation detected in different countries and societies, the fake news that can condition political action and the use of election-influencing bots. Moreover, it will allow us to shed light on the options in which we the people have to participate actively and ethically in political life in the coming years.

The way in which technological innovation influences not only how messages are transmitted but also how they are produced is the authors' starting point, but they do not succumb to technological determinism. Rather, they analyse digital political communication as the central element of communication. In lieu of merely describing how each tool is used, the authors present them as part of a comprehensive system.

We hope this book will serve as a guide for political communication directors, citizens, activists, students or scholars and provide them with a multidisciplinary, longitudinal analysis of the actors and trends of the past 25 years.

This compendium of research is a geographically and culturally diverse undertaking by researchers from various countries who have spent more than 20 years studying politics.

We have divided the book into two parts. In two highly differentiated sections, the researchers put forth a kaleidoscopic perspective complete with a wide range of approaches to the present subject matter. The research comes from diverse fields of knowledge with distinct hermeneutics and approaches to reality, some focusing on theory and others on case studies which illustrate the initial hypotheses.

In the first part, we look at the key players in digital communication. In the second, we deal with some of the latest trends. There are 12 chapters which can be read in any order.

In the first part, the authors discuss traditional media phenomena and actors, how they have adapted to digital political communication and how they have affected the same. In the second chapter, Eva Campos-Domínguez (University of Valladolid, Spain) and Irene Ramos-Vielba (Department of Political Science at the Danish Centre for Studies in Research and Research Policy, Aarhus University, Denmark) explain the important role played by parliaments in reinventing democracy with the inclusive participation of different political actors. They review 25 years of milestones in parliamentary communication and the transformation of parliamentary governance. The authors analyse and provide examples of the key trends and challenges along the road to hybrid parliament.

In the third chapter, Ainara Larrondo-Ureta (Universidad del País Vasco/Euskal Herriko Unibertsitatea, Spain) and Koldobika Meso-Ayerdi (idem) guide us through the evolution of political party strategies over the past few decades. The researchers describe, discuss and provide examples of major advances in organisational communication 2.0, in which messages tailor-made to the digital medium are used to drive audience participation. The chapter will deal with cross-platform, cross-media and transmedia storytelling, as well as personalisation, emotionalisation, big data and AI, in an effort to propose challenging new fields of research.

In the fourth chapter, Xosé López-García (University of Santiago de Compostela, Spain), João Canavilhas (University of Beira Interior, Portugal), María-Cruz Negreira-Rey (University of Santiago de Compostela, Spain) and Jorge Vázquez-Herrero (idem) study digital media and their relationship with the public sphere and reflect on the conceptualisation and practice of political journalism within a recent phenomenon: digital native media. The authors identify trends, emerging phenomena, and the evolving role of journalists and local and hyperlocal media in democratic participation and the reinvention of democracy.

The fifth chapter focuses on lobbies. As researchers Antonio Castillo-Esparcia (University of Málaga, Spain), Ana Almansa-Martínez (Idem) and Gisela Gonçalves (University of Beira Interior, Portugal) indicate, lobbies have been one of the least transparent and most influential actors. The authors analyse lobbies' actions and impacts, their influence on public policy and the conceptual boundaries of different issues in various countries, dealing with them as channels of political communication and organisational political communication.

The sixth chapter takes on a gender-based perspective and is dedicated to a political figure made invisible by political parties and the media: the victims of femicide. Through a review of the situation in Latin America and a case study, Santiago Gallur Santorum of the Technological Institute of Santo Domingo (INTEC), who has analysed femicide in several countries for more than 20 years, shines a light on this phenomenon and helps us understand what drives it. The divide between reality, public policy and opinions published in the media demonstrates how certain figures manage to keep certain issues hidden.

To close the first section of this book, Sandra Flores-Guevara (Autonomous University of the State of Hidalgo, México) and Laura Georgina Ortega-Luna (idem) reflects on the intersection of social movements and party systems as it pertains to the fluidity of political actors. Throughout her study the reader will see the relationship between traditional and new political actors who together weave the fabric of democracy. To illustrate this phenomenon, the author analyses the situation in

Mexico in recent years, where again we see connections branching out between different movements.

In the second part of the book, we reflect on some of the strategies and trends seen in most of the phenomena discussed in the first part (the use of emotions, 360° reality, social audiences and live-tweeting), and discuss their effects on the representation of ethnic minorities and election campaigns in Latin America.

In the eighth chapter, Sara Pérez-Seijo (USC), Pavel Sidorenko Bautista (University of Francisco de Vitoria) and María José Benítez de Gracia (Universidad Isabel I de Castilla) reflect on changes in communication brought on by VR technologies and 360° video. They use case studies to analyse the opportunities and challenges that this type of storytelling presents for the various actors within political communication. Citizen engagement and the ability to create a sense of presence are two of the strengths analysed. That said, this chapter will also discuss the dilemmas posed by this technology, above all from an ethical point of view.

In Chap. 9, researchers Nieves Lagares Diez (University of Santiago de Compostela, Spain), Erika Jaráiz Gulías (idem) and Gina Sibaja (University of Costa Rica) discuss engagement in politics and the importance of emotional framing, especially negative emotional framing, as a generator of political commitment. This chapter reviews the concept of engagement, the debate around the concept itself and its relationship to political participation through social media. Finally, the use of emotion is discussed as a fundamental point of cross-cutting political communication strategies in recent years.

Chapter 10 focuses on audience participation in one of the most relevant milestones in televised political communication: candidate debates. José Sixto-García, Ana-Isabel Rodríguez-Vázquez and Alba Silva Rodríguez, researchers from the University of Santiago de Compostela, analyse the actions the audience takes in real time as political parties and the media—two traditional actors in political communication—transmit their messages. Co-production again emerges as both a strength of and threat to political communication in a traditional medium such as television.

In Chap. 11, Magomed-Emin Aliev and Deborah Castro (University of Rotterdam, Holland) deal with fiction as a means of transmitting values and ideology through the creation of political imaginaries. Their starting point is society's racial dichotomy: the diversity, equality and visibility seen, on the one hand, in more black-owned media and an

African-American president in the United States, but, on the other, black- and female-led content suffering online trolling and hatred at the hands of white, predominantly male groups. In this context they present a case study on a fictional series as an element of analysis.

Lastly, Paulo Carlos López-López (University of Santiago de Compostela, Spain), Daniel Barredo Ibáñez (University of Rosario, Colombia; Fudan University, China) and María Pereira López (USC, Spain) analyse cyberpolitics in Latin America through the agenda and image of the region's candidates. The authors present extensive research on more than a dozen electoral contests that took place in Latin America between 2015 and 2020 in which some of the actors and strategies analysed in the preceding chapters emerge. Among their most important conclusions is the flourishing of digital social networks, complete with filter bubbles and echo chambers.

5 Upcoming Challenges

The post-COVID-19 era could mark a turning point in the panorama described thus far, and therefore present new opportunities for echo chambers to become more polyphonic. With this book we hope to contribute to the scientific literature and propose seven major challenges for the coming years:

1. Train citizens in digital democracy to make the next stage of history inclusive;
2. Foster the citizenry's agency in building cognitive frameworks and alternative meanings, and foster participation in the co-creation of information;
3. Create new hermeneutic perspectives to understand reality through hybrid intelligence;
4. Strengthen the values of truthfulness and credibility in public debate;
5. Leverage higher education to create evolving professions and skillsets;
6. Reflect on the need for new regulations for new paradigms;
7. Promote and disseminate ethical codes and best practices in companies and institutions.

We close by expressing our deepest gratitude to all the authors who made this book possible, especially Professor Manuel Castells for supporting the project and writing the preface. We hope that you enjoy it and that it may spur reflection and critical thinking in all those who read it. As we set forth in the preface, we remain steadfast in our conviction that a better world (for everyone) is possible.

Funding This chapter has been developed within the research project "Digital Native Media in Spain: Storytelling Formats and Mobile Strategy" (RTI2018-093346-B-C33) funded by the Ministry of Science, Innovation, and Universities and co-funded by the European Regional Development Fund (ERDF).

References

Anastasiadou, M., Santos, V., & Montargil, F. (2021). Which technology to which challenge in democratic governance? An approach using design science research. *Transforming Government: People, Process and Policy*. https://doi.org/10.1108/TG-03-2020-0045

Badawy, A., Addawood, A., Lerman, K., & Ferrara, E. (2019). Characterizing the 2016 Russian IRA influence campaign. *Social Network Analysis and Mining, 9*(1), 1–11. https://doi.org/10.1007/s13278-019-0578-6

Baishya, A. K. (2021). The conquest of the world as meme: Memetic visuality and political humor in critiques of the Hindu right wing in India. *Media, Culture & Society*, 43(6), 1113-1135. https://doi.org/10.1177/0163443720986039

Bessi, A., & Ferrara, E. (2016). Social bots distort the 2016 U.S. presidential election online discussion. *First Monday, 21*(11).

Bimber, B. (2014). Digital media in the Obama campaigns of 2008 and 2012: Adaptation to the personalized political communication environment. *Journal of Information Technology & Politics, 11*(2), 130–150. https://doi.org/10.1080/19331681.2014.895691

Bol, D., Giani, M., Blais, A., & Loewen, P. J. (2021). The effect of COVID-19 lockdowns on political support: Some good news for democracy? *European Journal of Political Research, 60*(2), 497–505. https://doi.org/10.1111/1475-6765.12401

Bossetta, M. (2019). Political campaigning games: Digital campaigning with computer games in European National Elections. *International Journal of Communication, 13*(22), 3422–3442.

Boulianne, S., Koc-Michalska, K., & Bimber, B. (2020). Right-wing populism, social media and echo chambers in western democracies. *New Media & Society, 22*(4), 683–669. https://doi.org/10.1177/1461444819893983

Bradshaw, S., & Howard, P. (2018). *Challenging truth and trust: A global inventory of organized social media manipulation* (Online Supplement to Working Paper). Project on Computational Propaganda. University of Oxford.

Campbell, D., & Lambright, K. (2020). Terms of engagement: Facebook and Twitter use among nonprofit human service organizations. *Nonprofit Management and Leadership, 30*, 545–568. https://doi.org/10.1002/nml.21403

Campos-Domínguez, E., & García-Orosa, B. (2018). Algorithmic communication and political parties: Automation of production and flow of messages. *Profesional de la Informacion, 27*(4), 769–777. https://doi.org/10.3145/epi.2018.jul.06

Carballo, M., López-Escobar, E., & McCombs, M. (2018). Communication, public opinion, and democracy: New challenges. *Communications Society, 31*(4), 121–133. https://doi.org/10.15581/003.31.4.121-133

Cardenal, A. S., Aguilar-Paredes, C., Galais, C., & Pérez-Montoro, M. (2019). Digital technologies and selective exposure: How choice and filter bubbles shape news media exposure. *The International Journal of Press/Politics, 24*(4), 465–486. https://doi.org/10.1177/1940161219862988

Casero-Ripollés, A. (2018). Research on political information and social media: Key points and challenges for the future. *El Profesional de la Información, 27*(5), 964–974. https://doi.org/10.3145/epi.2018.sep.01

Castells, M. (2009). *Comunicación y poder*. Madrid: Alianza Editorial.

Clarke, S., Hoggett, P., & Thompson, S. (2006). *Emotions, politics and society*. UK: Palgrave Macmillan.

Dean, J. (2019). Sorted for memes and gifs: Visual media and everyday digital politics. *Political Studies Review, 17*(3), 255–266. https://doi.org/10.1177/1478929918807483

Dellermann, D., Ebel, P., Söllner, M., & Leimeister, J. M. (2019). Hybrid intelligence. *Business and Information Systems Engineering, 61*(5), 637–643. https://doi.org/10.1007/s12599-019-00595-2

Dillet, B. (2020). Speaking to algorithms? Rhetorical political analysis as technological analysis. *Politics*. https://doi.org/10.1177/0263395720968060

Falasca, K., Dymek, M., & Grandien, C. (2019). Social mediaelection campaigning: who is working for whom? A conceptual exploration of digital political labour. *Contemporary Social Science, 14*(1), 89–101. https://doi.org/10.1080/21582041.2017.1400089

Ferrara, E. (2017). Disinformation and social bot operations in the run up to the 2017 French presidential election. *First Monday*, 22(8). https://doi.org/10.5210/fm.v22i8.8005

Field, L. (2020). Irish General Election 2020: Two-and-a-half party system no more? *Irish Political Studies, 35*(4), 615–636. https://doi.org/10.1080/07907184.2020.1762284

Filer, T., & Fredheim, R. (2017). Popular with the robots: Accusation and automation in the argentine presidential elections, 2015. *International Journal of Politics, Culture and Society, 30*(3), 259–274. https://doi.org/10.1007/s10767-016-9233-7

Fletcher, R., Cornia, A., & Nielsen, R. K. (2020). How polarized are online and offline news audiences? A comparative analysis of twelve countries. *The International Journal of Press/Politics, 25*(2), 169–195. https://doi.org/10.1177/1940161219892768

Forelle, M. C., Howard, P. N., Monroy-Hernandez, A., & Savage, S. (2015). Political bots and the manipulation of public opinion in Venezuela. *SSRN Electronic Journal*, 1–8. https://doi.org/10.2139/ssrn.2635800

Frey, C. B., Berger, T., & Chen, C. (2018). Political machinery: Did robots swing the 2016 US presidential election? *Oxford Review of Economic Policy, 34*(3), 418–442. https://doi.org/10.1093/oxrep/gry007

Gaber, I., & Fisher, C. (2021). "Strategic Lying": The case of Brexit and the 2019 UK election. *The International Journal of Press/Politics.* https://doi.org/10.1177/1940161221994100

García-Orosa, B. (2017). Profile of the Cyber Media Audience: Discursive Representation and Praxis of Receiver 2.0. *Palabra Clave, 21*(1), 111–133. https://doi.org/10.5294/pacla.2018.21.1.6

García-Orosa, B., & López-García, X. (2019). Language in social networks as a communication strategy: Public administration, political parties and civil society. *Communications Society, 32*(1), 107–125. https://doi.org/10.15581/003.32.1.107-125

García-Orosa, B., Vázquez-Sande, P., & López-García, X. (2017). Narrativas digitales de los principales partidos políticos de España, Francia, Portugal y Estados Unidos. *El Profesional de la Información (EPI), 26*(4), 589–600. https://doi.org/10.3145/epi.2017.jul.03

García-Orosa, B., Gamallo, P., Martín-Rodilla, P., & Martínez-Castaño, R. (2021). Hybrid intelligence strategies for identifying, classifying and analyzing political bots. Social Sciences, 10–10, 357. https://doi.org/10.3390/socsci10100357

Glowacki, M., Narayanan, V., Maynard, S., Hirsch, G., Kollanyi, B., Neudert, L.-M., Howard, P., Lederer, T., & Barash, V. (2018). *News and political information consumption in Mexico: Mapping the 2018 Mexican presidential election on Twitter and Facebook*, 1–6.

Grossman, G., Kim, S., Rexer, J., & Thirumurthy, H. (2020, April 22). Political partisanship influences behavioral responses to Governors' recommendations for COVID-19 prevention in the United States. Available at SSRN: https://ssrn.com/abstract=3578695 or https://doi.org/10.2139/ssrn.3578695

Hagen, L., Neely, S., Keller, T. E., Scharf, R., & Vasquez, F. E. (2020). Rise of the machines? Examining the influence of social bots on a political discussion network. *Social Science Computer Review.* https://doi.org/10.1177/0894439320908190

Haw, A. L. (2020). What drives political news engagement in digital spaces? Reimagining 'echo chambers' in a polarised and hybridised media ecology. *Communication Research and Practice, 6*(1), 38–54. https://doi.org/10.1080/22041451.2020.1732002

Hernández, E., Daza, J., & Meyer, F. J. (2019). Memes and politics. Why some political memes go viral and others don't? *IC-Revista Científica de Información y Comunicación, 16*, 579–613.

Howard, P. N., & Kollanyi, B. (2017). Bots, #Strongerin, and #Brexit: Computational propaganda during the UK-EU referendum. *SSRN Electronic Journal.* https://doi.org/10.2139/ssrn.2798311

IJsselsteijn, W. A., & Riva, G. (2003). Being there: The experience of presence in mediated environments 2. In G. Riva, F. Davide, & W. A. Ijsselsteijn (Eds.), *Being there: Concepts, effects and measurement of user presence in synthetic environments* (pp. 1–14). IOS Press.

Kamar, E. (2016). Direction in hybrid intelligence: Complementing AI system with human intelligence. *Proceedings of the 25th International Joint on Artificial Intelligence (IJCAI)*, 4070–4073.

Keller, T. R., & Klinger, U. (2019). Social bots in election campaigns: Theoretical, empirical, and methodological implications. *Political Communication, 36*(1), 171–189. https://doi.org/10.1080/10584609.2018.1526238

Kligler-Vilenchik, N., Baden, C., & Yarchi, M. (2020). Interpretative polarization across platforms: How political disagreement develops over time on Facebook, Twitter, and WhatsApp. *Social Media + Society, 6*(3). https://doi.org/10.1177%2F2056305120944393

Kreiss, D., & Mcgregor, S. (2018). Technology firms shape political communication: The work of Microsoft, Facebook, Twitter, and Google with campaigns during the 2016 U.S. presidential cycle. *Political Communication, 35*(2), 155–177. https://doi.org/10.1080/10584609.2017.1364814

Kušen, E., & Strembeck, M. (2020). You talkin' to me? Exploring human/bot communication patterns during riot events. *Information Processing and Management, 57*(1). https://doi.org/10.1016/j.ipm.2019.102126

Lai, M., Tambuscio, M., Patti, V., Ruffo, G., & Rosso, P. (2019). Stance polarity in political debates: A diachronic perspective of network homophily and conversations on Twitter. *Data and Knowledge Engineering, 124.* https://doi.org/10.1016/j.datak.2019.101738

Landman, T., & Splendore, L. (2020). Pandemic democracy: Elections and COVID-19. *Journal of Risk Research, 23*(7–8), 1060–1066. https://doi.org/10.1080/13669877.2020.1765003

Lewis, S. C., Guzman, A. L., & Schmidt, T. R. (2019). Automation, journalism, and human–machine communication: Rethinking roles and relationships of humans and machines in news. *Digital Journalism, 7*(4), 409–427. https://doi.org/10.1080/21670811.2019.1577147

Lilleker, D. G., Tenscher, J., & Štětka, V. (2015). Towards hypermedia campaigning? Perceptions of new media's importance for campaigning by party strategists in comparative perspective. *Information, Communication & Society, 18*(7), 747–765. https://doi.org/10.1080/1369118X.2014.993679

López Urrea, L. M., Páez Valdez, J. E., & Cuellar Rodríguez, A. D. (2016). El Discurso Político Mediado Por Ordenadores. *Revista Nexus Comunicación*, 19. https://doi.org/10.25100/nc.v0i19.666

Luceri, L., Badawy, A., Deb, A., & Ferrara, E. (2019). Red bots do it better: Comparative analysis of social bot partisan behavior. *The Web Conference 2019 – Companion of the World Wide Web Conference, WWW 2019*, 1007–1012. https://doi.org/10.1145/3308560.3316735

Mancini, P. (2020). Comparing media systems and the digital age. *International Journal of Communication, 14*, 5761–5774.

Mare, A., Mabweazara, H. M., & Moyo, D. (2020). "Fake news" and cyber-propaganda in Sub-Saharan Africa: Recentering the research agenda. *Africa Journalism Studies, 40*, 1–2. https://doi.org/10.1080/23743670.2020.1788295

Marsh, D., & Stoker, G. (1998). *Teoría y métodos de la ciencia política*. Madrid: Alianza.

McNair, B. (2017). *An introduction to political communication*. UK: Routledge.

Montal, T., & Reich, Z. (2017). I, Robot. You, Journalist. Who is the Author?: Authorship, bylines and full disclosure in automated journalism. *Digital Journalism, 5*(7), 829–849. https://doi.org/10.1080/21670811.2016.1209083

Morstatter, F., Wu, L., Nazer, T. H., Carley, K. M., & Liu, H. (2016). A new approach to bot detection. *IEEE/ACM International Conference on Advances in Social Networks Analysis and Mining (ASONAM)*, 533–540.

Murthy, D., Powell, A. B., Tinati, R., Anstead, N., Carr, L., Halford, S. J., & Weal, M. (2016). Bots and political influence: A sociotechnical investigation of social network capital. *International Journal of Communication, 10*(June), 4952–4971.

Perdana, R. S., Muliawati, T. H., & Alexandro, R. (2015). Bot spammer detection in Twitter using tweet similarity and time interval entropy. *Jurnal Ilmu Komputer Dan Informasi, 8*(1), 19. https://doi.org/10.21609/jiki.v8i1.280

Pilet, J. B. (2020). Hard times for governing parties: The 2019 federal elections in Belgium. *West European Politics*. https://doi.org/10.1080/01402382.2020.1750834

Popa, S. A., Fazekas, Z., Braun, D., & Leidecker-Sandmann, M. M. (2020). Informing the public: How party communication builds opportunity structures. *Political Communication, 37*(3), 329–349. https://doi.org/10.1080/10584609.2019.1666942

Post, S. (2019). Polarizing communication as media effects on antagonists. Understanding communication in conflicts in digital media societies. *Communication Theory, 29*(2), 213–235. https://doi.org/10.1093/ct/qty022

Puyosa, I. (2017). Political bots on Twitter in #Ecuador2017 presidential campaigns. *Contratexto*, 27, 39–60.

Ramalingam, D., & Chinnaiah, V. (2018). Fake profile detection techniques in large-scale online social networks: A comprehensive review. *Computers and Electrical Engineering, 65*(3), 165–177. https://doi.org/10.1016/j.compeleceng.2017.05.020

Römmele, A., & Gibson, R. (2020). Scientific and subversive: The two faces of the fourth era of political campaigning. *New Media & Society, 22*(4), 595–610. https://doi.org/10.1177/1461444819893979

Sablosky, J. (2021). Dangerous organizations: Facebook's content moderation decisions and ethnic visibility in Myanmar. *Media, Culture & Society*. https://doi.org/10.1177/0163443720987751

Salge, C. A. D. L., & Karahanna, E. (2018). Protesting corruption on Twitter: Is it a bot or is it a person? *Academy of Management Discoveries, 4*(1), 32–49. https://doi.org/10.5465/amd.2015.0121

Salikov, A. (2019). The digital transformation of the public sphere, its features in the context of various political regimes, and its possible influence on political processes. *Russian Sociological Review, 18*(4). https://doi.org/10.17323/1728-192x-2019-4-149-163

Santana, L. E., & Huerta Cánepa, G. (2019). ¿Son bots? Automatización en redes sociales durante las elecciones presidenciales de Chile 2017. *Cuadernos.info, 44*, 61–77. https://doi.org/10.7764/cdi.44.1629

Schuchard, R., Crooks, A. T., Stefanidis, A., & Croitoru, A. (2019). Bot stamina: Examining the influence and staying power of bots in online social networks. *Applied Network Science, 4*(1). https://doi.org/10.1007/s41109-019-0164-

Seiffert-Brockmann, J., Diehl, T., & Dobusch, L. (2018). Memes as games: The evolution of a digital discourse online. *New Media & Society, 20*(8), 2862–2879. https://doi.org/10.1177/1461444817735334

Shomova, S. (2021). "Hieroglyphs of protest": Internet memes and the protest movement in Russia. *Problems of Post-Communism*, 1–10. https://doi.org/10.1080/10758216.2020.1864217

Siddarth, D., Shankar, R., & Pal, J. (2021). 'We do politics so we can change politics': Communication strategies and practices in the Aam Aadmi Party's institutionalization process. *Information, Communication & Society*, 1–21. https://doi.org/10.1080/1369118X.2020.1856910

Slater, M., & Sanchez-Vives, M. V. (2016). Enhancing our lives with immersive virtual reality. *Frontiers in Robotics and AI, 3*(4), 1–47. https://doi.org/10.3389/frobt.2016.00074

Smith, J. N. (2018). The social network?: Nonprofit constituent engagement through. *Social Media, Journal of Nonprofit & Public Sector Marketing, 30*(3), 294–316. https://doi.org/10.1080/10495142.2018.1452821

Smokvina, T. K., & Pavleska, T. (2019). Igra mačke z mišjo: medijska regulacija v Evropski uniji v času algoritmizacije komuniciranja. *JAVNOST-THE PUBLIC, 26*, S82–S99.

Stromer-Galley, J. (2019). *Presidential campaigning in the Internet age*. Oxford: Oxford University Press.

Tamir, E., & Davidson, R. (2020). The good despot: Technology firms' interventions in the public sphere. *Public Understanding of Science, 29*(1), 21–36. https://doi.org/10.1177/0963662519879368

Tianru, G. (2020). Comparative political communication research in the digital epoch: A typology of national communication spaces. *The Information Society, 36*(2), 59–70. https://doi.org/10.1080/01972243.2019.1703866

Van der Kaa, H., & Krahmer, E. (2014). Journalist versus news consumer: The perceived credibility of machine written news. *The Computation Journalism Conference New York*, 1–4.

Vasilkova, V. V., & Legostaeva, N. I. (2019). Social bots in political communication. *RUDN Journal of Sociology, 19*(1), 121–133. https://doi.org/10.22363/2313-2272-2019-19-1-121-133

Waddell, F. (2018). A robot wrote this? *Digital Journalism, 6*(2), 236–255. https://doi.org/10.1080/21670811.2017.1384319

Wang, W., Shang, Y., He, Y., Li, Y., & Liu, J. (2020). BotMark: Automated botnet detection with hybrid analysis of flow-based and graph-based traffic behaviors. *Information Sciences, 511*, 284–296. https://doi.org/10.1016/j.ins.2019.09.024

Wölker, A., & Powell, T. E. (2018). Algorithms in the newsroom? News readers' perceived credibility and selection of automated journalism. *Journalism, 22*(1), 86–103. https://doi.org/10.1177/1464884918757072

Yarchi, M., Baden, C., & Kligler-Vilenchik, N. (2020). Political polarization on the digital sphere: A cross-platform, over-time analysis of interactional, positional, and affective polarization on social media. *Political Communication, 1*(42). https://doi.org/10.1080/10584609.2020.1785067

Yurievich, M. A., Alexander, K., Igorevna, M. O., Aleksandrovich, O. V., & Viktorovich, T. V. (2019). Transformation of the socio-political sphere in digital era: Some problems of value-normative harmonization. *Journal of Politics and Law, 12*(3). https://doi.org/10.5539/jpl.v12n3p11

Zheng, L., Albano, C. M., Vora, N. M., Feng, M. A. I., & Nickerson, J. V. (2019). The roles bots play in Wikipedia. *Proceedings of the ACM on Human-Computer Interaction, 3*(CSCW). https://doi.org/10.1145/3359317

CHAPTER 2

Parliaments and Key Transformations in Digital Communication

Eva Campos-Domínguez and Irene Ramos-Vielba

1 Examining Parliaments' Digital Communication

This chapter examines the development of parliaments' digital communication over the last 30 years, which is continuously being transformed and redefined. The connections between the main parliaments' functions—legislation, representation and government scrutiny—and the institutional democratic legitimation derived from parliaments' relationship with society (Barker, 2007) are now more complex and multifaceted (Leston-Bandeira & Thompson, 2018). Signs of political disaffection have

E. Campos-Domínguez (✉)
Department of Modern, Contemporary and American History, Journalism, Audiovisual Communication and Publicity, University of Valladolid, Valladolid, Spain
e-mail: eva.campos@uva.es

I. Ramos-Vielba
Department of Political Science, Danish Centre for Studies in Research and Research Policy, Aarhus University, Aarhus, Denmark
e-mail: iravi@ps.au.dk

B. García-Orosa (ed.), *Digital Political Communication Strategies*, The Palgrave Macmillan Series in International Political Communication, https://doi.org/10.1007/978-3-030-81568-4_2

developed in parallel to a growing social demand for both broader monitoring and increased involvement in the public sphere through participatory processes. These approaches might allow citizens to better assess performance in relation to central qualities of parliament, such as representativeness, transparency, accessibility, responsibility and efficiency (Beetham, 2006). The use of digital tools for these purposes can also help to articulate parliaments' accountability to the public within parliamentary management practices, including benchmarking of parliamentary information and public outreach, to ensure that parliaments' basic responsibilities to the people are met (Joseph, 2016).

In line with this, new forms of parliamentary communication have also been displayed via digital media use, aimed at promoting better and more fluid external communication (Schwanholz et al., 2017). These efforts have been supported by the consideration that communication flows and dialogue between members of the parliaments and citizens may contribute to improve democratic values. Furthermore, technological developments in parliaments have been associated with the advancement towards fulfilling the United Nations Sustainable Development Goal 16 about 'peace, justice and strong institutions', as it is believed that the application of technologies could enhance both democratic practices and inclusiveness through effective interaction between parliamentary representatives and society (Niebel et al., 2013; Oni et al., 2021). This would be associated with a reduction in perceived deficiencies that feed citizen scepticism over parliamentary institutions leading to potential improvements in terms of democratic deficit.

Therefore, recent parliamentary communication has witnessed gradual development in the internet age, as a consequence of the implementation of various digital tools that have fostered the transformation of both communication objectives and characteristics. This change has been mediated by intensified communication processes linked to global trends such as increasing ideological and affective polarisation or the crisis of intermediation of traditional social actors. The spread of an open-source culture has also contributed to the normalisation of datafication in society, providing new rationales to support the empowerment and the agency of a datafied public (Baack, 2015). Yet, the contexts in which data sets are generated and, particularly, the neutrality of such paradigm within the ecosystem of connective media have been critically questioned (Van Dijck, 2014). In addition to this, further considerations on interactions among social groups, understood as epistemic communities, would emphasise the role of discourse reproduction in connection with speakers' authority to convey content to recipients (Van Dijk, 2014). Simultaneously, new communicative conditions, stemming from new technological resources and electronic means, have been progressively 'eroding the institutional monopoly on large-scale coordination' (Shirky, 2008: 143). This has significantly influenced the organisational structures responsible for digital communication, making a new scenario of 'organisation without organisations' possible, as observed in electoral campaigns management (Mevdic, 2011). Ultimately, the outreach of current parliaments' digital communication lies in the combination of messages that are created, disseminated and mobilised by a variety of digital users and a network of societal participants.

Since the 1990s, there has been a growing scholarly interest in these phenomena, which has resulted in an extensive academic literature that analyses the use of digital resources by parliamentary institutions, parliamentary representatives and grassroots citizens. From a communication characteristics perspective, most studies to date have focused on analysing how parliaments and parliamentarians produce or disseminate content through the Internet in different geographical contexts (Scherpereel et al., 2018; Spierings et al., 2019; Esteve del Valle & Borge Bravo, 2018; Odeyemi & Abioro, 2018). Additionally, a stream of academic contributions has concentrated on various factors underpinning parliaments' public engagement, ranging from decision-making processes or procedural justice to new social media use or Twitter conversations on e-petitions debated in parliament (Asher et al., 2019; Kelly & Bochel, 2018; Leston-Bandeira, 2014). Other studies—as part of a project by the Hansard Society undertaken in the UK, Canada, Chile and Australia—also considered the prospects of an effective use of technologies not only to foster engagement but also to transform the future of internal parliamentary processes and to improve public access to parliamentary information (Williamson & Fallon, 2011).

Technological advancements then pose important challenges for analytical approaches to parliaments' digital communication with a focus on the use of each specific digital tool separately. A new focus should now be placed on parliamentary communication as a process that integrates numerous digital tools simultaneously. Further attention to processes of content creation could also expand our understanding beyond descriptive analyses of parliamentarians' activities and perceptions—revealing, for instance, the role of parliamentary assistants in supporting social media presence (Lev-On et al., 2017). Likewise, exploration into the informal space where parliamentarians interact can provide a better glimpse of information exchange and mobilisation of political support that is expanded into virtual space; despite this, interactions between members are less observable than their interaction via social media with constituents (Norton, 2019).

Nevertheless, the scientific literature on parliaments' digital communication still presents some limitations to gain fine-grained understanding of the relevance of all these issues for civic engagement. In line with this, Norton (2017) highlighted that one challenging task for contemporary parliament is to fight against citizen mistrust and scepticism within a democratic context in which digital information is increasingly accessible and society is increasingly polarised. Communication flows in parliamentary Twitter networks, for example, seem to present different degrees of polarisation along ideological lines and cross-party interactions (Esteve del Valle & Borge Bravo, 2018; Esteve del Valle et al., 2021). In a similar vein, the Parliamentary Office of Science and Technology (POST) considered disinformation to be an issue of most interest to UK Parliament for future legislation (POST, 2019). Among rapidly evolving areas, bots, trolls and 'content polluters' are hijacking discussions on social media networks for political purposes. The POST report also noted that although the efforts in the detection of fake news have improved—mainly through the use of human fact checkers and the development of algorithms—disinformation campaigns still play a significant role for citizens' trust in parliament that legislative institutions should not ignore.

This overall situation, therefore, demands a deeper understanding of key elements in contemporary parliaments' digital communication in fragmented democratic societies, with increasing political disengagement and declining trust in public institutions. To contribute to such an aim, this chapter conducts an overview of the main trends in parliaments' digital communication over the last three decades that inform current challenges.

2 Main Trends in Parliaments' Digital Communication (1990–2021)

The development of parliamentary communication in the last 30 years has been largely driven by the changing digital media landscape. The range of digital tools available and the set of new communicative possibilities associated with them have progressively shaped the evolution of parliaments'

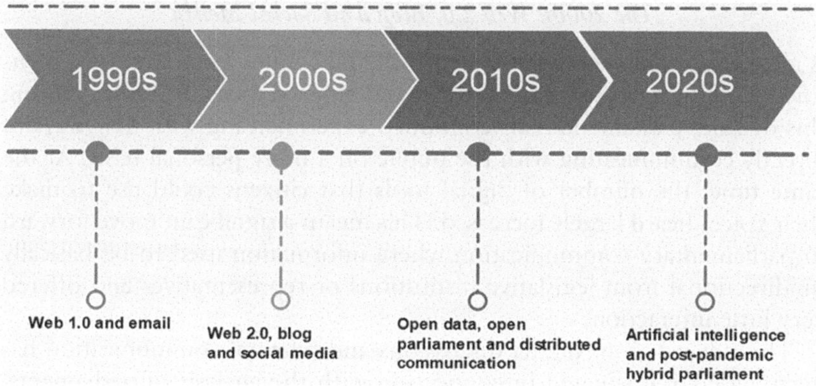

Fig. 2.1 Development of parliaments' digital communication

digital communication to date. In this summary review, key digital-related elements are considered to be permeating parliamentary communication practices and, subsequently, academic analyses in this field of study. This section focuses on a set of essential digital-related transformations for each decade from 1990 to the present that are illustrated in Fig. 2.1.

The 1990s: Web 1.0 and Email

In the 1990s, parliaments started to adopt a variety of information and communication technologies (ICT) in their daily work, mainly for internal processes. The basic purpose was to make internal administration and management more efficient. One important part of this change involved expanding information digitisation into computer-readable formats or data encoding to make data processing, storage and transmission more reliable and, thereafter, decrease bureaucracy.

During this decade, parliaments also experimented with new media available at that time with the aim of being more accessible to citizens. Parliamentarians received some guidance in how to use Web 1.0 applications to communicate their parliamentary work and activities to society. This helped them to explore the prospects of new digital means to move its traditional communications towards digital formats, mainly through email and website content (Dai, 2007).

The 2000s: Web 2.0, Blog and Social Media

A next important step in parliaments' digital communication can be identified with the emergence of Web 2.0 and blogs in the early 2000s. During this decade, parliamentarians continued experimenting with new ways of directly communicating with the public on a more personal basis. At the same time, the number of digital tools that citizens could use to make their voices heard largely increased. This meant a significant move forward in parliamentary communication where information used to be basically unidirectional from legislative institutions or representatives and offered very little interaction.

This advance into digital discussions and bilateral communication has been widely investigated in connection with the analysis of parliaments' engagement with the public (Kelly & Bochel, 2018; Leston-Bandeira, 2014). It has been argued that the adoption of such digital tools led parliamentary representatives to a communication operating model progressively based on more decentralised structures. This also represented a significant evolution in citizens' digital uses as they moved from a predominant passive role of receiving information posted on basic websites to an increasing active role in producing and exchanging messages. Such a crucial change challenged the focus of the professional top-down communication approach that had dominated since the post-war period (Gibson, 2013). At the same time, this new situation raised questions regarding the mechanisms connecting 'the granular information environments of web 2.0 citizen activity' with real decision-making processes (Chadwick, 2009: 40).

Parliaments around the world also started to use different social networking platforms (e.g. Twitter, Facebook, YouTube) to share text, images and videos online. Content production, dissemination and *viralisation* through these tools have been widely addressed and analysed in a variety of academic research studies from a digital communication perspective (e.g. Scherpereel et al., 2018; Spierings et al., 2019; Esteve del Valle & Borge Bravo, 2018; Odeyemi & Abioro, 2018). Before the advent of internet-based social media, the possibilities for online communication were essentially limited to email and contact forms. Now, with the proliferation of social media, digital tools could then be used to generate direct dialogue between citizens and parliamentarians. This idea spread into parliamentary communication studies, which noted that representatives, however, often have little involvement in social media deliberations (Lev-On et al., 2017).

The 2010s: Open Data, Open Parliament and Distributed Communication

The open data movement that emerged from diverse grassroots activist groups, including open source advocates, civic technology developers and open knowledge campaigners, became broadly visible through two international conferences held in 2010. These conferences—one in the US hosted by the Department of Commerce and one in London organised by the civil society—contributed to the progressive institutionalisation of the open data movement worldwide. The call for governments and public institutions to provide access to valuable open data—for example, geospatial data, land registers, contracting or parliamentary voting—was aimed at facilitating further reuse and then generating economic, social and democratic benefits. Inspired by these ideas, open data started to be promoted through public transparency portals as a form of strengthening accountability to citizens. An ecosystem of electronic devices, programs and applications became available to society to develop the collective capacity of citizens for public oversight, monitoring and reporting. These conditions were increasingly acknowledged as a contribution to the common good and the general interest of society.

Within this frame of reference, the principles of an open government that is more accessible, responsive and accountable to society were consolidated through the international programme Open Government Partnership that was launched in 2011 to provide a platform for helping multiple national and local governments to co-create reforms in a set of policy areas in collaboration with civil society organisations. This initiative then sparked further transformation possibilities applied to parliaments. Along the same lines, 53 countries signed the 2012 Parliamentary Opening Declaration, aimed at encouraging both the opening of parliaments and their commitment to citizen involvement in parliamentary work. This scheme was promoted by civil society parliamentary monitoring organisations (PMOs) that had two main objectives: to improve parliamentary accountability as well as the capacity of citizens to participate in parliamentary processes (Ramos-Vielba et al., 2013).

Studies subsequently focused on the implementation of open parliament measures in different contextual settings with special interest in the promotion of both transparency and accountability to favour access to information about parliamentary activities. This also enabled interaction processes between the society and parliament. One of these analyses evaluated the application of an open parliament policy in the Brazilian Chamber of Deputies (Faria & Rehbein, 2016). This research included the observation of the virtual discussion between citizens and parliamentarians through a digital participation platform launched by the Brazilian parliament. Such platform tools facilitated collaboration, for example, for the joint edition of legislative texts or collaborative activities to use parliamentary open data (hackathons). In addition to this, a mediated interaction between deputies, experts and citizens and the creation of a permanent space dedicated to open parliament practices were also observed.

This stage of development is then influenced by the incorporation of varied digital technology applications, in a context where citizens play an increasingly participatory role in consultations or decision-making processes. Normative views on public participation, however, suggest benefits associated to citizens' empowerment but often neglect the role of power, as some participation mechanisms may also serve to endorse party's values and legitimise policy orientation or political decisions (Bouchard, 2016). Similar ambivalent effects seem to be embedded in variegated bottom-up digital initiatives that, based on the economy of enthusiasm and collaboration (Zafra, 2017), seek to challenge the status quo and bring added value. This may be the case of *prosumption* efforts produced by activism and social movements that try to develop an ability to disrupt institutions in creative manners (Chen, 2015). As a result, institutions might be legitimised and reinforced by these actions. Likewise, in digital political campaigns, a new grassroots-based mode of 'citizen initiated campaigning' (CIC) is built upon an informal network structure in which supporters register to use online tools to campaign on behalf of electoral candidates (Gibson, 2013). Studies of 'citizen campaigners' show that the participation of non-members in informal political discussions online may revitalise party activities (Vaccari & Valerini, 2016). These types of 'satellite' campaigns originating beyond party structures and control can be supported by a range of different organisations or 'democratic intermediaries' (Dommett & Temple, 2018), revealing the existence of more layers of complexity in the interactions between societal and institutional spheres.

The spread of widely distributed forms of communication is also reflected in parliamentary environments, where some intermediary organisations attempt to articulate and aggregate societal demands, for example, through interest groups and online-based organisations, which may at the same time act as a catalyst for communication. In this spirit, some PMOs provide selective parliamentary information to the public, with the purpose of paving the way for responsive and interactive parliament-society interconnections.

The 2020s: Artificial Intelligence and Post-pandemic Hybrid Parliament

Recent parliamentary uses point out how artificial intelligence (AI) and machine learning can be explored as an auxiliary tool in legislation towards improving the efficiency, transparency and accountability of parliament within existing legislative frameworks (Furst, 2018). In some initial steps, parliaments around the world have started to embrace technological assistance through the application of AI-led technology in their legislative process. AI has been used, for example, in the parliament and state legislatures in India to handle a large number of bills and committee reports in order to study potential patterns among them and streamline some procedures (Tripathi, 2018). The US Congress has developed an AI engine to automatically compare legislation and analyse text differences to help in the understanding of the changes (Ackley, 2019). The Austrian parliamentary administration has implemented an AI monitor system to find and deliver reliable information to parliamentarians (Reichstaedter & Lanzerstorfer, 2019). Such cases of preliminary experimentation show the potentiality of further AI developments for parliamentary work.

These types of AI applications, however, raise major concerns about ethical dilemmas associated with the trustworthiness of the technology in its implementation upon legislation, including the potential emergence of a biased algorithm, the supplied data to the AI or how the AI is programmed and trained (Saari, 2020). Other important questions about likely AI implementation by public institutions—for example, in government delivery of next-generation citizen services—refer to privacy issues and the gradual reduction of human involvement due to the accelerating pace in the rate of automation over time (Mehr, 2017). There is thus a pressing need for reaching a proper balance between regulating AI utilisation to mitigate ethical risks and maximising the advancement of possible solutions that benefit societies yet avoiding complete AI decision-making (Schwab & Davis, 2018). Considering the role of AI from a democratic perspective, the public interest would benefit from the creation of large public databases to foster the development of AI, ensuring algorithmic transparency and liability with the support of a standing audit body (Bunz & Janciute, 2018).

These reflections take place in a global context in which digital tools have progressively moved from being complementary instruments in informing and shaping public opinion to be part of a more segmented and on-demand communication scheme. Citizens being treated as a homogenised mass have given way to a more differentiated and individualised approach. Based on large data analysis, computer systems have acquired new skills and can now perform tasks that previously required human intelligence, from image and speech recognition to automatic and immediate translation of languages. Advanced computational communication techniques combine the use of bots, AI systems, artificial agents with social intelligence and the so-called affective computing. Some examples of cutting-edge experiments with systems that learn how sentiments are articulated have been already implemented in diverse areas, such as brand management, film reviews, financial market analysis or homeland security (Ahmad, 2011). Key developments are based on monitoring big data, including biological data—through brain scans, portable biosensors, eye tracking or facial analyses—to adapt messages to the behaviour of citizens and to better understand their potential consequences and further repercussions.

Parliament has also undergone further digital reinforcement triggered by the coronavirus (COVID-19) outbreak, which was declared a global pandemic by the World Health Organization on 11 March 2020. This situation brought significant technical, political and procedural challenges for parliaments worldwide that led to rethinking parliamentary activities under urgent and unexpected conditions. To respond to this new reality, parliaments moved some procedures online and adapted legislative instruments to comply with social distancing and restrictions placed on physical access to their premises. Suitable digital solutions were then needed to make a parliament work remotely. Those parliaments with cloud-based back-office tools enabled staff members to continue core operations from home, while at the same time some parliaments (e.g. Spain, Brazil, Norway or Finland) amended their regulation to allow for remote sittings (Williamson, 2020). Among the adaptation of parliamentary procedures and practices, virtual meetings, remote committees or online engagement sessions with petitioners were implemented, for instance, in the UK Parliament. Representational activities of individual parliamentarians were also affected, as observed in Canada, which then required more time and attention towards direct COVID-19-related service to constituents. This meant, in practice, interesting learning experiences involving the use of new media that shaped parliamentarians' representational behaviours to be more flexible and responsive to the changing demands posed by the pandemic (Koop et al., 2020).

In most cases, the result of such additional upheaval to the operation of the institution has been the emergence of a hybrid parliament form, combining elements of both physical and virtual parliament, like in Ireland (Murphy, 2020). It is still too early to determine how efficient such a new hybrid manner of conducting parliamentary affairs may be in many aspects. Negotiations or critical decisions might lose some effectiveness when done remotely. Despite this, it has been considered that virtual parliamentary functioning may reduce major barriers to involvement in political life and could mean a considerable step for gender equality and greater diversity in representation in the future (Pankhurst, 2020). However, other factors beyond technology use, such as discrepancies in terms of status relationships or caring roles, for instance, would indicate that political representation is strongly linked to structural conditions that perpetuate social inequalities and gender imbalances. In general terms, the promotion of flexible work practices to respond to changing needs and accommodate diverse personal situations has been associated with a predominantly positive view of remote working to date. Even so, important challenges for the well-being of remote workers remain, depending on virtual work characteristics, levels of social support or a series of individual differences that make teleworking not necessarily suitable for all (Wang et al., 2021). Further exploration of mixed working formulas could be then considered in post-pandemic scenarios.

It is yet unclear whether a semi-virtual parliament will stay or if some elements will be preserved for certain circumstances (Whale, 2020). Nevertheless, this hybrid nature seems to already be influencing the culture embedded in the parliamentary institution and expanding its digital technological capabilities. In line with this, parliaments face a series of challenges regarding, on the one hand, the security in the access and use of the systems by all members of parliament, including advisers and supporting staff, and, on the other hand, the veracity of the process through transparent and auditable mechanisms (Williamson, 2020). For these goals, it seems that previous parliaments' investment in innovation and digital infrastructure over the last ten years facilitated the adaptation to the new context caused by the pandemic. The long-term effects of the COVID-19 pandemic upon public institutions and society are still undetermined. It may contribute to exacerbating some underlying tensions between the multi-dimensions and roles of parliaments (Malloy, 2020), but this corona crisis may yet be an incentive to embrace technological approaches and develop a culture of experimentation (Van Lier, 2020).

3 Final Remarks

Over the last 30 years, parliaments' digital communication has undergone a constant transformation driven by intertwined technological advancement and societal developments that seem to act like push and pull forces. Cumulative technological innovation has promoted changes in how parliaments develop their functions and carry out their activities. The incorporation of new digital tools, ranging from Web 1.0 applications in the 1990s to AI and machine learning in the 2020s, has been primarily intended to further improve the efficiency of internal parliamentary processes. It has been also suggested that the parliaments that encouraged technological efforts have then adapted to incoming challenges and unexpected conditions more easily. Technology has come to pervade many aspects in parliaments' evolution, including their external communication to the public.

Both parliamentary institutions and individual parliamentarians have experimented with new digital formats available in each decade—email and website, blog and social media, open data and open platforms—which have contributed to shaping parliaments' public engagement over time. These sets of tools have been used in the first place for unidirectional outreach work to facilitate better understanding of parliamentary procedures or to disseminate parliamentary information to society. Additionally, digital instruments and online communication have facilitated progressive steps into more interactive exchanges with the outside world through debates with virtual communities or the integration of different fora for public participation (e.g. learning programmes, workshops, e-petitions, public committees or parliamentary apps).

These transformations have not been registered in isolation in the parliamentary institution, but they have simultaneously affected how grassroots citizens and social groups became involved in different forms of democratic engagement. The possibilities of channelling the representation function through digital means inspired general demands for representatives' responsiveness, institutional transparency and availability of parliamentary data. Complementary moves by social media users and technology activists sought to enhance monitoring capacities for civic oversight in connection with the parliamentary duty of accountability. This also led to some initiatives to encourage citizens to participate in parliamentary processes that motivated parliaments to introduce new interaction mechanisms.

This continuous reshaping of parliamentary-society interconnections takes place in volatile contexts where increasingly complex societies become more difficult to represent. Traditional forms of representation and accountability show some signs of wear concurrently with the spread of feelings of individual indifference, disinterest, disengagement or political apathy. Distributed forms of digital communication emerge and the use of social media seems to play an important role in citizens' confidence in political institutions. Expected leading strategies in parliaments' public engagement may also generate some tension between participatory initiatives and representative democracy due to the limited number of participants. Moreover, advancement in transparency and accountability does not necessarily imply improvements in public understanding of parliament, public participation or increased public trust (Hazell et al., 2012). Further experimentation and creative responses, including the combination of online and offline settings in hybrid parliamentary forms, would be encouraged to continue exploring possibilities for parliaments' digital communication in the coming decades.

References

Ackley, K. (2019). Confused by Congress' bills? Maybe AI can help. Retrieved from: https://www.rollcall.com/news/congress/congress-artificial-intelligence-clerk

Ahmad, K. (2011). *Affective computing and sentiment analysis. Emotion, metaphor and terminology*. Springer.

Asher, M., Leston-Bandeira, C., & Spaiser, V. (2019). Do parliamentary debates of e-petitions enhance public engagement with parliament? An analysis of Twitter conversations. *Policy and Internet, 11*, 149–171. Retrieved from: https://doi.org/10.1002/poi3.194

Baack, S. (2015). Datafication and empowerment: How the open data movement re-articulates notions of democracy, participation, and journalism. *Big Data and Society, 2*(2). Retrieved from: https://doi.org/10.1177/2053951715594634

Barker, R. (2007). Democratic legitimation: What is it, who wants it, and why? In A. Hurrelmann, S. Schneider, & J. Steffek (Eds.), *Legitimacy in an age of global politics* (pp. 19–34). Palgrave Macmillan.

Beetham, D. (2006). *El parlamento y la democracia en el siglo veintiuno. Una guía de buenas prácticas.* Unión Interparlamentaria. Retrieved from: http://www.ipu.org/pdf/publications/democracy_sp.pdf

Bouchard, N. (2016). The dark side of public participation: Participative processes that legitimize elected officials' values. *Canadian Public Administration, 59*(4), 516–537.

Bunz, M., & Janciute, L. (2018). *Artificial intelligence and the Internet of Things: UK policy opportunities and challenges* (Policy Briefs, 2). Communications and Media Research Institute, University of Westminster.

Chadwick, A. (2009). Web 2.0: New challenges for the study of e-democracy in an era of informational exuberance. *A Journal of Law and Policy for the Information Society, 5*(1), 9–41.

Chen, K. (2015). Prosumption: From parasitic to prefigurative. *The Sociological Quarterly, 56*(3), 446–459. Retrieved from: https://doi.org/10.1111/tsq.12103

Dai, X. (2007). Prospects and concerns of e-democracy at the European Parliament. *The Journal of Legislative Studies, 13*(3), 370–387. Retrieved from: https://doi.org/10.1080/13572330701500789

Dommett, K., & Temple, L. (2018). Digital campaigning: The rise of Facebook and satellite campaigns. *Parliamentary Affairs, 71*(1.1), 189–202. Retrieved from: https://doi.org/10.1093/pa/gsx056

Esteve del Valle, M., & Borge Bravo, R. (2018). Echo chambers in parliamentary Twitter networks: The Catalan case. *International Journal of Communication, 12*, 1715–1735.

Esteve del Valle M., Broersma M., & Ponsioen A. (2021). Political interaction beyond party lines: Communication ties and party polarization in parliamentary Twitter networks. *Social Science Computer Review*, First Published February. Retrieved from: https://doi.org/10.1177/0894439320987569

Faria, C., & Rehbein M. (2016). Open parliament policy applied to the Brazilian Chamber of Deputies, *The Journal of Legislative Studies, 22*(4): 559–578. Retrieved from: https://doi.org/10.1080/13572334.2016.1235333

Furst, K. (2018). Why the legislative and election process needs artificial intelligence. Retrieved from: https://ai-supremacy.com/news/2018/10/7/why-the-legislative-and-election-process-needs-artificial-intelligence

Gibson, R. (2013). Party change, social media and the rise of 'citizen-initiated' campaigning. *Party Politics, 21*, 183–196.

Hazell, R., Bourke, G., & Worthy, B. (2012). Open House? Freedom of information and its impact on the UK Parliament. *Public Administration, 90*, 901–921. Retrieved from: https://doi.org/10.1111/j.1467-9299.2012.02024.x

Joseph, J. A. (2016). Building on the CPA benchmarks to establish a parliamentary accountability and management framework: The case of Canada. In M. O'Brien, R. Stapenhurst, & L. von Trapp (Eds.), *Benchmarking and self-assessment for Parliaments* (pp. 227–240). World Bank Group.

Kelly, R., & Bochel, C. (2018). *Parliament's engagement with the public*. Briefing Paper, 8279. House of Commons Library. Retrieved from: https://research-briefings.files.parliament.uk/documents/CBP-8279/CBP-8279.pdf

Koop, R., Blidook, K., & Fuga, L. A. (2020). Has the COVID-19 pandemic affected MPs' representational activities? *Canadian Journal of Political Science, Revue Canadienne de Science Politique, 53*(2), 287–291.

Leston-Bandeira, C. (2014). The pursuit of legitimacy as a key driver for public engagement: The European Parliament case. *Parliamentary Affairs, 67*(2), 415–436. Retrieved from: https://doi.org/10.1093/pa/gss050

Leston-Bandeira, C., & Thompson, L. (2018). *Exploring parliament*. Oxford University Press.

Lev-On, A., Sabag Ben-Porat, C., & Lehman-Wilzig, S. (2017). A Facebook post is born: Exploring the process of generating MPs' social media presence. *The Journal of Legislative Studies, 23*(4), 549–565. Retrieved from: https://doi.org/10.1080/13572334.2017.1394738

Malloy, J. (2020). The adaptation of parliament's multiple roles to COVID-19. *Canadian Journal of Political Science, Revue Canadienne de Science Politique, 53*(2), 305–309. Retrieved from: https://doi.org/10.1017/S0008423920000426

Mehr, H. (2017). *Artificial intelligence for citizen services and government*. Ash Center for Democratic Governance and Innovation, Harvard Kennedy School. Retrieved from: https://ash.harvard.edu/files/ash/files/artificial_intelligence_for_citizen_services.pdf

Mevdic, S. (2011). Campaign management and organization. The use and impact of information and communication technology. In S. Mevdic (Ed.), *New directions in campaign elections* (pp. 59–78). Routledge.

Murphy, M. C. (2020, July 9). Ireland's new Parliament: Political and physical change coincide amid COVID-19 crisis. *Hansard Society*. Retrieved from: https://www.hansardsociety.org.uk/blog/irelands-new-parliament-political-and-physical-change-coincide-amid-covid-19

Niebel, D., Kopp, G., & Beerfeltz, H. (2013). *Information and communications technology (ICT): Key technologies for sustainable development* (BMZ Strategic Paper, 2). Federal Ministry for Economic Cooperation and Development.

Norton, P. (2017). Speaking for parliament. *Parliamentary Affairs, 70*(2), 191–206. Retrieved from: https://doi.org/10.1093/pa/gsw031

Norton, P. (2019). Power behind the scenes: The importance of informal space in legislatures. *Parliamentary Affairs, 72*(2), 245–266. Retrieved from: https://doi.org/10.1093/pa/gsy018

Odeyemi, T., & Abioro, T. (2018). Digital technologies, online engagement and parliament-citizen relations in Nigeria and South Africa. In O. Fagbadebo & F. Ruffin (Eds.), *Perspectives on the legislature and the prospects of accountability in Nigeria and South Africa*. Springer.

Oni, S., Oni, A. A., Gberevbie, D. E., & Ayodele, O. T. (2021). E-parliament and constituency representation in Nigeria. *Cogent Arts and Humanities, 8*(1), 1878590.

Pankhurst, H. (2020, April 21). Zoom parliament: A huge step for gender equality and greater diversity. *The House*. Retrieved from: https://www.politicshome.com/thehouse/article/zoom-parliament-a-huge-step-for-gender-equality-and-greater-diversity

POST. (2019). *Research for parliament preparing for a changing world*. Parliamentary Office of Science and Technology. Retrieved from: https://researchbriefings.files.parliament.uk/documents/POST-PB-0033/POST-PB-0033.pdf

Ramos-Vielba, I., Gonzalo Rozas, M., & Campos-Domínguez, E. (Eds.). (2013). *Parlamentos abiertos a la sociedad. Participación y monitorización*. Fundación Ideas; Friedrich Ebert Stiftung-Madrid.

Reichstaedter, P., & Lanzerstorfer, R. (2019). Austria uses AI to keep MPs informed. Retrieved from: https://www.ipu.org/austria-uses-ai-keep-mps-informed

Saari, M. (2020). IR 4.0 in Parliament: Conceptualising the application of artificial intelligence and machine learning in the Parliament of Malaysia's parliamentary questions. *International Journal of Law Government and Communication, 5*(20), 124–137. Retrieved from: https://doi.org/10.35631/IJLGC.5200010

Scherpereel, J., Wohlgemuth, J., & Lievens, A. (2018). Does institutional setting affect legislators' use of Twitter? *Policy and Internet, 10*, 43–60.

Schwab, K., & Davis, N. (2018). *Shaping the future of the fourth industrial revolution*. World Economic Forum.

Schwanholz, J., Theiner, P., & Busch, A. (2017). The interactive parliament. Evolving use of digital media by national legislatures in the EU. In J. Brichzin, D. Krichewsky, L. Ringel, & J. Schank (Eds.), *Soziologie der Parlamente* (pp. 337–368). Springer.

Shirky, C. (2008). *Here comes everybody: The power of organizing without organizing*. Penguin Books.

Spierings, N., Jacobs, K., & Linders, N. (2019). Keeping an eye on the people: Who has access to MPs on Twitter? *Social Science Computer Review, 37*(2), 160–177.

Tripathi, K. (2018). AI push: Parliament, assemblies to use artificial intelligence and machine learning under E-Vidhan project. Retrieved from: https://www.financialexpress.com/india-news/ai-push-parliament-assemblies-to-use-artificial-intelligence-and-machine-learning-under-e-vidhan-project/1426380/

Vaccari, C., & Valerini, A. (2016). Party campaigners or citizen campaigners? How social media deepen and broaden party-related engagement. *International Journal of Press/Politics, 21*, 294–312.

Van Dijck, J. (2014). Datafication, dataism and dataveillance: Big Data between scientific paradigm and ideology. *Surveillance and Society, 12*(2), 197–208.

Van Dijk, T. A. (2014). *Discourse and knowledge: A sociocognitive approach*. Cambridge University Press.

Van Lier, F. A. (2020, May 12). Towards virtual parliaments? *Open Democracy*. Retrieved from: https://www.opendemocracy.net/en/can-europe-make-it/towards-virtual-parliaments/

Wang, B., Liu, Y., Qian, J., & Parker, S. K. (2021). Achieving effective remote working during the COVID-19 pandemic: A work design perspective. *Applied Psychology, 70*(1), 16–59.

Whale, S. (2020, April 23). Is the 'hybrid' parliament here to stay? *The House*. Retrieved from: https://www.politicshome.com/thehouse/article/is-the-hybrid-parliament-here-to-stay

Williamson, A. (2020, April 8). How are parliaments responding to the Coronavirus pandemic? *Hansard Society*. Retrieved from: https://www.hansardsociety.org.uk/blog/how-are-parliaments-responding-to-the-coronavirus-pandemic

Williamson, A., & Fallon, F. (2011). Transforming the future parliament through the effective use of digital media. *Parliamentary Affairs, 64*(4), 781–792. Retrieved from: https://doi.org/10.1093/pa/gsr028

Zafra, R. (2017). *El entusiasmo. Precariedad y trabajo creativo en la era digital*. Anagrama.

CHAPTER 3

Political Communication Evolution in the Digital Hybrid Media System: Innovation and Experimentation as Strategies Towards a New Paradigm

Ainara Larrondo-Ureta and Koldobika Meso-Ayerdi

1 Introduction

Nowadays, societies have at their disposal multiple media possibilities, mainly derived from the technological advances of the last few decades, hence, the clear "mediatisation" of politics. Since the arrival of the Internet as the fourth great media platform, politics has become hyper-visible, generating a sensation of greater knowledge of, or proximity to political organisations and public institutions, a transparency that is open to being exploited, above all in electioneering terms.

A. Larrondo-Ureta (✉) • K. Meso-Ayerdi
Universidad del País Vasco/Euskal Herriko Unibertsitatea, Leioa, Spain
e-mail: ainara.larrondo@ehu.eus; koldo.meso@ehu.eus

B. García-Orosa (ed.), *Digital Political Communication Strategies*, The Palgrave Macmillan Series in International Political Communication, https://doi.org/10.1007/978-3-030-81568-4_3

Throughout its history, politics has gone through continual adaptations derived from its presence in different media and channels that have influenced its communication, from written, visual, sound and audiovisual channels to digital online channels (websites, social media, etc.) (Shah et al., 2015). On these channels, political communication has explored new narratives that influence the social perception of contemporary politics. Indeed, whilst politics and political communication are two epistemologically different fields, it is a fact that politics is developed and defined to a large extent via mediated communication. As a matter of fact, it is important to highlight that current political communication has its own place in a multiple communicative scenario, a media system defined as "hybrid" (Chadwick, 2013; Kalsnes et al., 2017).

In this introduction, it is also important to draw attention to other factors that have contributed to the evolution of the traditional political paradigm or of the pre-Internet phase. Among these, the so-called affective turn (Arias, 2016) has been decisive. It refers to the influence that emotions and feelings have on the paradigm of the social sciences, one of which is political communication. It is true that the combination of digital communicative strategies and affective strategies has proved successful in recent political initiatives that have now become paradigmatic examples of effective communication management in the post-modern context (Casero-Ripollés et al., 2016). Analysis has shown that traditional political parties have fewer flexible structures and discourses that are not spontaneous, which, ideologies aside, make these organisations seem more distant, above all among young people.

It is worth remembering that online political communication has important consequences for political action, above and beyond the changes in the methods and forms of communicating. Firstly, this type of political communication provides the media with greater power and a greater control of the message. After all, digital communication resources (websites, social media, etc.) allow political organisations and their leaders to communicate directly with the public, without the mediation of the mainstream media. The traditional rules that governed the politician-journalist-citizen relationship have become outmoded (Casero-Ripollés et al., 2016). Secondly, this same change of "media regime" (Delli-Caprini & Williams, 2011) means that politics is up against the empowerment that the same platforms or networks give to the connected public so they can "monitor" the system (Gutiérrez-Rubí, 2011: 2014). This has taken shape within a context of crisis in public confidence towards leaders and their organisations, which, over the last decade, has led to a proliferation of civic forms of communication that also call for political action in a more visible and powerful way (Sampedro, 2012), but using other styles and resources that are fresher and more spontaneous (WhatsApp, videoblogs, viral videos, memes, etc.). The issues covered by political discourse are thus being conditioned, to a large extent, by the digital political conversation (Stromer-Galley & Wichowski, 2011; Wright, 2011), and political parties try, paradoxically, to make their leaders appear less political (Ornstein & Mann, 2000).

The impact of digital activism has led organisations to even simulate citizen participation in order to boost support of the party's principles and arguments, for example via the recruitment of "digital activists" who help to build a better image of the party on social media (García-Orosa et al., 2017).

In short, the Internet has proved to be the ideal place for citizen participation, an area in which political parties and institutions have lost the privilege of political action (Krueger, 2006: 760), which implies the development of an even more efficient communication if that is possible. This efficiency is now understood in other terms, as a consequence of the difficult demarcation between emitters (the media, political parties and the general public) and receivers (the public and political parties), between facts and opinions, between public and private and between information and entertainment. The need to expand in an area of information overload and crossed messages is added to the need to provide an outlet for different interpersonal and mass communication options, which, far from substituting each other, coexist and complement each other.

With this aim in mind, over the last decade, political parties have opted for integrated communication plans that regard different online actions in an increasingly synergic manner. Likewise, it is also important to add to these changes the trend of promoting a more personal and affective discourse (Delli-Caprini & Williams, 2011).

2 The Digital Political Message

Whilst the changes undergone by political communication cannot be reduced to a mere change in the form of the political message, it is true that the manner of conceiving these messages and transmitting them to the public via different platforms and different communicative modalities (websites, channels 2.0, apps, storytelling, transmedia, etc.) is an essential aspect to be taken into account when analysing the evolution of political communication up to the present day (Larrondo, 2017).

On the other hand, while analysis of the communicative dimension of political parties has been largely confined to its development in specific electoral contexts in which communication is based on clear political marketing strategies, it is true that political parties are living a permanent campaign since their arrival on the Internet. This initial institutional foray by political communication into the digital environment took place in the early and mid-1990s, starting with the development of organisational or corporate websites. Later, coinciding with the start of a new century, other channels and media arrived, characterised by their social nature, the so-called platforms 2.0 among which can be found formats such as the blog and the videoblog, podcasts, video browsers (YouTube), social aggregators, social media (Facebook) and the microblogging platforms (Twitter), to which other more recent social media have been added (Instagram, TikTok, etc.), and instant messaging services or channels known as OTT (over-the-top) (WhatsApp and Telegram). Since their emergence in the first decade of 2000, social media have played an important role in political communication strategy (Maarek, 2014; Kalnes, 2009). They increase the visibility of political parties and their candidates and contribute to generating a bidirectional communicative process that modifies the participative flow, making them especially useful channels for reaching specific groups of voters (Woolley & Howard, 2016).

Similarly, some organisations have developed specific online versions (apps) for mobile devices (Gutiérrez-Rubí, 2015). A recent example is that of America First, the official party app of the candidate to the 2020 US presidential election, Donald Trump, launched to campaign on his behalf (latest news, events register, crowdfunding, story shares and experiences, etc.).

Whilst the website has been considered an autonomous communication space, political communication on social media is still dependent on the messages distributed via other channels. In fact, it has been shown that the digital strategy seeks, above all, to spread the party message among the highest number of channels in order to prolong its impact and circulation. This is important because, while the arrival of the Internet and the development of the website forced political communication departments at that time to adapt, these changes did not produce a great transformation in their usual methods and routines. On the other hand, social media have brought with them changes in form and substance, which is why the challenges arising in the shadow of the evolution of the Internet from 1.0 to 2.0 are the most relevant for research and practice in this field.

In this sense, an exploitation has begun of the trends in the social media context, such as the personalisation and emotionalisation of leaders' messages or experimentation of the storytelling technique. More specifically, political parties have begun to experiment with the so-called transmedia political narrative (TPN) (D'Adamo & García-Beaudoux, 2016). This has nothing to do with the usual combination of different offline and online closed messages that produce distinguished narratives such as multi-platform or cross-media. Transmedia narratives adopt the storytelling format and are eminently interactive, being based on the concept of the "open message" and so are accepting social media—mainly Twitter—as their main propagation channel.

This means that these narratives move away from the ideal of absolute control of the political message and its impact (García-Orosa et al., 2017). It also means that they are appropriate for putting into practice tendencies such as the emotionalisation and personalisation of the political message (Bennet, 2012). As with cross-media narratives, transmedia narratives can also make use of different offline and online channels, but with the aim of providing different content in each one which is complemented with that on the other channels. This results in a unitary account made up of multiple parts among which there is continuity or some kind of nexus, a dynamic which the connected public adds to with all kinds of contributions (comments, tweets, re-tweets, likes, etc.). Although there are notable examples that value the interest and usefulness of TPNs, these have not achieved a total expansion as yet due to their complexity; thus, existing developments are of special interest, as shall be seen later.

In the last few years, political communication has wanted to go further, also experimenting with other advanced forms, such as transmedia or immersive narratives, and the communicative products based on *big data*, "an extremely rich informative source for the planning of strategies with personalised messages and channels" (Campos-Domínguez & García-Orosa, 2018). The use of big data proved to be one of the main innovations in the US campaign of 2016, thanks to Cambridge Analytica, a company steeped in controversy due to its fraudulent use of Facebook user data.

3 The Digital Office

With the arrival of the Internet at the beginning of the 1990s, the traditional offices of political organisations became online offices directed at the media, thanks to the development of organisational websites. While initially these websites repeated the textual, visual and sound message of offline formats (press conferences and dossiers, etc.) over time, they began to adapt these messages starting from the use of communicative elements specific to the digital environment, taking advantage of the resource of hyper-textuality via the use of links, the combined use of text, video, audio and so forth (multi-mediality), and resources for dialogue with the audience—chats, forums, comments, direct messages and more.

Beyond serving as mere shop windows, these websites began to take on all the functions of a communication department, giving greater autonomy to political parties and generating a change in their role of journalistic source and, in general, in the relationship with journalists. The development of the so-called Virtual Press Rooms (VPRs) contributed to this (García-Orosa, 2009). These rooms include high-quality images, raw footage videos so that journalists can edit them, voice recordings and an archive of all press releases. Together with other less-specific spaces aimed at a more general audience, Virtual Press Rooms are designed so that journalists can find specific material. In fact, VPRs usually integrate videos of virtual press conferences, both live and recorded.

Coinciding with the arrival of the new century, this evolution has led to the creation of online departments aimed at the community, characterised by their participative nature and for the development of different kinds of spaces to meet users. Proof of this evolution is the migration of the press office towards what is now known as the *social media newsroom* (SMNR). This confirms that the routines of the communication departments are adapting not only to attract journalists and find a space in the media but also to capture the interest of the general public.

Analysis of organisational websites has proved to be an empirical procedure, useful for inferring the communicative usages that political parties make of new technologies on a daily basis (De Landtsheer, 2012; Gibson & Ward, 2000) and also in the context of e-campaigns, as is shown in the extensive international comparative study coordinated by Steven Ward et al. (2008). These usages are related to design (usability and accessibility), content form (hyper-textuality and multi-mediality), quality (updating, search engine type services, newspaper archive, etc.) and interactivity (communicative exchange, email, social media, etc.). These usages may be grouped into three parameters or dimensions that describe the primary functions of political websites, which has allowed us to discover whether or not said functions are fulfilled and to what extent (Larrondo, 2017):

Communication: a dimension referring to those resources that provide information and opinion with a journalistic end, whether it be in textual, visual, audio-visual, sound or multimedia format, together with those resources that contribute to the usability of the website (browsability and usability).

Mobilisation: a dimension relating to all those resources used by the website to mobilise the public or encourage them to actively participate in the party and its activities, and so a considerable part of these resources could be considered propagandistic.

Interaction: a dimension linked to all the options that allow the user to interact, according to three basic options of interactivity: selective, communicative and productive. This last dimension derives from the necessary consideration of organisational websites as something more than mere informative platforms for connecting with the audience and the general public, taking into account the existence of a new model of corporate communication that is eminently interactive and social—something extremely useful for achieving the communicative aims of political parties.

From the middle of the first decade of the 2000s, it can be seen that political parties begin to take online campaigning seriously, over and beyond websites, and we see politicians starting to use blogs, a tool which allows the greatest interaction with the audience and even creates a certain following or fidelity (Stanyer, 2006). These second-generation organisational websites give great importance to interaction with the public, although they continue to prioritise the informative and propagandistic function (Norris, 2003; Römmele, 2003; Gibson et al., 2003; Schweitzer, 2005).

In the last decade, we have been able to observe that the key in this scenario of unquestionable professional opportunities appears to be the *digital attitude*, that is, the positive predisposition in the face of continuous change and towards a growing sophistication. This has been achieved from development within communication departments of profiles specialised in usability and web design, in management of the relationship with the audience and in search engine optimisation and analytics and online reputation (Larrondo, 2017).

4 Towards a New Paradigm

Politics in social media reached its maximum expression during US president Barack Obama's 2008 electoral campaign, which stands out as the first to take full advantage of the resources available on the Internet 2.0 (Aaker & Chang, 2010). In fact, this successful campaign symbolised the growing interest on behalf of politicians in approaching a younger audience, revealing the possibility of introducing, for the first time in many years, profound structural changes in the communicative and promotional behaviour of political parties.

Recent studies have concluded that politicians opt for Twitter more than other social media, especially at particular points in the campaign (Enli & Skogerbø, 2013; Larsson & Moe, 2012; Pătruţ & Pătruţ, 2014; Vergeer, 2015; Larrondo, Pérez & Meso, 2016). From a general point of view, political leaders have accepted the need to build follower loyalty and generate engagement through constant updating and messages that add value to active audiences for different reasons (emotion, personalisation, social condemnation, etc.).

Similarly, interaction rates have improved in recent years and politicians are showing greater interest in re-tweeting and drawing third parties into the conversation. There is also a growing use of links, videos and hashtags. Despite everything, political representatives appear reluctant to use their profiles outside the programme or agenda marked by their party. One illustrative case in this sense is the scarce advantage taken of Twitter by the candidates in the 2016 elections to the Basque Parliament to personally defend those campaign issues linked to particularly sensitive subjects of interest to women, such as gender equality, the fight against sexist violence, the gender wage gap or the feminisation of poverty, among others (Larrondo et al., 2019).

More recently, the expansion of the social Internet via platforms such as Instagram or TikTok means that there are great possibilities for politics on social media, in demanding more than ever before a specific communicative strategy, because simply 'being' is no longer the most relevant thing. No political party is considering excluding these new forms of communication from their political strategy, in order to establish links with their supporters and generate complicity that could materialise in the form of votes—a tendency that has been called into question by those who believe that the political use of social media should seek to give answers, create interest and debate about the issues and problems of public interest (Sweester & Lariscy, 2008).

In this sense, narrative techniques, such as storytelling or transmedia political narratives, are more proximate to the desired aim of listening, compared with other spokesperson practices or traditional narrative techniques. In fact, transmediality is directly connected to the recognition that political parties dedicate, a priori, to those who listen to their political messages: If the listener or receiver should be at the centre of communicative strategy design, the best way of giving them importance is by recognising them and giving them greater presence and responsibility in the political story.

The efficacy of storytelling as a communication technique lies in its capacity for attracting the attention and interest of the audience to the story and what it says. From a cognitive viewpoint, human beings tend to pay more attention to, understand better and remember more effectively, information or explanations that have a narrative format (D'Adamo & García-Beaudoux, 2016).

Messages created with this technique are characterised for presenting specific stories with a beginning, middle and end structure. These stories tend to use analogy to convey more visually the idea being transmitted. They can also raise conflicts or questions to awaken curiosity and interest right to the end of the story, where a moral is usually presented. But perhaps the most relevant aspect of storytelling is that these stories are created to activate emotions, usually positive ones (joy and hope), in order to motivate and incite action or performance (Hyvärinen, 2008).

One of the first significant changes in the type of storytelling used by political parties is that of personalising the message. Rather than the parties, it was the main political leaders who began with this tendency of taking centre stage in the messages constructed by the organisations (Gutiérrez-Rubí, 2015).

Storytelling is most at home during electoral campaigns. Previous contributions about storytelling and the feminisation of politics reveal the intra-tensions that this technique can generate in the bosom of a political party, between the message that the candidate wishes to convey and that of the party, that of a brand weighed down with traditions and values (Larrondo & Orbegozo, 2019). The transmedia campaign Ezpain Gorrien Iraultza (The Red Lip Revolution, or RLR) may be a representative of this tendency. This campaign took place in the context of a regional election (the Basque Parliamentary Elections of 2016 in Spain) and was generated from a press article of the same name, later becoming the hashtag #EzpainGorrienIraultza on Twitter. Using a key symbol of the normative construction of femininity in popular culture—red lipstick and the act of putting it on—this transmedia storytelling made a contribution to understanding how women and egalitarian claims can intervene in masculinised and mediatized electoral spaces, transforming an area that has traditionally been one of clear male domination (Larrondo & Orbegozo, 2021).

The #EzpainGorrienIraultza conversation was created from the interventions of political parties, sympathisers, political representatives and citizens without links to any party. This narrative thus placed on the same level rhetorical subjects traditionally situated on different levels in the creation and receiving of messages: parties, spokespeople, the audience, the media, etc. In this sense, the RLR case symbolises a new way of thinking about political communication—that which truly gives a new role to the audience or the general public. Indeed, it participates in the creation of political meanings from more private perspectives, more personal and emotional viewpoints that later become common with other users, among which can be found the political leaders themselves (in this case the female politicians). The RLR case is also interesting as it shows how Twitter promotes collectivity and decentralises information flows that are difficult to control, influencing or even pressuring the traditional authorities and the communication strategies of political parties (Larrondo & Orbegozo, 2021).

In this review, another essential aspect of online politics nowadays is that relating to those actions derived from the use of big data. Political parties turn to Analytics Companies (SMA) that offer them data about user interaction on social media. This is an immense source of information with a huge potential for explaining collective action processes and, in general, social processes linked to politics that are important to political parties, including those which are most predictive, in this case from automated learning (AL) (Morales i Gras, 2020). Thus, new methods arise to measure the effects of political messages on social media, a field in which Campos-Domínguez and García-Orosa (2018) emphasise the importance of the use of algorithms and data as an element of analysis.

The so-called algorithmic communication already forms part of the strategy of every political party and becomes important with the automation of the production and circulation of political messages. In fact, together with the now habitual use of big data in campaign strategies in different political contexts and countries, including Spain (Dader &

Campos, 2017), companies contract analytics 2.0 services with the aim of obtaining the personal data of the electorate during the pre-campaign phase (Konitzer et al., 2019; Kreiss, 2016). This allows parties to segment their messages and establish political affinities among the public, which allows them to better take advantage of their political discourse. Likewise, the use of big data has been successful in the automated construction of information and opinion via computer programmes by parties and candidates. This type of action comes under the umbrella term 'robotic political communication' (Campos-Domínguez & García-Orosa, 2018; Kreiss & Jasinski, 2016; Innerarity & Colomina, 2020). The computational management of digital campaigns, like the 2008 US presidential campaign that took Barack Obama to victory, marked the starting signal for the growing use of this kind of strategy.

In this context, it is also worth drawing attention to *bots* or algorithms which, via artificial intelligence and *machine learning*, learn to simulate human behaviour (Hwang, 2017; Persily, 2017; Vosoughi et al., 2018). *Bots* are able to contribute not only to computational propaganda but also to the flow of misinformation on the Internet, and their electoral use complicates the work of campaign regulators as it is difficult to determine the identity of *bot* creators and sometimes impossible to decipher, even using sophisticated methods (Bradshaw & Howard, 2017).

The attention of the political parties is now focussed therefore on social media, which centres its efforts on behaviour metrics and algorithmic classification, using *bots* to segment the population and measure the state of opinion, together with tracking other parties or for sending personalised messages. These social *bots*—algorithms that automatically produce content and interact with humans on social media—seek to emulate and alter the behaviour of the general public (Ferrara et al., 2016).

Similarly, political entities launch *chatbots* as a tool that automatically interacts with the electorate with the aim of guiding them towards the desired action. Not only these virtual assistants are a tool for improving the quality of the public's political experience in relation to the parties and candidates, but they also afford a whole series of possibilities (Gutiérrez Rubí, 2018), such as providing information about the political and public agenda of the representatives, about the parliamentary agenda and legislative initiatives, about the electoral programme and so on.

5 Final Remarks

The capacity of media politics has increased exponentially and continues to have considerable communication power, but it struggles against the crisis of legitimacy in formal politics. New patterns arise within this political framework influenced by technoculture and by a new online sociability (Govil & Baishya, 2018).

All this has determined the evolution of mediated politics in the last decades, as we have attempted to show briefly in this chapter. We have made reference to successive adaptations in digital political communication and, above all, to the fundamental implications that these adaptations have brought to the manner of being and practising traditional politics; a politics that can still be felt in many current experiences of mediatized politics, even those considered to be very advanced or modern. But many of the new schemes developed by political communication under the protection of the Internet appear to be still under construction, as is the case with storytelling and transmedia narratives.

With every media and technological innovation, political communication has faced continuous challenges; after all it has only been in the last few years that we have been able to see more clearly how political parties are repeating the 'mantra' of innovation in their most recent campaigns. It can be seen that there is a zeal to use each new communicative technology and resource, provided that it is the newest in relation to previous campaigns which on many occasions leads political offices and those responsible for communication to focus their interest on the form rather than the substance. Facebook Live, mobile games, collaborative electoral spots, augmented reality, virtual reality and videos 360°, campaigns centred on data and microtargeting and more are realities which political communication analysts are already looking at in order to understand how political parties will react in response to the 'democratisation of the audience' in a regime of increasing "volatility" in every sense. All the signs suggest that they will do so with opportunism rather than strategy, in line with an increasingly less committed electorate, individuals who do not feel represented (Innerarity, 2018).

Political parties have begun to articulate messages aimed at mobilising this electorate and at replicating party discourse in an automated manner on a grand scale. Online political communication reveals a new dimension based on the use of big data, which helps to build predictive models of citizen behaviour that calculate the probability of one particular type of electorate supporting a specific candidate, voting for one party or supporting a certain programme (Howard et al., 2018).

Ultimately, the new paradigm of political communication faces the challenge of defying phenomena and scenarios which are uncertain for democracy (Bradshaw & Howard, 2018), by moving away from big data and robotic communication which are not transparent, as is the case with opportunistic automated information via algorithms which challenge truth and trust, especially in contexts of political communication (fake news, etc.).

References

Aaker, J., & Chang, V. (2010). Obama and the power of social media and technology. *The European Business Review*, 16–21.

Arias, M. (2016). *La democracia sentimental. Política y emociones en el siglo XXI*. Barcelona: Página Indómita.

Bennet, W. L. (2012). The personalization of politics: Political identity, social media, and changing patterns of participation. *The Annals of the American Academy of Political and Social Science, 644*(1), 20–39.

Bradshaw, S., & Howard, P. N. (2017). Troops, trolls and troublemakers: A global inventory of organized social media manipulation. *The Computational Propaganda Project*, 12.

Bradshaw, S., & Howard, P. N. (2018). Challenging truth and trust: A global inventory of organized social media manipulation. *The Computational Propaganda Project*, 1.

Campos-Domínguez, E., & García-Orosa, B. (2018). Comunicación algorítmica en los partidos políticos: automatización de producción y circulación de mensajes. *Profesional de la Información, 27*(4), 769–777.

Casero-Ripollés, A., Feenstra, R. A., & Tormey, S. (2016). Old and new media logics in an electoral campaign: The case of Podemos and the two-way street mediatization of politics. *The International Journal of Press/Politics, 21*(3), 378–397.

Chadwick, A. (2013). *The hybrid media system: Politics and power*. Oxford University Press.

D'Adamo, O., & García-Beaudoux, V. (2016). Comunicación Política: narración de historias, construcción de relatos políticos y persuasión. *Comunicación y Hombre, 12*, 23–39.

Dader, J. L., & Campos, E. (Coords.). (2017). *La búsqueda digital del voto. Cibercampaña electorales en España. 2015–16*. Tirant lo Blanch.

De Landtsheer, C. (2012). Towards a methodology for evaluating the quality of political websites. In *Democratic thought in the age of globalisation*. University Maria Curie Sklodowska Press.

Delli-Caprini, M., & Williams, B. A. (2011). *After broadcasting news*. Cambridge University Press.

Enli, G. S., & Skogerbø, E. (2013). Personalized campaigns in party-centred politics: Twitter and Facebook as arenas for political communication. *Information, Communication & Society, 16*(5), 757–774.

Ferrara, E., Varol, O., Davis, C., Menczer, F., & Flammini, A. (2016). The rise of social bots. *Communications of the ACM, 59*(7), 96–104.

García-Orosa, B. (2009). *Gabinetes de comunicación on line*. Comunicación Social.

García-Orosa, B., Vázquez-Sande, P., & López-García, X. (2017). La narrativa transmedia en los principales partidos políticos de España, Francia, Portugal y Estados Unidos. *El Profesional de la Información, 26*(4), 589–601.

Gibson, R. K., & Ward, S. (2000). A proposed methodology for studying the function and effectiveness of party and candidate websites. *Social Science Computer Review, 18*(3), 301–319.

Gibson, R. K., Margolis, M., Resnick, D., & Ward, S. J. (2003). Election campaigning on the WWW in the USA and UK: A comparative analysis. *Party Politics, 9*(1), 47–75.

Govil, N., & Baishya, A. K. (2018). The bully in the pulpit: Autocracy, digital social media, and right-wing populist technoculture. *Communication, Culture andCritique, 11*(1), 67–84.

Gutiérrez-Rubí, A. (2018). *"¿Asistentes virtuales también para partidos y políticos?"*. El País, February 26. Available at: https://elpais.com/politica/2018/02/26/micropolitica/1519636154_945042.html.

Gutiérrez-Rubí, A. I. (2011). *La política vigilada. La comunicación política en la era de Wikileaks*. UOC.

Gutiérrez-Rubí, A. I. (2015). *La transformación digital y móvil de la comunicación política*. Ariel.

Howard, P., Woolley, S., & Calo, R. (2018). Algorithms, bots, and political communication in the US 2016 election: The challenge of automated political communication for election law and administration. *Journal of Information Technology and Politics, 15*(2), 81–93.

Hwang, T. (2017). Rethinking countermeasures in the age of computational propaganda. In S. Powers & M. Kounalakis (Eds.), *Can public diplomacy survive the internet? Bots, echo chambers, and disinformation*. U.S. Advisory Commission on Public Diplomacy.

Hyvärinen, M. (2008). Analyzing narratives and story-telling. In P. Alasuutari, L. Bickman, J. Brannen, (Eds.), *The SAGE handbook of social research methods* (pp. 447–460) SAGE.

Innerarity, D. (2018). *El año de la volatilidad*. El País Opinión. Danielinnerarity.es.

Innerarity, D., & Colomina, C. (2020). La verdad en las democracias algorítmicas. *Revista CIDOB d'Afers Internacionals, 124*, 11–23.

Kalnes, Ø. (2009). E-ruptions in Party Politics? The case of Web 2.0 and Norwegian Parties. *Cuaderns del CAC, 33*, 63–76.

Kalsnes, B., Larsson, A. O., & Enli, G. S. (2017). The social media logic of political interaction: Exploring citizens' and politicians' relationship on Facebook and Twitter. *First Monday, 22*(2–6).

Konitzer, T., Rothschild, D., Shawndraw, H., & Kenneth, C. W. (2019). Using big data and algorithms to determine the effect of geographically targeted advertising on vote intention: Evidence from the 2012 U.S. presidential election. *Political Communication, 36*(1), 1–16.

Kreiss, D. (2016). *Prototype politics: Technology-intensive campaigning and the data of democracy*. Oxford University Press.

Kreiss, D., & Jasinski, C. H. (2016). The tech industry meets presidential politics: Explaining the democratic party's technological advantage in electoral campaigning, 2004–2012. *Political Communication, 33*(4), 544–562.

Krueger, B. S. (2006). A comparison of conventional and Internet political mobilization. *American Politics Research, 34*(6), 759–776.

Larrondo, A. (2017). Regional parties' web strategies in the age of virtual dialogue and closeness. *Electronic Government. An International Journal, 13*(3), 183–199.

Larrondo, A., & Orbegozo, J. (2019). The feminization of politics and its influence on organizational communication strategy. A case study. In I. Ruiz-Mora, G. Gonçalves, & I. Somerville (Eds.), *Organisational and strategic communication research global trends* (pp. 199–222). Labcom.

Larrondo, A., & Orbegozo, J. (2021). Hashtivism's potentials for mainstreaming feminism in politics: The Red Lips Revolution transmedia narrative. *Feminist Media Studies*, online preprint.

Larrondo, A., Pérez, J., & Meso, K. (2016). How effective is the online political communication? Analysis of the Basque political parties' interaction network in Twitter. *Textual & Visual Media, 9*, 37–54.

Larrondo, A., Peña, S., & Orbegozo, J. (2019). Palabra de candidata. La limitada influencia del género en el discurso electoral en Twitter. *Comunicación y Medios*, 40.

Larsson, A. O., & Moe, H. (2012). Studying political microblogging: Twitter users in the 2010 Swedish election campaign. *New Media & Society, 14*(5), 729–747.

Maarek, P. (2014). Politics 2.0: New forms of digital political marketing and political communication. *Trípodos, 34*, 13–22.

Morales i Gras, J. (2020). Cognitive biases in link sharing behavior and how to get rid of them: Evidence from the 2019 Spanish general election Twitter conversation. *Social Media + Society, 6*(2).

Norris, P. (2003). Preaching to the converted?: Pluralism, participation and party websites. *Party Politics*, 9–21.

Ornstein, N. J., & Mann, T. E. (2000). *The permanent campaign and its future.* American Enterprise Institute Press.

Pătruţ, B., & Pătruţ, M. (Eds.). (2014). *Social media in politics. Case studies on the political power of social media* (pp. 63–80). Springer.

Persily, N. (2017). Can democracy survive the internet? *The Journal of Democracy, 28*(2), 63–75.

Römmele, A. (2003). Political parties, party communication and new information and communication technologies. *Party Politics, 9*(1), 7–20.

Sampedro, V. (2012). New trends and challenges in political communication. *International Journal of Press/Politics, 16*(4), 431–439.

Schweitzer, E. J. (2005). Election campaigning online: German party websites in the 2002 national elections. *European Journal of Communication, 20*(3), 327–351.

Shah, D., Culver, K. B., Hanna, A., Macafee, T., & Yang, J. (2015). Computational approaches to online political expression: Rediscovering a science of the social. In S. Coleman & Freelon, D. (Eds.), *Handbook of digital politics* (pp. 281–305) Edward Elgar Publishing.

Stanyer, J. (2006). Online campaign communication and the phenomenon of blogging. *Aslib Proceedings: New Information Perspectives, 58*(5), 404–415.

Stromer-Galley, J., & Wichowski, A. (2011). Political discussion online. In M. Consalvo & C. Ess (Eds.), *The handbook of Internet studies* (pp. 168–187). Blackwell Publishing.

Sweester, Kay D. & Lariscy, Ruthann W. (2008). Candidates make good friends: An analysis of candidates' uses of facebook. *International Journal of Strategic Communication, 2*(3), 175–198.

Vergeer, M. (2015). Twitter and political campaigning. *Sociology Compass, 9*(9), 745–760.

Vosoughi, S., Roy, D., & Aral, S. (2018). The spread of true and false news online. *Science, 359*, 1146–1151. https://doi.org/10.1126/science.aap9559

Ward, S., Owen, D., Davis, R., & Taras, D. (Eds.). (2008). *Making a difference: A comparative view of the role of the Internet in election politics.* Lexington Books.

Woolley, S. C., & Howard, P. N. (2016). Political communication, computational propaganda, and autonomous agents. *International Journal of Communication, 10*, 4882–4890.

Wright, S. (2011). Politics as usual? Revolution, normalization and a new agenda for online deliberation. *New Media & Society, 14*(2), 244–261.

CHAPTER 4

Political Journalism in Digital Native Media

Xosé López-García, João Canavilhas, María-Cruz Negreira-Rey, and Jorge Vázquez-Herrero

1 Introduction

At the beginning of the third decade of the millennium, the transformation of the communicative ecosystem in the digital era has created a scenario for technologically mediated communication where media and digital platforms have positioned themselves as indispensable intermediaries of a growing number of human practices (Casero-Ripollés, 2020a), generating a platformisation of society (van Dijck et al., 2018). Platforms occupy a central place due to their distributed nature and being intertwined with institutions, markets and technologies (de Reuver et al., 2018), while the media struggles to maintain its relevant role by offering information of public interest through both those that have migrated to

X. López-García (✉) • M.-C. Negreira-Rey • J. Vázquez-Herrero
University of Santiago de Compostela, Santiago de Compostela, Spain
e-mail: xose.lopez.garcia@usc.es; cruz.negreira@usc.es; Jorge.vazquez@usc.es

J. Canavilhas
Universidade da Beira Interior, Covilhã, Portugal

B. García-Orosa (ed.), *Digital Political Communication Strategies*, The Palgrave Macmillan Series in International Political Communication, https://doi.org/10.1007/978-3-030-81568-4_4

the new digital scenario (Boczkowski, 2004) and the new media, which was conceived and designed for the network society (Nossek & Adoni, 2017).

Contemporary societies are characterised by a very intense mediatisation in which all performances in our social world are closely related to digital media and the underlying structures (Couldry & Hepp, 2017). In a scenario of ubiquitous mediations (Aguado, 2020), media have become omnipresent, shaping the entire scope of social domains and playing a fundamental role in the transformation of culture and society (Casero-Ripollés, 2020a). In recent years, algorithms and automation have also become ubiquitous (Thurman et al., 2019), creating new complexities and challenges for technologically mediated communication and journalism.

Digital journalism—in this context of communicative ubiquity and the rise of misinformation (Tandoc et al., 2019)—seeks to settle its role after more than 27 years, after being constituted as a scientific discipline and shaping a field in constant growth (Salaverría, 2019). Journalism and media are undergoing a radical change due to the disruptive processes of technology and global uncertainty—caused by the 2008 financial crisis (Pavlik, 2013) and, later, by the effects of the COVID-19 pandemic with an ambivalent impact (Casero-Ripollés, 2020b)—and both play an important role for democracy and the existence of an informed citizenry (Olsen et al., 2020).

2 Digital Native Media and Political Journalism

The emergence of new actors on the periphery of journalism (Tandoc, 2019), who are already in the journalistic field with their own voice (Hermida & Young, 2019), and of new journalistic actors who exist hand-in-hand with digital native media and explore renewed territories (García-Orosa et al., 2020), has expanded the journalistic offer in the digital scenario in recent years. Over the years, digital native media have not only become a flourishing phenomenon worldwide (Salaverría, 2020), but a good number of the journalistic projects that are contemplated for the immediate future are framed in this category of new media, understood as an alternative media ecosystem to the traditional one, which innovates, uses new narrative formats, and has a new relationship with the audience (Cabrera-Méndez et al., 2019).

This diversity of digital media models, which many citizens use as a platform to coordinate and mobilise (Gil de Zúñiga & Chen, 2019), has become a referent of political life for many citizens who access content to inform themselves through different devices and channels in a mobile society scenario (Westlund & Färdigh, 2015). Although digital communication transformations have affected the relationship between society, journalism and politics in different contexts in various ways and intensities (Jebril et al., 2020), the fact remains that journalists continue to exercise important roles in everyday and political life (Hanitzsch & Vos, 2018). Hence, the importance gained not only by legacy media, which continue to have an important influence, but also by digital natives doing political reporting.

The incorporation of current technologies into journalistic practices in digital media has opened new dimensions for political information (Humprecht & Esser, 2018). At the same time that traditional media has adapted to the new environment, new digital native media initiatives have emerged that bet on regeneration through models of political-economic self-sufficiency and citizen patronage (Osuna-Fernández, 2017). The transformations, in both journalism and politics, and their mutual links have motivated new research questions (Waisbord, 2012) and have placed the new media, which face renewed challenges in the field of information, in a new social, political and economic context. The abundance of information has shown that it also generates instabilities, conflicts and contradictions in the political scenario and that a greater quantity is not necessarily equal to a greater quality (Casero-Ripollés, 2018).

In this scenario, new political media has evolved rapidly over the last three decades and continues to provide novel forms (Owen, 2018). New native headers of political information have also appeared. The consolidation of *Mediapart* (France) or *Politico* (United States) demonstrated the viability of a new avenue for political information from digital native media in the context of new initiatives (Nielsen, 2016). But these were not the only cases as—in times of real-time journalism—analytical and slow journalism defined its space (Le Masurier, 2015) and enriched the field of quality and political journalism in the network society. In fact, there are currently a large number of digital native media that renew narratives and intervene in the political field, some with state and/or global vocation and others from the hyperlocal field—attached to proximity to intervene in the social and political field—which is now a trend in the digital society.

From the political field, research is redefined as the keys to rethink the public sphere altered by digital changes (Bennett & Pfetsch, 2018). Meanwhile, in a necessary challenge to better understand the network society, digital native media intervene in the public space with narrative proposals developed with current technologies, some more disruptive than others. Journalism from digital native media is expanding despite the crisis (Negredo et al., 2020), and from them come proposals for political and social journalism, as well as dynamics of communicative intervention in proximity spaces. In addition, they do so through multimedia and interactive narratives, with the participation of the audiences (Peters & Witschge, 2015), which results in constant renewal and innovative proposals. These emerging forms show that there are renewed ways for the work of journalists to remain relevant to people's lives (Deuze, 2019).

3 Mobile Devices as a Disruptive Element

News media plays a fundamental role because it informs citizens, providing them with the necessary knowledge to evaluate political proposals and make decisions that are of common interest (Strömbäck, 2005). The higher the penetration rate of the media, the greater is the impact of its messages on the community.

In this context, mobile phones have gained a central place in contemporary society by becoming the public's preferred medium for receiving news (Walker, 2019). Therefore, journalism for this type of device is the one that has grown the fastest (Perreault & Stanfield, 2019), with authors arguing that digital journalism is becoming mobile (Bui & Moran, 2020).

This success is justified not only by the characteristics of the mobile medium itself, such as portability, ubiquity and permanent connection to the Internet (Aguado & Martínez, 2006), among others, but also because the media bet on 'push news' to keep their consumers linked (Wheatley & Ferrer-Conill, 2020), something valued in the fast-paced society in which we live today.

Through news apps or web browsing, news consumption on mobile devices facilitates new ways for citizens to engage in politics (Martin, 2015) by enabling newsgathering and discussion on issues of public interest (Lee et al., 2014), which reinforces the importance of smartphones in the relationship of citizens with political journalism.

Moreover, these devices also allow users to become actively involved in their mission of reporting to authorities or providing information to journalists, reinforcing their role as watchdogs (Hellmueller et al., 2016). As devices that always accompany their user (Gant & Kiesler, 2001) and have powerful multimedia capabilities, smartphones have empowered citizens by allowing them to take geolocated photos and videos and send them directly to the authorities or to the news media. As the first case, the BOS:311 app in Boston is one of the many examples of the potential of these devices as an instrument of citizenship by allowing citizens to report anomalies to the mayor's office. The second case is TIMBY, a platform that brings together activists, journalists and other professionals in a joint mission to give visibility to issues that were not reaching public opinion. In this platform, the reporter app is fundamental in the collection of information coming from various unofficial sources, including citizens. Both cases are examples of how mobile phones have changed the journalistic ecosystem.

4 Democracy and Social Involvement from the Hyperlocal Space

Proximity spaces remain fundamental in linking citizens with local authorities, and they are also the place where community actors connect for social action. Although the conception and dimension of the local have evolved with lifestyles and the functioning of the economy or politics (Nielsen, 2015), media of proximity maintains its role in satisfying the right to information of small social groups, contributing to preserving and developing the identity of their communities or favouring social cohesion (Camponez, 2002; Leupold et al., 2018).

Since the first decade of the 2000s, hyperlocal media has proliferated in various countries and media contexts (Harte et al., 2018; Gulyas & Baines, 2020) and has renewed local media ecosystems. Such media is characterised by covering the smallest geographic and social areas (Radcliffe, 2012), their community orientation, and their informative purpose of occupying spaces forgotten by the mainstream media (Metzgar et al., 2011). Moreover, hyperlocal media includes news projects that have discovered the possibility in the network of developing their activity at a lower cost, which has favoured many of them becoming digital natives (Metzgar et al., 2011).

The growth of hyperlocal media at the international level occurs as a reaction to the crisis of the traditional media model and the closure of numerous local newspapers (Franklin, 2006). The crisis of local journalism raises concerns about its possible consequences on the democratic development of local communities, which suffer in the absence of quality local information (Wahl-Jorgensen, 2019). Even if the rise of hyperlocal media helps to reverse the expansion of media deserts (Bucay et al., 2017), Nygren et al. (2018) assert that it is difficult to assess whether such growth compensates—in terms of its democratic role—the crisis of traditional local media. Although hyperlocal media gives voice to the community and acts as a platform for social cohesion and action, its limited human and economic resources may hinder its role as a watchdog for power.

Local media combines its informative mission with a series of functions at the social level. Firmstone (2016) points out that local media must provide citizens with attractive and sufficient information to motivate them to become involved in the issues affecting their city. In fulfilling their democratic role, the author also indicates that they should take an active role in social campaigns, represent all the points of view of those involved in the information, monitor power and publish content produced by citizens. On the other hand, Barnett and Townend (2015) indicate that hyperlocal media also represents citizens and promotes public interest campaigns to call for political intervention. However, the studies conducted to date on the coverage and promotion of these social campaigns reflect a disparate degree of involvement among the media (Barnett & Townend, 2015; Williams et al., 2015), conditioned in turn by their funding models (Harlow & Chadha, 2018).

In the development of their daily activity, hyperlocal media professionals interact with other 'superior' actors in the community, such as other local and regional media or the local government. The political power often sees hyperlocal media as unreliable, critical and negative for the community (Radcliffe, 2012). Despite this, such media is seen by governors as an information service that fills a social need (Carson et al., 2016) and helps to move their discourse (Chen et al., 2017).

The news agendas of the hyperlocal media tend to be dominated by social issues and topics of interest for the community's day-to-day life. Nevertheless, local political information continues to occupy a more or less relevant space. Kerkhoven and Bakker (2014) reveal that the most frequently recurring topic in hyperlocal digital media in the Netherlands is politics, followed by events, human and social stories, economy, culture and sport. Leckner et al. (2019) identify news about local activities, culture, entertainment and municipal politics as the most common across

Swedish hyperlocals. D'Heer and Paulussen (2013) point out that news about events, social and cultural activities, sports and education are the most frequently occurring based on a case study of a Belgian hyperlocal, highlighting that political and economic information barely represents 2% of the total.

Research on Spanish local and hyperlocal digital media (Negreira-Rey, 2020) shows that the priority topics on their agendas are social, cultural, sports, political and town planning issues. The promoters of these media outlets explain that political issues lose weight in the face of human stories, but they provide assurances that politics still retains an important place when it relates to the local level and directly affects the community. This informative position is also reflected in the sources that are most frequently cited in the news. Among the hyperlocal digital media, sources belonging to associations or social entities predominate, as well as those referring to individual citizens. However, in local digital media outlets—which are more attached to institutions and municipal governments—official sources—mostly belonging to the local government—tend to predominate.

5 Multimedia Storytelling, Politics and Social Change

Narrative through new media responds to people's need to expand knowledge about themselves and to collectively reimagine who they can become (Murray, 2017). The role of storytelling in society plays a significant role in deepening our understanding and representation of the world. With the acquisition of characteristics specific to the digital medium, narrative formats have evolved towards hyper-textuality, multi-mediality and interactivity, consolidating as current forms of storytelling (George-Palilonis, 2012; Jacobson et al., 2016). Several dimensions of digital journalism have been favoured, such as long-form journalism (Lassila-Merisalo, 2014), transmedia journalism (Moloney, 2011), immersive journalism (Uskali et al., 2020), as well as complex formats such as interactive documentary (Aston et al., 2017) and newsgames (Bogost et al., 2012).

These projects require up-to-date and specialised professional skills, as well as a strong commitment to innovation. Several digital native media have experimented with interactive multimedia formats as part of a strategic line of innovation. In *El Confidencial* (Spain), they have a media lab—ElConfidencial.LAB—where one of the objectives is the exploration of new products, formats and services, transferring the innovative spirit through processes that affect all areas of the organisation. One of the most outstanding works in recent years, dealing with a topic closely related to politics, is *El bueno, el malo y el tesorero* [The Good, the Bad and the Treasurer]. This newsgame deals with corruption by placing the user in the role of a treasurer of a city council. Through decision-making, affected by various parameters and contextualised with information, the user experiences different corruption practices deeply instilled in the political system and increasingly known. From the United States, *Politico* stands out for the publication of interactives—generally data visualisations—on topics such as elections or political journalism investigations. Digital native media such as *Observador* (Portugal) and *Mediapart* (France) have a tradition in the development of special coverage and visual formats. Also *elDiario.es* (Spain) has several examples of long-form reportages and webdocs, such as *Detrás del paraíso* [Beyond the Paradise], which analyses the social reality behind major tourist destinations, or the journalistic investigation *Las muertes de Ceuta* [The Deaths of Ceuta].

The development of multimedia, interactive and immersive projects has an important experimental and innovative component that occasionally moves away from traditional models, driving a very significant creative climate in actors outside the conventional media system. Production from the periphery means abandoning centrality in terms of funding and moving away from the stigmas of the mainstream media (Irigaray, 2015). Diverse entities such as universities, NGOs and independent production companies—which in many cases promote joint collaborations—take part in the production. This independence offers a space for conversation and participation where users can intervene in matters of a public nature which, together with the characteristics of the digital media, allows collaborative and interactive construction.

The strategies for public involvement are diverse and, in some cases, even seek a connection with physical events and narrative expansion to the territory. Some outstanding cases are *Quipu*, *0 responsables* [0 Accountable], *Mujeres en venta* [Women for Sale] or *El feriante* [The Stallholder]. In these examples, the purpose was to open a debate and elicit a social and political change, involving the audience in the process. Social issues as a focus of attention and local scope converge to tell stories of proximity that transfer realities, needs, injustices and conflicts through the interactive documentary (Vázquez-Herrero & Moreno, 2017)—one of the formats with the greatest multimedia and interactive deployment in the media. Its characteristics—such as decision-making—drive the degree of audience involvement (Vázquez-Herrero et al., 2017): in denunciation, in uniting citizenship and in the construction of memory. Its impact has been studied not only from the perspective of citizen political participation (Cortés-Selva & Pérez-Escolar, 2016) but also from transmedia activism, as 'forms of action that interweave physical, mental or social participatory processes' (Ortuño & Villaplana, 2017, p. 140).

Interactive narratives are revealed as promoting forms of social change (Miller & Allor, 2016; Peralta & Ouariachi, 2015; Rose, 2017) and political involvement (Watson, 2017). Nash (2017) considers co-creation of a resource for citizens to exercise their political role, which is present in collaborative projects. Other authors highlight the potential of bringing together multiple voices (Dovey & Rose, 2012; Green et al., 2017). Patricio Irisarri, director of *El feriante*, states that the effects of the project were tangible in its social, cultural and political impact, and he adds that these narratives enable processes of political intervention (Vázquez Herrero, 2019). However, the steps taken by journalism in this field are still developing.

6 Conclusion

In the contemporary communication ecosystem, where the media struggles to maintain its role in society, new media and new ways of connecting journalism and politics have emerged. Both spheres, unquestionably linked by the role of journalism in democracy, are continuously subject to change and influenced by factors such as misinformation, self-communication and platformisation.

Technological development and crises create a situation conducive to the emergence of digital native media and peripheral actors. In the new models of digital journalism, political information retains a leading role, with outstanding examples in the international arena that focus on it as an activity that affects society.

Particularly relevant is the role played by local and hyperlocal media in bringing political life closer to citizens. The sense of community in small areas forgotten by the mainstream media turns the hyperlocal media into custodians of the democratic role and promoters of political intervention at the closest level to the citizen.

Political journalism is not left out of the trends, such as the popularisation of the smartphone as the main device for information consumption. This forces the media to make strategic decisions to direct its production towards the mobile, through websites, apps, notifications and social networks.

With regard to narratives, digital native media explores new ways to convey political issues to the audience, favouring their involvement through interactive, immersive and gamified formats. However, productions of great interest are identified, due to their collaborative and transmedia nature, which are born from other organisations.

Political journalism is developed in digital native media and through current forms of journalism in order to build bridges between citizens and government institutions. In a context marked by the rise of new platforms, the mobile scenario and misinformation, journalistic actors cannot remain on the side lines of the debates but exercise their role with the greatest effort and adaptation to the current communicative context.

Acknowledgements This research has been developed within the research project 'Digital Native Media in Spain: Storytelling Formats and Mobile Strategy' (RTI2018–093346-B-C33), funded by the Ministry of Science, Innovation and Universities (Government of Spain) and the ERDF structural fund.

References

Aguado, J. M. (2020). *Mediaciones ubicuas: Ecosistema móvil, gestión de identidad y nuevo espacio público.* Gedisa.

Aguado, J. M., & Martínez, I. J. (2006). El proceso de mediatización de la telefonía móvil: de la interacción al consumo cultural. *Zer, 11*(20), 319–343.

Aston, J., Gaudenzi, S., & Rose, M. (2017). *i-Docs: The evolving practices of interactive documentary.* Columbia University Press.

Barnett, S., & Townend, J. (2015). Plurality, policy and the local. Can hyperlocals fill the gap? *Journalism Practice, 9*(3), 332–349. https://doi.org/10.1080/17512786.2014.943930

Bennett, W. L., & Pfetsch, B. (2018). Rethinking political communication in a time of disrupted public spheres. *Journal of Communication, 68*(2), 243–253. https://doi.org/10.1093/joc/jqx017

Boczkowski, P. J. (2004). *Digitizing the news. Innovation in online newspapers.* The MIT Press.

Bogost, I., Ferrari, S., & Schweizer, B. (2012). *Newsgames. Journalism at play.* The MIT Press.

Bucay, Y., Elliott, V., Kamin, J., & Park, A. (2017). America's growing news deserts. *Columbia Journalism Review*.

Bui, M., & Moran, R. (2020). Making the 21st century mobile journalist: Examining definitions and conceptualizations of mobility and mobile journalism within journalism education. *Digital Journalism, 8*(1), 145–163. https://doi.org/10.1080/21670811.2019.1664926

Cabrera-Méndez, M., Codina, L., & Salaverría-Aliaga, R. (2019). What is new media? The views of 70 Hispanic experts. *Revista Latina de Comunicación Social, 74*, 1506–1520. https://doi.org/10.4185/RLCS-2019-1396-79en

Camponez, C. (2002). *Jornalismo de Proximidade*. Minerva Coimbra.

Carson, A., Muller, D., Martin, J., & Simons, M. (2016). A new symbiosis? Opportunities and challenges to hyperlocal journalism in the digital age. *Media International Australia, 161*(1), 132–146. https://doi.org/10.1177/1329878X16648390

Casero-Ripollés, A. (2018). Research on political information and social media: Key points and challenges for the future. *El profesional de la información, 27*(5), 964–974. https://doi.org/10.3145/epi.2018.sep.01

Casero-Ripollés, A. (2020a). Journalism and Media: A new journal to expand knowledge in a dynamic field. *Journalism and Media, 1*(1), 177–178. https://doi.org/10.3390/journalmedia1010012

Casero-Ripollés, A. (2020b). La Covid-19 en el periodismo: um impacto ambivalente. *RAE-IC, 7*(14), 2–26. https://doi.org/10.24137/raeic.7.14.1

Chen, N. N., Ognyanova, K., Zhang, C., Wang, C., Ball-Rokeach, S., & Parks, M. (2017). Causing ripples in power relations. The meso-level influence of a hyperlocal news website. *Journalism Studies, 18*(6), 710–731. https://doi.org/10.1080/1461670X.2015.1078738

Cortés-Selva, L., & Pérez-Escolar, M. (2016). Civic participation and interactive documentaries: A contribution to the open government model. *El profesional de la información, 25*(4), 578–587. https://doi.org/10.3145/epi.2016.jul.07

Couldry, N., & Hepp, A. (2017). *The mediated construction of reality*. Polity Press.

D'heer, E., & Paulussen, S. (2013). The use of citizen journalism for hyperlocal news production. *Recherches en Communication, 39*, 151–164.

de Reuver, M., Sørensen, C., & Basole, R. C. (2018). The digital platform: A research agenda. *Journal of Information Technology, 33*(2), 124–135. https://doi.org/10.1057/s41265-016-0033-3

Deuze, M. (2019). What journalism is (not). *Social Media + Society, 5*(3). https://doi.org/10.1177/2056305119857202

Dovey, J., & Rose, M. (2012). We're happy and we know it: Documentary, data, montage. *Studies in Documentary Film, 6*(2), 159–173. https://doi.org/10.1386/sdf.6.2.159-1

Firmstone, J. (2016). Mapping changes in local news. *Journalism Practice, 10*(7), 928–938. https://doi.org/10.1080/17512786.2016.1165136

Franklin, B. (2006). *Local journalism and local media. Making the local news.* Routledge. https://doi.org/10.4324/9780203969205

Gant, D., & Kiesler, S. (2001). Blurring the boundaries: Cell phones, mobility, and the line between work and personal life. In B. Brown, N. Green, & R. Harper (Eds.), *Wireless world: Social and interactional aspects of the mobile age* (pp. 121–131). Springer-Verlag.

García-Orosa, B., López-García, X., & Vázquez-Herrero, J. (2020). Journalism in digital native media. Beyond technological determinism. *Media and Communication, 8*(2), 5–15. https://doi.org/10.17645/mac.v8i2.2702

George-Palilonis, J. (2012). *The multimedia journalist. Storytelling for today's media landscape.* Oxford University Press.

Gil de Zúñiga, H., & Chen, H.-T. (2019). Digital media and politics: Effects of the great information and communication divides. *Journal of Broadcasting & Electronic Media, 63*(3), 365–373. https://doi.org/10.1080/08838151.2019.1662019

Green, D. P., Bowen, S., Hook, J., & Wright, P. (2017). Enabling polyvocality in interactive documentaries through "structural participation". In G. Mark & S. Fussell (Eds.), *Proceedings of the 2017 CHI conference on human factors in computing systems* (pp. 6317–6329). ACM. https://doi.org/10.1145/3025453.3025606

Gulyas, Á., & Baines, D. (2020). *The Routledge companion to local media and journalism.* Routledge.

Hanitzsch, T., & Vos, T. P. (2018). Journalism beyond democracy: A new look into journalistic roles in political and everyday life. *Journalism, 19*(2), 146–164. https://doi.org/10.1177/1464884916673386

Harlow, S., & Chadha, M. (2018). Looking for community in community news: An examination of public-spirited content in online news sites. *Journalism.* https://doi.org/10.1177/1464884918805255

Harte, D., Howells, R., & Williams, A. (2018). *Hyperlocal journalism: The decline of local newspapers and the rise of online community news.* Routledge.

Hellmueller, L., Mellado, C., Blumell, L., & Huemmer, J. (2016). The contextualization of the watchdog and civic journalistic roles: Reevaluating journalistic role performance in U.S. newspapers. *Palabra Clave, 19*(4), 1072–1100. https://doi.org/10.5294/pacla.2016.19.4.6

Hermida, A., & Young, M. L. (2019). From peripheral to integral? A digital-born journalism not for profit in a time of crises. *Media and Communication, 7*(4), 92–102. https://doi.org/10.17645/mac.v7i4.2269

Humprecht, E., & Esser, F. (2018). Mapping digital journalism: Comparing 48 news websites from six countries. *Journalism, 19*(4), 500–518. https://doi.org/10.1177/1464884916667872

Irigaray, F. (2015). Navegación territorial: entramado narrativo urbano. In F. Irigaray & A. Lovato (Eds.), *Producciones transmedia de no ficción. Análisis, experiencias y tecnologías.* UNR Editora.

Jacobson, S., Marino, J., & Gutsche, R. E. (2016). The digital animation of literary journalism. *Journalism, 17*(4), 527–546. https://doi.org/10.1177/1464884914568079

Jebril, N., Jukes, S., Iordanidou, S., & Takas, E. (2020). *Journalism, society, and politics in the digital media era*. Intellect.

Kerkhoven, M., & Bakker, P. (2014). The hyperlocal in practice: Innovation, creativity and diversity. *Digital Journalism, 2*(3), 296–309. https://doi.org/10.1080/21670811.2014.900236

Lassila-Merisalo, M. (2014). Story first – Publishing narrative long-form journalism in digital environments. *Journal of Magazine & New Media Research, 15*(2), 1–15.

Le Masurier, M. (2015). What is slow journalism? *Journalism Practice, 9*(2), 138–152. https://doi.org/10.1080/17512786.2014.916471

Leckner, S., Tenor, C., & Nygren, G. (2019). What about the hyperlocals? The drivers, organization and economy of independent news media in Sweden. *Journalism Practice, 13*(1), 68–89. https://doi.org/10.1080/17512786.2017.1392254

Lee, H., Kwak, N., Campbell, S. W., & Ling, R. (2014). Mobile communication and political participation in South Korea: Examining the intersections between informational and relational uses. *Computers in Human Behavior, 38*, 85–92. https://doi.org/10.1016/j.chb.2014.05.017

Leupold, A., Klinger, U., & Jarren, O. (2018). Imagining the city: How local journalism depicts social cohesion. *Journalism Studies, 19*(7), 960–982. https://doi.org/10.1080/1461670X.2016.1245111

Martin, J. (2015). Mobile news use and participation in elections: A bridge for the democratic divide? *Mobile Media & Communication, 3*(2), 230–249. https://doi.org/10.1177/2050157914550664

Metzgar, E., Kurpius, D., & Rowley, K. (2011). Defining hyperlocal media: Proposing a framework for discussion. *New Media & Society, 13*(5), 772–787. https://doi.org/10.1177/1461444810385095

Miller, L., & Allor, M. (2016). Choreographies of collaboration: Social engagement in interactive documentaries. *Studies in Documentary Film, 10*(1), 53–70. https://doi.org/10.1080/17503280.2016.1171686

Moloney, K. T. (2011). *Porting transmedia storytelling to journalism* (MA thesis). University of Denver.

Murray, J. (2017). *Hamlet on the Holodeck*. The MIT Press.

Nash, K. (2017). i-Docs and the documentary tradition: Exploring questions of engagement. In J. Aston, S. Gaudenzi, & M. Rose (Eds.), *i-Docs: The evolving practices of interactive documentary* (pp. 9–25). Columbia University Press.

Negredo, S., Martínez-Costa, M. P., Breiner, J., & Salaverría, R. (2020). Journalism expands in spite of the crisis: Digital-native news media in Spain. *Media and Communication, 8*(2), 73–85. https://doi.org/10.17645/mac.v8i2.2738

Negreira-Rey, M. C. (2020). *Cibermedios locais e hiperlocais en España: mapa, modelos e produción informativa* (PhD dissertation). Universidade de Santiago de Compostela.

Nielsen, R. K. (2015). Introduction: The uncertain future of local journalism. In R. K. Nielsen (Ed.), *Local journalism. The decline of newspapers and the rise of digital media* (pp. 1–25). I.B. Tauris, Reuters Institute for the Study of Journalism, University of Oxford.

Nielsen, R. K. (2016). The business of news. In T. Witschge, C. W. Anderson, D. Domingo, & A. Hermida (Eds.), *The Sage handbook of digital journalism* (pp. 51–67). Sage.

Nossek, H., & Adoni, H. (2017). Coexistence of "old" and "new" news media in a transitional media system: News repertories in Israel. *Participations, 14*(2), 399–415.

Nygren, G., Leckner, S., & Tenor, C. (2018). Hyperlocals and legacy media. Media ecologies in transition. *Nordicom Review, 39*(1), 33–49. https://doi.org/10.1515/nor-2017-0419

Olsen, R. K., Pickard, V., & Westlund, O. (2020). Communal news work: Covid-19 calls for collective funding of journalism. *Digital Journalism, 8*(5), 673–680. https://doi.org/10.1080/21670811.2020.1763186

Ortuño, P., & Villaplana, V. (2017). Activismo transmedia. Narrativas de participación para el cambio social. *Obra Digital, 12*, 123–144.

Osuna-Fernández, C. M. (2017). *Periodismo de regeneración profesional en Internet: Alternativas de autosuficiencia económico-política y mecenazgo ciudadano* (PhD dissertation). Universidad Complutense de Madrid.

Owen, D. (2018). *The new media's role in politics.* BBVA OpenMind, Penguin Random House. Retrieved from https://www.bbvaopenmind.com/wp-content/uploads/2018/03/BBVA-OpenMind-Diana-Owen-The-New-Medias-Role-in-Politics.pdf

Pavlik, J. V. (2013). Innovation and the future of journalism. *Digital Journalism, 1*(2), 181–193. https://doi.org/10.1080/21670811.2012.756666

Peralta, L., & Ouariachi, T. (2015). The educational potential of the digital narratives in the communication for social change. Youth Against Climate Change as a case study. *Obra Digital, 8*, 40–61.

Perreault, G., & Stanfield, K. (2019). Mobile journalism as lifestyle journalism? *Journalism Practice, 13*(3), 331–348. https://doi.org/10.1080/17512786.2018.1424021

Peters, C., & Witschge, T. (2015). From grand narratives of democracy to small expectations of participation. *Journalism Practice, 9*(1), 19–34. https://doi.org/10.1080/17512786.2014.928455

Radcliffe, D. (2012). *Here and now: UK hyperlocal media today.* Nesta.

Rose, M. (2017). Not media about, but media with: Co-creation for activism. In J. Aston, S. Gaudenzi, & M. Rose (Eds.), *i-Docs: The evolving practices of interactive documentary* (pp. 49–65). Columbia University Press.

Salaverría, R. (2019). Digital journalism: 25 years of research. Review article. *El profesional de la información, 28*(1). https://doi.org/10.3145/epi.2019.ene.01
Salaverría, R. (2020). Exploring digital native news media. *Media and Communication, 8*(2), 1–4. https://doi.org/10.17645/mac.v8i2.3044
Strömbäck, J. (2005). Search of a standard: Four models of democracy and their normative implications for journalism. *Journalism Studies, 6*(3), 331–345. https://doi.org/10.1080/14616700500131950
Tandoc, E. C. (2019). Journalism at the periphery. *Media and Communication, 7*(4), 138–143. https://doi.org/10.17645/mac.v7i4.2626
Tandoc, E. C., Lim, D., & Ling, R. (2019). Diffusion of disinformation: How social media users respond to fake news and why. *Journalism, 21*(3), 381–398. https://doi.org/10.1177/1464884919868325
Thurman, N., Lewis, S., & Kunert, J. (2019). Algorithms, automation, and news. *Digital Journalism, 7*(8), 980–992. https://doi.org/10.1080/21670811.2019.1685395
Uskali, T., Gynnild, A., Jones, S., & Sirkkunen, E. (2020). *Immersive journalism as storytelling: Ethics, production, and design*. Routledge.
van Dijck, J., Poell, T., & de Waal, M. (2018). *The platform society: Public values in a connective world*. Oxford University Press.
Vázquez Herrero, J. (2019). *Narrativas digitales de no ficción interactiva: análisis de la experiencia del usuario* (PhD dissertation). Universidade de Santiago de Compostela.
Vázquez-Herrero, J., & Moreno, G. (2017). Documental interactivo iberoamericano: proximidad y transformación social. *Doc On-line, 2017SI*, 109–130. https://doi.org/10.20287/doc.esp17.dt05
Vázquez-Herrero, J., Negreira-Rey, M.-C., & Pereira-Fariña, X. (2017). Interactive documentary contributions to the renewal of journalistic narratives: Realities and challenges. *Revista Latina de Comunicación Social, 72*, 397–414. https://doi.org/10.4185/RLCS-2017-1171en
Wahl-Jorgensen, K. (2019). The challenge of local news provision. *Journalism, 20*(1), 163–166. https://doi.org/10.1177/1464884918809281
Waisbord, S. (2012). Repensar la agenda de investigación sobre periodismo y política en la academia globalizada. In S. Berrocal & E. Campos (Eds.), *La investigación en Periodismo político en el entorno de los nuevos medios de comunicación*. Sociedad Española de Periodística.
Walker, M. (2019). Americans favor mobile devices over desktops and laptops for getting news. *Pew Research Center*. Retrieved from https://www.pewresearch.org/fact-tank/2019/11/19/americans-favor-mobile-devices-over-desktops-and-laptops-for-getting-news/
Watson, R. (2017). Affective radicality: Prisons, Palestine, and interactive documentary. *Feminist Media Studies, 17*(4), 600–615. https://doi.org/10.1080/14680777.2017.1326560

Westlund, O., & Färdigh, M. A. (2015). Accessing the news in an age of mobile media: Tracing displacing and complementary effects of mobile news on newspapers and online news. *Mobile Media & Communication, 3*(1), 53–74. https://doi.org/10.1177/2050157914549039

Wheatley, D., & Ferrer-Conill, R. (2020). The temporal nature of mobile push notification alerts: A study of European news outlets' dissemination patterns. *Digital Journalism*. https://doi.org/10.1080/21670811.2020.1799425

Williams, A., Harte, D., & Turner, J. (2015). The value of UK hyperlocal community news: Findings from a content analysis, an online survey and interviews with producers. *Digital Journalism, 3*(5), 680–703. https://doi.org/10.1080/21670811.2014.965932

CHAPTER 5

Lobbies: The Hidden Side of Digital Politics

Antonio Castillo-Esparcia, Ana Almansa-Martínez, and Gisela Gonçalves

1 Introduction

Contemporary societies, characterized by their complexity, are shaped by numerous social interests that must be present in the political system (Almond, 1958; Burdeau, 1982). These interests are the expression of citizens' demands on public affairs, which must be addressed by those in power (Bentley, 1983; Berry, 1977). These are also translated into the political system through specialized organizations, which traditionally have consisted of political parties. But interests are also conveyed through lobbies, in the form of organizations that develop activities aimed at public authorities in order to influence decisions that affect their interests.

A. Castillo-Esparcia (✉) • A. Almansa-Martínez
University of Málaga, Málaga, Spain
e-mail: acastilloe@uma.es; anaalmansa@uma.es

G. Gonçalves
University of Beira Interior, Covilhã, Portugal
e-mail: gisela.goncalves@labcom.ubi.pt

B. García-Orosa (ed.), *Digital Political Communication Strategies*, The Palgrave Macmillan Series in International Political Communication, https://doi.org/10.1007/978-3-030-81568-4_5

In any social organization, pressure groups appear as an inseparable element of the political structure with a representation in the long and complex process of forming decisions, either by integrating the demands or by setting the hierarchy and the order of propositions or requests, which may be addressed in the political dialogue.

The starting point for the analysis of social groups and political life was the research conducted by Bentley, in his study of the different social manifestations. Thus, it included his famous statement that implies recognition of the significance of associations in contemporary societies:

> The main work while studying all forms of social life is the analysis of the groups, which can be classified in multiple manners. If only groups are defined properly, everything is already set. And when I say everything, I mean each and every one of the things. (1983: 256)

Regarding the concept of lobbying, the Venice Commission defines it as "the oral or written communication by private individuals or groups, each with varying and specific interests, with a public official to influence legislation, policy or administrative decisions" (CDL-AD, 2013.011-eReport on the Role of Extra-Institutional Actors in the Democratic System -Lobbying-. Adopted by the Venice Commission at its 94th Plenary Session, Venice, 8–9 March 2013).

The UK Parliament defines the lobby as "when an individual or a group tries to persuade someone in Parliament to support a particular policy or campaign. Lobbying can be done in person, by sending letters and emails or via social media".

For its part, the European Union, through its Transparency Register, defines lobbying as "any activity with the aim of directly or indirectly influencing the formulation or implementation of policies and decision-making processes".

2 Features of Lobbying

The key issues that a lobbyist must address have changed over time. This mutation directly relates to the exchange of techniques used by these agents of mediation. The so-called old lobby has been joined by the new lobby. While the former refers to bribery, corruption, etc., the latter emphasizes the action performed on public opinion. Nowadays, this shift has enabled "instrumental lobbyist", who besides being an expert in direct techniques of influencing public decision-makers, must also be knowledgeable in training or education of the public.

Routes of origin for professional lobbyists are diverse: a former Member of Parliament or Government, which has close relations to it, as the main shareholder or beneficiary, with private interests, employees of firms or managers of private associations, as well as advertising and public relations specialists, and lastly journalists.

However, experts point to different backgrounds for lobbyists (e.g., lawyers or PR firms), such as Berry (1989: 91–93), who emphasizes law firms and public relations offices. By contrast, Hrebenar and Scott (1990: 71–88) added former congressmen and members of the administration. Another source of lobbyists is through outgoing high-level government officials, who become part of business management or lawyer firms (the revolving door concept).

Good lobbyists should be able to run and demonstrate a range of features to complete their activity satisfactorily. All these actions and activities can be summarized in ten points, which express the main features of the job:

1. They must know how to advise, inspire, prepare, and coordinate the activities of organizations that represent groups in the different branches of government (legislative, executive, and judicial), as well as public-focused actions.
2. The relationship between the people who achieve the goals at work should be deep, friendly, private, and fruitful, especially with key players. They also must have a wide network of contacts at the highest levels.
3. The contacts that they maintain should be enabled throughout their activities in order to get quick and easy access.
4. They should be aware of and be able to communicate the views of supporters in the various processes at the most appropriate time, timely and accurately prepare more appropriate judgments, and get positively highlighted circumstances. They must always resort to the truth, because if the data and arguments are not valid, any further action will be doomed to failure.
5. They must be aware at all times and promptly apply judicious techniques as well as be ready to come up with, in any case, the optimal and appropriate solution.

6. They must be able to inspire and even produce a large number of petitions, letters, and messages that could reach public decision-makers, as well as being able to define the best moment to act (grassroots lobbying).
7. They should possess sufficient scholar knowledge to define appropriate advice on the amount and type of pressure exerted on a given political actor.
8. Their knowledge of public relations techniques, information, and advertising should be maximized in order to improve the image of supporters constituents. They must have easy access to means of communication that enable the publication of information favorable to most of the represented interests.
9. They should be inspiring for publications and information to lean toward the political actor they are lobbying for in the political process.
10. They should have the appropriate training and expert knowledge in organizing conferences, visits, and so on, of public figures and stakeholders, in order to obtain more information about them.

3 Lobbying and Political Action

A dual phenomenon is taking place, namely the stateisation of society and the socialization of the state, both elements that interact in a reciprocal manner. Thus, there is a growing presence of public authorities in the resolution of social issues and conflicts. Likewise, the state and its powers increasingly rely on the opinions of social organizations in order to be able to develop regulations as closely as possible to the social reality (Chalmers & Macedo, 2020; De Bruycker & Beyers, 2019).

Hence, many analysts point to a direct relationship between the increase in state participation in society and the growing presence of lobbies in public institutions (Grant, 1989; Gray & Lowery, 1993; McFarland, 1987). In this sense, Almond and Powell (1972: 19) pointed out the need to attribute greater complexity to the traditional model of public powers (legislative, executive, and judicial), adding other functions such as the articulation of interests and the aggregation of interests. For Easton (1965: 116), lobbies, like political parties, act as structural regulators on the volume of demands by selecting and modulating the numerous social demands that are addressed to the public authorities. This synthesis and homogenization make it possible to regulate the quantity of demands, rendering them acceptable in the eyes of the system.

The techniques used by lobbyists have been systematized by Ziegler and Dye (1990: 227–230) into four categories:

(a) Access to power, to communicate relevant information to public decision-makers. A fundamental requirement is to have open access to the political system. Law firms, PR, and consulting agencies offer connections and potential clients, thus becoming real companies that carry out lobbying activities without being considered de jure but de facto.
(b) Information. A good lobbyist knows the legislative process, is an expert in political debate, and provides information about the group's position in different situations. In order to be able to do their job, they have to know how to use the right language, know the relevant people, know how to deal with different issues, and so on.
(c) Grassroots mobilization through letters, messages, or phone calls from citizens to the relevant people, always under the appearance of being spontaneous.
(d) Grassroots support campaigns for all of the above actions and on all issues. This support is carried out with the intention of creating a public image favorable to groups or individuals or to create a concrete public demand.

For interest groups, it is essential to take part in public policy processes, although not all have the same capacity for access and action due to various factors (Gallagher Cunningham et al., 2017 and Klüver, 2013). If we look at this imbalance of lobbying forces, a series of values can be shown that strengthen these capabilities for political influence, such as:

(a) The ability to mobilize lobby supporters or members as a sign of social support in the context of public opinion, which has a relevant value in the democratic system. Thus, there are interest groups that mobilize their members through public demonstrations, support in the form of messages in different formats, explaining the number of followers or valuing the economic volume generated in the sector, among other things (Branton et al., 2015; Mergeai & Gilain, 2020; Rasmussen et al., 2018).

(b) The lobby's financial capacity allows it to carry out a set of activities that cannot be carried out by lobbies with scarce economic resources. Hence, business or employers' lobbies have greater resources than those that generate income from the volume of their membership, such as NGOs, consumer associations, professional associations, or trade unions. These resources, in turn, can be projected onto other capacities available to lobbies (Carty, 2010; Dempsey, 2009; Dür, 2008; Schnakenberg, 2017).

(c) Access to public authorities is essential to be able to engage in dialogue processes with decision-makers, as it is difficult to gain the support for a proposal just by handing over documentation or through grassroots campaigns. This capacity is part of the revolving door concept, since those who have been part of the public authorities maintain a network of contacts that allows them to interact more easily. Likewise, being aware of the gatekeepers in the administration or the legislature is essential to know who to act on, a responsibility that does not necessarily fall on the person with the highest hierarchical rank (Dür et al., 2015).

(d) Advocacy helps when there is a fit with social values, since it is easier for those in power to make decisions with social demands in line with what is acceptable to the population as a whole (Biliouri, 1999; Rasmussen et al., 2018).

(e) Having a favorable social image facilitates the lobby's work, as its proposals seem to have a higher level of legitimacy (Klüver et al., 2015; Lowery, 2013; Marshall, 2015; Rasmussen, 2015).

(f) Occupying a strategic space in society or in the economy also confers greater weight in dialogue processes. This would be the case of the role of the financial system in the economic system, which is realized in an expression widely used in European institutions, as "systemic elements", that is, underpinning the system.

In essence, lobbying is linked to the political culture of each society and is a reflection, to a certain extent, of its ability to structure and manage social demands toward the political system. Furthermore, based on the political organization in which the lobby carries out its activity, it is possible to plan activities and actions to influence different institutional players, such as:

(a) The government, since this is the institution with the initiative to propose legislation, because it has a considerable administrative structure and information
(b) The Parliament, because it is the body in which laws are discussed and approved, so lobbies must participate in the whole political process
(c) The judiciary, as it is the body that oversees the legality of regulations and is an area in which lobbies have an influence
(d) Political parties, as they are organizations that play a fundamental role in the political process

These actors are aware of how they can be influenced by lobbyists. Which of them acts on the other is something that depends on the organizational, legislative, cultural, and social contexts, so each lobbyist must be aware of these balances of power and influence those that are most operational and effective.

4 Lobbying and Communication

In its modern form, the political game is increasingly organized and structured, both by public opinion and by symbolic political struggle. The latter tends to cut down, significantly, to a public opinion battle. As the representatives of public opinion and advocates for society's claims, lobbyists seek to capture the intentions of the public in order to report them to public authorities.

One of the key points of political domination is based on the mainly symbolic mechanisms, since the most important political action is shown surreptitiously and overlappingly, as well as it mostly consists of the enforcement of the world rating systems.

This symbolic structuring has an impact on individual and collective ideologies and, specifically, on journalists and their companies, as entities that interact in a given social system, and therefore cannot be removed from it. In this sense, the abovementioned system influences perceptions and thoughts of individuals, including media professionals.

The communication flow that is established from the societal system toward political bodies has been defined by Meynaud (1962: 116–118) as the action carried out by pressure groups, which collect the information circulating in society and transmit it to political decision-makers. In this way, they integrate the aspirations of individuals who, without these organizations, would not have formal channels, political parties excluded, with dangerous consequences in the form of disorderly and violent petitions.

For a lobby, the communication strategy could focus on two different perspectives:

1. Proactive strategy, in which the lobby takes the initiative in the definition, elaboration, and approval of public policies, which allows it to raise flags and anticipate issues that may affect the interest group. Being able to raise issues that may affect the interests of the lobby facilitates the structuring of the issue, sets the conceptual boundaries of the discussion, and influences the approach to the solution (Carty, 2010; De Bruycker, 2016; Schnakenberg, 2017).
2. Reactive strategy, which is established through a passive action of the lobby, which is only put into action when a decision affecting the lobby's interests is being considered, discussed, or approved. This action does not allow solutions to be proposed, but it is based on defensive activity, which greatly reduces the lobby's scope for action (Chari & Hillebrand O'Donovan, 2011 and Rasmussen et al., 2018).

Currently, one of the most significant resources is actions on public opinion (grassroots mobilization). This technique has been widely studied in American political science, particularly since the emergence of the so-called new lobbying, as reflected in studies by Fowler and Shaiko (1987), and Whiteley and Winyard (1987). The set of strategies aimed at public opinion is structured into a series of functions:

1. To diffuse its deprecations, proposals, and demands over the citizens as a whole (diffusion function).
2. Mobilizing aspect on its adherents and supporters (mobilizing function).
3. Psychological variant in relation to its members, providing an image of psychological support. Thus, in a society of increasingly isolated individuals, the group followers have the image of belonging to an association that has a social presence, with the colligations manifesting themselves as welcoming instances for individuals (psychic cohesion function).

When we talk about the actions of lobbies, it is necessary to appeal to the strong presence of communication in their actions, because relations with public authorities involve information supply, the presence of deliberative bodies, and personal relations with those who participate in the process of discussing public policies. From the lobbies' perspective, their strategies fall into two main types: direct access to decision-makers (direct lobbying) or the creation of social mobilization campaigns in support of their demands (indirect lobbying).

Direct lobbying, understood as direct communication with politicians and public officials (either within or outside institutional premises) and which can take the form of:

1. Advice or presentations to officials, either on an ad hoc or on periodic basis
2. Providing draft reports to civil servants in which specific details of the policy itself are drafted
3. Seeking informal contacts with individual politicians or branches of civil society, including having simple telephone conversations with such staff
4. Formal or invited consultation through institutionalized channels
5. Participation in hearings, such as parliamentary committees
6. Participation in a delegation or conference
7. Requested, or unsolicited, information or documents sent to politicians and civil servants

Indirect or grassroots lobbying is one of the current trends in public affairs, in which a set of communication actions are produced on the political leader or officials, through presence in the media, by direct requests from citizens or by creating social media spaces. In its most benign form, this type of citizen participation can be enriching for citizens. However, this technique can also be more reprehensible when it becomes astroturfing, the controversial practice of lobbyists hiding behind front organizations to give the appearance of popular support for a cause that is in fact funded by private interests. The activities associated with these offline and online campaigns are as follows:

1. Direct online citizens' petitions
2. Letters to government or parliamentarians
3. Public debates
4. Leaflets and posters

5. Demonstrations, among other activities, in order to put pressure on politicians to listen to them
6. Use of related organizations such as advocacy associations
7. Use of other entities such as think tanks
8. Blogging
9. Cyber activists posting on social media

One of the essential aspects of lobbies in their public opinion–shaping activity is to present themselves to those in power as defenders of socially relevant demands and with the need to adopt political solutions. However, it should not be forgotten that it is necessary to perform audience management, as lobbying, being a communicative activity, must be aware of the channels and sources of information of those who must make the decision. In this sense, the results of the FleishmanHillard consultancy firm on the main information channels of European parliamentarians are relevant (Graph 5.1).

It is striking that search engines and online newspapers, along with European media and social media conversations are the most frequently used tools. In contrast, blogs and stakeholder websites, together with Wikipedia and stakeholder social media, are the least frequently used.

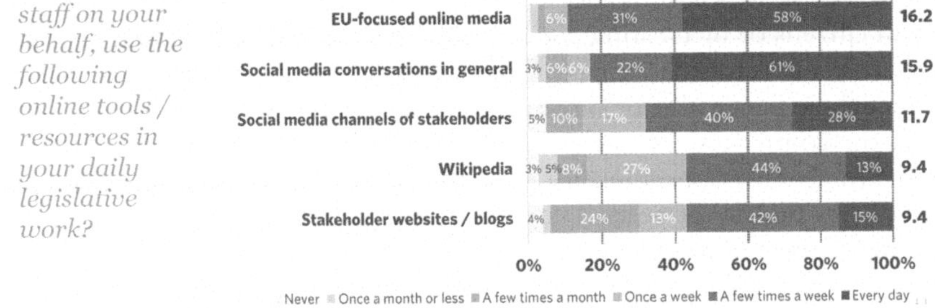

Graph 5.1 Search engines, newspapers, and EU and social media essential to legislative work. (Source: FleishmanHillard (2015): 3rd European Parliament Digital Trends Survey online, Brussels)

5 Lobbying in the European Union

The European Union has become a body in which the participation of lobbies has acquired significant relevance due to the generation of European regulations that directly and indirectly affect national policies. One consequence is the profusion of interest groups from European countries, but also from outside Europe, which try to influence the EU legislative process.

In order to regulate stakeholder participation, the Transparency Register was created. In 2011, both the European Parliament and the European Commission created their Transparency Register through an agreement between both institutions. This is a commitment that aims to establish a transparency framework in the relations between stakeholders and both institutions. In order to manage this Transparency Register, both the European Parliament and the European Commission created their own structure, called the Common Secretariat of the Transparency Register.

The original idea of the Transparency Register is that any organization or person whose purpose is to influence and participate in the processes and implementation of public policies of the European Union can participate in the whole process. By creating the Register, it is possible to know what kind of organizations want to participate, what interests they intend to defend or legitimize, which organizations participate in the defense of these interests and the economic and personal resources they have to carry out this representation activity. All organizations participating in the Register must adhere to a Code of Conduct. The creation of this Register allows for greater public scrutiny of the work of interest groups, as it enables the media, citizens, or any other actor in the European Union to be aware of the activities of interest groups and the influence they can have on the legislative and executive process of the European Union.

The evolution of the Transparency Register shows an upward curve, which shows the lobbies' interest in participating in EU policies (Graph 5.2).

Inclusion in the register entails a number of prerogatives for lobbyists. In the European Parliament, the advantages include access to the premises, speaking at public hearings of its committees, receiving notifications about committee activities, co-organizing events with Parliament's parties, among others. In the case of the Commission, you can have meetings with Commissioners, members of Cabinets and Directors-General; public

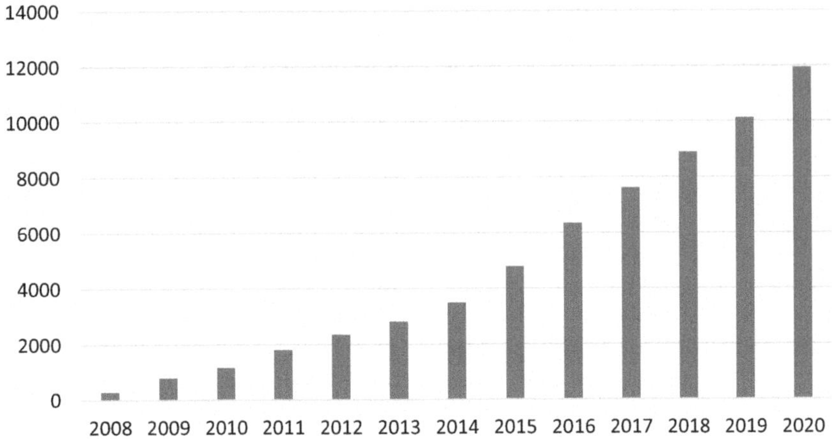

Graph 5.2 Evolution of the number of lobbies in the EU. (Source: Transparency Register (2020). Chart created for this study)

consultations (you receive automatic notification of consultations and roadmaps in the areas you have indicated); expert group (Register registration is required for the appointment of certain types of expert group members); contacts with officials, for a meeting or an event.

As an example of the transparency policy of the European Union and the importance it has for citizens and its own institutions, the Registry Secretariat offers information courses on how the Register works and the most relevant aspects of interest groups. Thus, within the European Parliament, 16 training sessions were held in 2019 for the Parliament's own staff with the title "Who are interest representatives? Introduction to the Transparency Register". Similarly, the European Commission has organized four training courses in 2019 for its own staff, under the title Dealing appropriately and effectively with interest representatives.

There have been numerous attempts to bring clarity to the actions of lobbies and recurring initiatives by the European institutions themselves or by independent bodies, such as Transparency International, which has carried out studies on the role of lobbies, as in the case of its 2015 report, entitled Lobbying in Europe: Hidden Influence, Privileged Access, in which it calls for a series of initiatives:

(a) Require public institutions and representatives to proactively record and publish information on their interactions with lobbyists, including summaries of meetings, calendars, agendas, and documentation received.
(b) Ensure that a "legislative footprint" is created for each proposal, in order to ensure full transparency of decision-making processes.
(c) Ensure that records apply to both direct and indirect lobbying efforts, targeting all institutions and individuals who play a role in public decisions.
(d) Introduce a legal obligation for public authorities to strive for a balanced composition of advisory and expert bodies, representing a diversity of interests and views.
(e) Hold open calls to constitute the advisory/expert groups and ensure that common selection criteria are used to balance different interests.
(f) Publish legislative footprints to track, in a uniform manner, contacts and input received on draft policies, laws, and amendments.
(g) Ensure greater transparency on the composition and activities of expert groups by publishing information on the selection process of members, as well as the publication of detailed meeting minutes.

The European institutions have produced initiatives to improve transparency for the lobbying work, which are based on two main principles:

1. The legislative footprint as a mechanism that focuses on the traceability of committee legislation in Parliament and consists of a mechanism in which it is possible to observe how a piece of legislation has been modified throughout the process and who has made these contributions. This mechanism provides clarity on the actors involved, how participation has taken place and the degree of co-creation in the policy decision.
2. The publication of public agendas makes it possible to know with whom official meetings are held by the members of the commission, an element that is already in place. In addition, some recommendations extend the mere listing of meetings to include information on the topics discussed, the documentation provided, and any agreements adopted through a meetings summary. The Commission has established that its members must make public information on the meetings they and members of their cabinets hold with lobbyists,

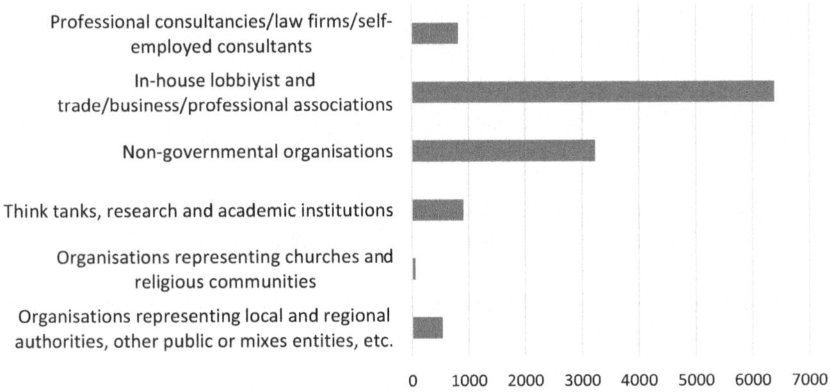

Graph 5.3 Typology of interest groups in the European Union. (Source: Transparency Register (2020). Chart created for this study)

providing information on the date of the meeting, the place where it is held, the name of the member of the Commission and/or cabinet member, the name of the organization or freelancer and the purpose of the meeting (Decision of 25 November 2014 on meetings held between members of the Commission and lobbyists) (Graph 5.3).

There are large differences in the number of lobbyists by sector. Undoubtedly, the largest group is in-house lobbyist and trade/business and professional association lobbyist, followed by nongovernmental organizations lobbyist. On the other hand, the smallest group is that of organizations lobbyist representing churches and religious communities (Graph 5.4).

Germany, France, and the UK (in the lead) together with the USA, the Netherlands, Italy, and Switzerland are the countries with the highest number of representatives. Spain, along with Denmark, Austria, Sweden, Finland, Ireland, Luxembourg, Norway, and Poland are at the other end of the spectrum (Graph 5.5).

To communicate, stakeholders mainly resort to one-on-one meetings, which are used very frequently. Stakeholder websites, issues-specific websites, and infographics are used with some frequency. Events, issues-specific websites, and sponsored media are used the least.

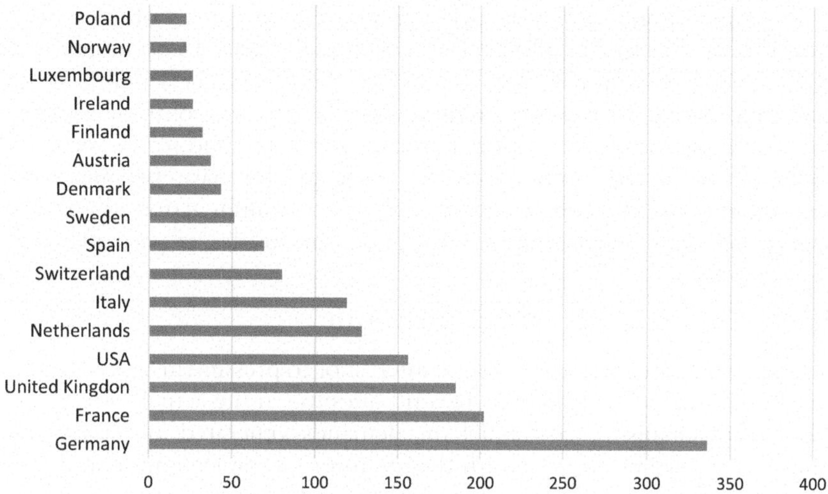

Graph 5.4 Countries with an office in Brussels. (Source: Transparency Register (2020). Chart created for this study)

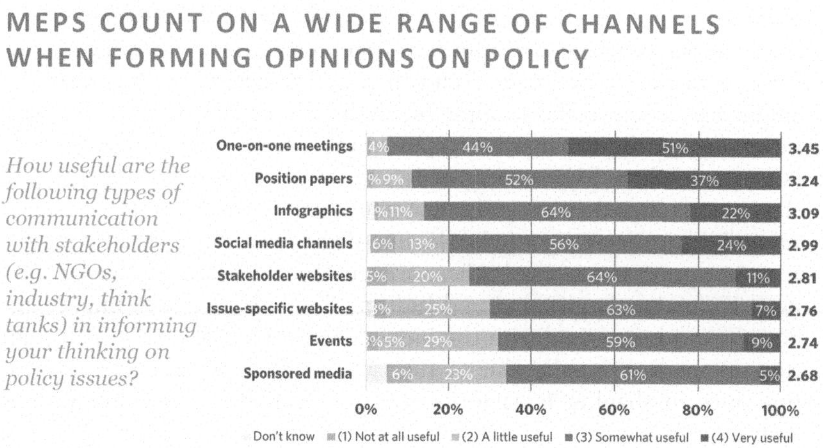

Graph 5.5 MEPs count on a wide range of channels when forming opinions on policy. (Source: FleishmanHillard (2015): 3rd European Parliament Digital Trends Survey online, Brussels)

All contemporary political society is a system composed of many relationships and processes of power, in which individuals do no longer play the main supporting role, but in its place there is rather a multitude of associations that measure its strength according to the controlled instruments, its social presence, to the purposes advocated and to the media of influence possessed, among others. These groups have become truly important political actors in developing one continuous action toward the whole society, in general, and toward public authorities, in particular.

6 Epilogue

The relevance attached to groups of interest or to pressure groups (according to the field of its activity) is beyond question in the actual society, just like the mechanisms to channel the demands generated in society and aimed at public authorities, with the intention of implementing and executing the appropriate decisions in favor of and according to the interests of the groups.

The pluralist societies demonstrate the collective management of conflicts through the interactions and mutual influence among the groups present in the community. This inter-associative relevance causes that proposals have to be negotiated mutually together with the continuous contributions from, to, and over each other. Nevertheless, the fact that this configuring structure shows some hierarchical imbalances, with the presence of some groups that possess some more capacity than others to postulate or to enforce its own proposals, should not be ignored.

Pressure groups develop and implement their activities on the organizations and institutions regarded as legitimate representative bodies of popular sovereignty, and similarly there are the three classic branches of state power: Executive, Legislative, and Judicial. Similarly, they also impact significantly and increasingly, on the individuals and social groups, through action on the mass media, due to the fact that they possess a remarkable significance in shaping behaviors, attitudes, and thoughts circulating in society.

The limited social performance of associations in the social, political, and economic dynamics restricts significantly its incidence. One of the elements applied by the pressure groups in the plentiful manner consists of an appeal to the media system in order to spread the demands and groups' petitions within society. Thus, the mass media have been informed by the particular configuration in symbolic, cognitive, and informative structuring as the receiving instances of various types of associative activities in order to adapt its editorial space to coalition goals.

The pressure groups need the media intermediation as one more mechanism in its global strategy of pressure on the public decision-makers. Owning and gaining access to a favorable and frequent presence in media conveys the feeling and perception of a large social support to the demands and claims of groups, arousing the focus of the social concerns on those issues, which are conducive to group requirements.

Thus, communication exerted by groups or companies is an important way of generating public opinion, either directly influencing the audience or trying to influence it in a more indirect way, presenting content on events and situations that concern the group in the media.

Hence, the mass media gather, interpret, assess and transmit information proceeding from social organizations as an expression of societal ecosystem needs. Similarly, through the information system, among other mechanisms, the political system perceives the petitions of society as being capable of reaching a solution.

Resorting to mass media allows the groups to reflect its demands publicly, with the consequent political existence, due to the fact that the policy is manifested increasingly as a symbolic struggle in which each association pursues to monopolize its views successfully and to promote new claims, these being the proceedings that contribute to the achievement of group's goals.

References

Almond, G. A. (1958). A research note: Comparative study of interest groups and the political process. *American Political Science Review, 52*(2), 270–282.

Almond, G. A., & Powell, G. B. (1972). *Política comparada*. Editorial Paidos.

Bentley, A. F. (1983). *Il Processo di Governo. Uno studio delle Pressione Sociali*. Giuffrè.

Berry, J. (1977). *Lobbying for the people. The political behavior of public interest groups*. Princeton University Press.

Berry, J. (1989). *The interest group society*. Scott Foresman/Little.

Bilouri, D. (1999). Environmental NGOs in Brussels: How powerful are their lobbying activities? *Environmental Politics, 8*(2), 173–182. https://doi.org/10.1080/09644019908414472

Branton, R., Martínez-Ebers, V., Carey, T. E., Jr., & Matsubayashi, T. (2015). Social protest and policy attitudes: The case of the 2006 immigrant rallies.

American Journal of Political Science, 59(2), 390–402. https://doi.org/10.1111/ajps.12159
Burdeau, G. (1982). *Traité de Science Politique*, Tom III (La Dynamique Politique), Vol. I (Les Forces Politiques). Librairie Génerale de Droit et Jurisprudence.
Carty, V. (2010). New information communication technologies and grassroots mobilization. Information. *Communications Society, 13*(2), 155–173. https://doi.org/10.1080/13691180902915658
Chalmers, A. W., & Macedo, F. S. (2020). Does it pay to lobby? Examining the link between firm lobbying and firm profitability in the European Union. *Journal of European Public Policy.* https://doi.org/10.1080/13501763.2020.1824012
Chari, R., & Hillebrand O'Donovan, D. (2011). Lobbying the European Commission: Open or secret? *Socialism and Democracy, 25*(2), 104–124. https://doi.org/10.1080/08854300.2011.579475
De Bruycker, I. (2016). Pressure and expertise: Explaining the information supply of interest groups in EU legislative lobbying. *JCMS: Journal of Common Market Studies, 54*(3), 599–616.
De Bruycker, I., & Beyers, J. (2019). Lobbying strategies and success: Inside and outside lobbying in European Union legislative politics. *European Political Science Review, 11*(1), 57–74.
Dempsey, S. E. (2009). NGOs, communicative labor, and the work of grassroots representation. *Communication and Critical/Cultural Studies, 6*(4), 328–345. https://doi.org/10.1080/14791420903348625
Dür, A. (2008). Measuring interest group influence in the EU: A note on methodology. *European Union Politics, 9*(4), 559–576.
Dür, A., Bernhagen, P., & Marshall, D. (2015). Interest group success in the European Union: When (and why) does business lose? *Comparative Political Studies, 48*(8), 951–983. https://doi.org/10.1177/0010414014565890
Easton, D. (1965). *Esquema para el análisis político.* Amorrortu Editores.
Fowler, L. L., & Shaiko, R. G. (1987). The grass roots connection: Environmental activists and senate roll calls. *American Journal of Political Science, 31*(3), 484–510.
Gallagher Cunningham, K., Dahl, M., & Frugé, A. (2017). Strategies of resistance: Diversification and diffusion. *American Journal of Political Science, 61*(3), 591–605. https://doi.org/10.1111/ajps.12304
Grant, W. (1989). *Pressure groups, politics and democracy.* Philip Allan.
Gray, V., & Lowery, D. (1993). The diversity of state interest group systems. *Political Research Quarterly, 46*(1), 81–98.
Hrebenar, R. J., & Scott, R. K. (1990). *Interest groups politics in America.* Prentice Hall.
Klüver, H. (2013). *Lobbying in the European Union: Interest groups, lobbying coalitions and policy change.* Oxford University Press.

Klüver, H., Braun, C., & Beyers, J. (2015). Legislative lobbying in context: Towards a conceptual framework of interest group lobbying in the European Union. *Journal of European Public Policy, 22*(4), 447–461. https://doi.org/10.1080/13501763.2015.1008792

Lowery, D. (2013). Lobbying influence: Meaning, measurement and missing. *Interest Groups & Advocacy, 2*(1), 1–26.

Marshall, D. (2015). Explaining interest group interactions with party group members in the European Parliament: Dominant party groups and coalition formation. *JCMS: Journal of Common Market Studies, 53*(2), 311–329.

McFarland, A. S. (1987). *Los grupos de presión en el Congreso norteamericano.* Gernika.

Mergeai, S., & Gilain, H. (2020). *Analyse comparative des stratégies employées par le lobby pharmaceutique, gazier et automobile visant à influencer les réglementations de l'UE.* Louvain School of Management, Université Catholique de Louvain.

Meynaud, J. (1962). *Nouvelles études sur les groupes de pression en France.* Armand Colin.

Rasmussen, A. (2015). Participation in written government consultations in Denmark and the UK: System and actor-level effects. *Government and Opposition, 50*(2), 271–299.

Rasmussen, A., Mader, L. K., & Reher, S. (2018). With a little help from the people? The role of public opinion in advocacy success. *Comparative Political Studies, 51*(2), 139–164.

Schnakenberg, K. E. (2017). Informational lobbying and legislative voting. *American Journal of Political Science, 61*(1), 129–145. https://doi.org/10.1111/ajps.12249

Whiteley, P. F., & Winyard, S. J. (1987). *Pressure for the poor. The poverty lobby and policy makings.* Methuen.

Ziegler, H., & Dye, T. R. (1990). *The irony of democracy. An uncommon introduction to American politics.* Cole Publishing Company.

CHAPTER 6

Feminism and Political Communication: How Femicide Is Treated in Digital Media: Santo Domingo Media Case Study During 2020

Santiago Gallur Santorum

1 Introduction

On December 30, 2020, Listín Diario, a digital media outlet of Santo Domingo city, in the Dominican Republic, reported that at least 58 femicides had been committed during the same year. This was in contrast to the limited number of news stories published during that period in the country. In Santo Domingo alone, there are 24 digital media outlets which, having reported periodically on the subject, would have provided a minimum of 1392 news stories, covering each of the murders of women committed in the whole country. Paradoxically, during 2020, not even half of those 1392 news items, which would be expected in the coverage

S. Gallur Santorum (✉)
Technological Institute of Santo Domingo (INTEC), Santo Domingo, Dominican Republic
e-mail: santiago.gallur@intec.edu.do

B. García-Orosa (ed.), *Digital Political Communication Strategies*, The Palgrave Macmillan Series in International Political Communication, https://doi.org/10.1007/978-3-030-81568-4_6

of femicide at the national level, were published. While there is no recent or past research on the media coverage of the phenomenon in the country, there is a collective memory that does recall regular information on femicides in the country (Allué & de Pedro, 2017; Candelario, 2005; García, 2014; Panadero, 2012; Romero Nova, 2018). However, the use of the term itself had already been accepted for years due to gender-based violence (Candelario, 2005), both by society and by the media themselves (Panadero, 2012).

Since 2005, various studies have been published in the Dominican Republic on gender-based violence in the country in the form of gender studies (Candelario, 2005). The issue of violence against women has been of great concern to the Caribbean nation, to the point of considering the need to implement gender mainstreaming in schools in the country in order to improve educational quality (Folgueiras & Marín, 2009). All of this contributed to spreading awareness of the social need to fight for a life free of violence for women (Panadero, 2012). However, despite attempts to combat this phenomenon, violence against women remained constant (Garcia, 2014). All of this has caused the topic to be studied in a specific way, even in cases of gender-based violence against girls and adolescents in the city of Santo Domingo (Allué & de Pedro, 2017). This situation motivates the extensive research offered here, in which, for the first time in the history of the Dominican Republic, a phenomenon is studied from inside the country itself, one that, despite having been invisibilized by the national media, has a real impact on the nation. There have been previous attempts to study the impact of the media on such important aspects as education (Leguizamón, 2018). However, although the determinants of gender-based violence in the national context has been studied (Romero Nova, 2018), the communication of femicide in the country has never been analyzed in detail before.

2 State of the Art

For almost two decades the Dominican Republic has been asking for a justified response to gender-based violence (Pola, 2003), with specific proposals for studies on the subject (Candelario, 2005). At the end of the first decade of the twenty-first century, the social reaction against femicide began to strengthen in Latin America (Prieto-Carrón et al., 2007). Despite this, gender stereotypes that conditioned the possibility of women's development in all areas were rooted even in political communication (Aalberg & Jenssen, 2007). Thus, political communication in Latin America began to be studied under a gender perspective (Edwards, 2009), in order to try to understand how to propose strategies to curb the advancement of femicide and gender-based violence. Thus, the media began to be held responsible for spreading stereotypes about women in news on crimes (Taylor, 2009) that led to victimization. Thus, political communication began to be seen as relevant to curbing femicide (Ahrens, 2009). Since the end of the 2000s in the Dominican Republic, the need has been raised to decrease the discrimination suffered by women through the implementation of the gender approach even in education itself (Folgueiras & Marín, 2009).

Studies on information on violence against women in Latin America began formally in the early 2010s (Hurtado & Fríes, 2010). Gradually, a number of countries in the subcontinent have been paying attention to femicide (Meneghel & Hirakata, 2011). Thus, the analyses of femicide news coverage become an important (Richards et al., 2011) and recurrent research topic (Rodríguez, 2012). Simultaneously, political communication on gender issues also began to be perceived as a must (Ross & Comrie, 2012), reporting on femicide (Munévar, 2012) in all countries including the Dominican Republic, where the phenomenon became increasingly visible (Panadero, 2012). Thus, gender has been constituted over the years as an issue of central importance in political communication (Flicker, 2013). The media had already been a key element in the inadequate dissemination of femicide news (Gillespie et al., 2013), having a direct impact on marital violence in the Dominican Republic (Garcia, 2014). At the same time, research on this subject continued to emerge in countries such as Italy (Gius & Lalli, 2014).

Despite the international diffusion of the problem of femicide and its dissemination and representation in the mass media, in the Latin American context various works have shown that the social perception of the phenomenon has not changed at all, in countries such as Nicaragua (Luffy et al., 2015). The only real change that all these incipient investigations succeeded in effecting was to turn a private crime into a public problem (Comas-d'Argemir, 2015) and to bring the attention of the authorities and society in countries like Turkey, where until then the situation had not been given much consideration (INCE Yenilmez & Demir, 2016). Therefore, femicide had already been constituted by mid-2010 as a significant social phenomenon and therefore of great interest for social investigations despite the fact that crimes against women remained unabated (Corradi et al., 2016). Femicide needed to be made visible (Weil, 2016).

In the very case of Latin America in 2017 the theory was raised that the continuity of the phenomenon could be due either to a legal vacuum or to a deficit in the rule of law (Saccomano, 2017). In surrounding countries such as Mexico, the rate of femicide was so high that the lack of adequate policy measures was on the agenda (Estrada, 2017). Meanwhile, the Dominican Republic did not present a much more satisfactory situation, but research on gender-based violence against women, girls and adolescents became increasingly frequent (Allué & de Pedro, 2017), highlighting particular aspects of the conditions that even affected intimate violence among couples in the Dominican context (Caridad Bueno & Henderson, 2017). All this ended up causing specific responses to this phenomenon to be sought in the functioning of the justice and protection system for women in Latin America (Joseph, 2017). Meanwhile, in the international context, common reflections were offered on the impact of media speeches on femicide in countries as different as Italy (Bandelli, 2017) and Jordan (Mahadeen, 2017).

It was clear at the end of the 2010s that the media and their speeches had a very strong impact on society, to the extent that they were seen as an element linked to education in the Dominican Republic, which even raised the need for a curricular renewal for this reason (Leguizamón, 2018). Thus, the international situation was beginning to have direct policy implications due to gender approaches and measures in social media and media in countries such as the United Kingdom (Djupe et al., 2018). After that, started the analysis of the news about femicide (Bouzerdan & Whitten-Woodring, 2018) and its impact on politics. Therefore, studies on the determinants of gender-based violence emerged in countries such as the Dominican Republic (Romero Nova, 2018). Among them was social media such as Twitter, where even political journalism could see gender discrimination (Usher et al., 2018).

In 2019, some academic voices were raised stating that the elimination of violence against women in Latin America and the Caribbean was essential to achieving sustainable development, equality and peace at the international level (Montiel, 2019). However, reality continued to provide a very different context in each country, beyond good international intentions. Thus, even though the #MeToo movement had reached countries like Brazil through social networks, femicide remained unstoppable (Paiva, 2019). It was found that the way in which the murders of women in Latin America were being reported was not only inadequate, but clearly failed because of the continuity and increase in cases (Castillo, 2019) of femicide (Corradi & Bandelli, 2019).

Femicide and its media diffusion was achieving a double effect at the international level. On the one hand, in countries such as Turkey, the phenomenon succeeded in awakening collective subjectivity by promoting feminist activism against femicide (Altuntaş, 2019). On the other hand, in nations such as Italy, attention was paid to the representations made by the media of men accused of femicide in the coverage of the situation (Masciave, 2019). These reactions coexist in the international context with less striking but equally significant ones, such as studies on femicide communication in the media in Kenya (Wasuna, 2019) or Greece (Al Agkmpari, 2020). This international research confirmed the idea of mediatization of femicide, with a very specific representation of gender violence through the media of countries such as Italy (Busso et al., 2020). However, everything previously commented did not stop a constant reality in diferents national context: female Dominican victims of trafficking in Puerto Rico were becoming victims of femicide (Harrison, 2020). The implications were so profound that in 2020 research on gender violence started to be published by public school teachers in the Dominican Republic, again highlighting the evident link between femicide, its media coverage and education (Mencía-Ripley, 2020).

3 Methodology

The hypothesis that motivated this research is as follows. The media in Santo Domingo, the capital of the Dominican Republic, have given minimal coverage to femicides that occurred in the national territory during 2020, while at the same time disseminating in a residual way any political proposals aimed at solving the issue of the murders of women. For this research, a methodology of content analysis by means of an analysis sheet was carried out based on the study of all news headlines published by all the digital newspapers of Santo Domingo city, during 2020 (January 1 to December 31 of that year). The choice of the time frame is due to the fact that analyzing the entire year 2020 mediatically allows us to determine if there has been any changes in routine information before and after the COVID-19 pandemic in the country (in March of that year).

A total of over 500 news items from the 24 media outlets in the country's capital city have been analyzed. The parameters studied have been the use of the term femicide in the header, the sources used, the type of news and whether it was national or international.

The 24 media outlets analyzed were as follows:

1. LISTÍN DIARIO: www.listin.com.do
2. EL NACIONAL: www.elnacional.com.do
3. HOY: www.hoy.com.do
4. EL CARIBE: www.elcaribe.com.do
5. DIARIO LIBRE: www.diariolibre.com
6. EL DÍA: www.eldia.com.do
7. EL NUEVO DIARIOS: www.elnuevodiario.com.do
8. METRO: www.metrord.do
9. CIUDAD ORIENTAL: www.ciudadoriental.com
10. ÚLTIMAS NOTICIAS: www.ultimasnoticias.com.do
11. ACENTO: www.acento.com.do
12. PRIMICIAS: www.primicias.com.do
13. AL MOMENTO: www.almomento.net
14. SANTO DOMINGO A DIARIO: www.santodomingoadiario.com
15. DIARIO DIGITAL RD: www.diariodigital.com.do
16. DIARIO DOM: www.diariodom.com
17. EL DINERO: www.eldinero.com.do
18. DIARIO HISPANIOLA: www.diariohispaniola.com
19. DIARIO DOMINICANO: www.diariodominicano.com
20. NOTICIAS DOMINICANAS: www.noticiasdominicanas.co
21. LAS ÚLTIMAS NOTICIAS: www.lasultimasnoticias.net
22. REMOLACHA: www.remolacha.net
23. EL PERIÓDICO: www.elperiodico.com.do
24. ZONA ESTE Santo Domingo www.zonaeste.com.do

4 Data Analysis

The analysis carried out using the methodological indications highlighted in the previous section has yielded a series of striking data in several respects. Thus, the first thing to highlight is the low number of news items published during 2020 on femicide in the Dominican Republic. We have noted that the 24 digital media outlets analyzed have published in total just over 500 news items. The number of femicides that occurred in the country during 2020 was 58, according to a news story published on

December 30, 2020 by Listín Diario. This indicates the first striking data in the analysis, since if there had been media coverage of femicide in the country, a ballpark figure of 1392 news items on the subject should have been published, in the 24 media outlets studied (using the simple logic of multiplying the 58 murders marked as femicide by the number of mentioned digital newspapers). Far from a near-expected figure, the slightly more than 500 news items analyzed indicate a possible expected coverage of less than half of the crimes committed against women in the country. However, the analysis developed indicates something even more worrying: the coverage of femicide by the digital media has been completely unequal, to the point of finding a medium that publishes a little more than 300 news items about femicide, while most are in the range of the 10 news items published on the subject.

This is why we can highlight a dynamic common to 23 of the 24 media outlets analyzed: minimum coverage of femicide, with an average of 10 news items published by each media outlet, which generates information covering only a little less than 15% of the 58 femicides that occurred in the country during 2020. In addition to the above, there is another dynamic that draws attention to the 23 media outlets (of the 24 analyzed) that published more than half of the 500 news items studied on femicide: most of them do not deal with crimes committed against women, but with situations related to femicide. That is, a minimum percentage of the 500 news items analyzed in total, just over 10 news texts (2% of the total), deal with political proposals to combat femicide and curb the murder of women and gender-based violence. Thus, only 2% of the total news items published during 2020 by the 24 media outlets analyzed refer to policies to stop femicide in the country. The total of this minimum percentage of news were statements made by politicians in the face of specific cases of femicide that alarmed the population.

The digital media that form the exception to the rule of the 24 media outlets studied have developed periodic coverage of femicide with news published on the subject every week. However, the main feature of such coverage is that this is not news of murders of women in the Dominican Republic but abroad (countries in the Latin American context). Thus, despite widespread coverage of the phenomenon of femicide, there is no follow-up on the murders of women in the country, but in others. We can therefore point out that 100% of the media outlets analyzed have not carried out coverage or monitoring of femicide at the national level. None of the media outlets have published on a regular basis on the subject, paying attention to the murders of women in the country. All these dynamics highlighted by the data analysis generate doubts about the real intention of the information published by the set of analyzed media outlets, since it can be stated categorically that femicide has not been a topic of interest for the digital media of Santo Domingo, even if it has been a specific situation to cover when society reacts to such crimes, whether in a national or international context.

5 Conclusion

After a thorough analysis of the just over 500 news items published by 24 digital media outlets on femicide, we can highlight a series of conclusions:

I. Femicide in the Dominican Republic was not a topic that the digital newspapers of the capital city paid attention to despite the 58 murders of women that occurred in 2020. On the contrary, it has become nothing more than a one-off news item when the phenomenon provokes a particular social reaction, and this situation is covered more than the murders of dozens of women.
II. Communication on political intentions to curb the murder of women in the country during 2020 was minimal in the 24 digital media outlets analyzed. In fact, the residual percentage of the news published on the subject indicates that they were specific statements and not the communication of real policies aimed at stopping the phenomenon of femicide.
III. The term femicide has been used generically in the headlines by the vast majority of the media outlets analyzed. However, the news headlines in which it appears have not in general referred to real situations of murders of women but to social or media dynamics resulting from this situation.
IV. In a residual way we can point out that, although one of the 24 digital newspapers analyzed has covered the phenomenon of femicide comprehensively, the published news dealt with the murders of women that occurred abroad, not in the Dominican Republic.
V. The scant presence of news about femicide in the Dominican Republic creates a doubly paradoxical perception. On the one hand, it appears that there have been no murders of women in

the country during 2020. On the other hand, reporting more frequently on crimes against women in the Latin American context gives the impression that the country is in a situation of greater protection for women than the surrounding countries.

VI. The media should report on events and phenomena affecting society. Femicide is a scourge that negatively impacts all aspects of Dominican society. Failure to adequately monitor such crimes or policies against them ends up generating an alarming sense of normalcy and impunity.

VII. Although it is not enough to publish news about femicide (since these stories must be adequately covered, written and published, respecting the rights of victims and their families), the fact that the phenomenon is barely covered plunges Dominican women into a situation of vulnerability, as their murder is very likely not to be made visible by the media.

VIII. Journalists, media and politicians need to be made aware that femicide must be disseminated through the media in order to make the situation visible, to prevent such crimes and to report the consequences of these crimes for the culprits.

References

Aalberg, T., & Jenssen, A. T. (2007). Gender stereotyping of political candidates: An experimental study of political communication. *Nordicom Review, 28*(1), 17–32.

Ahrens, K. (Ed.). (2009). *Politics, gender and conceptual metaphors.* Springer.

Al Agkmpari, F. (2020). *The portrayal of femicide in Greek media* (No. GRI-2020-28333). Aristotle University of Thessaloniki.

Allué, S. L., & de Pedro, A. I. I. (2017). Violencia de género contra niñas y adolescentes en Santo Domingo (República Dominicana). *Revista INFAD de Psicología. International Journal of Developmental and Educational Psychology, 2*(1), 211–220.

Altuntaş, D. (2019). Collective subjectivity in feminist activism against femicide in Turkey. Collective subjectivity as an intersectional strategy in the struggle against femicide in Turkey.

Bandelli, D. (2017). *Femicide, gender and violence: Discourses and counterdiscourses in Italy.* Springer.

Bouzerdan, C., & Whitten-Woodring, J. (2018). Killings in context: An analysis of the news framing of femicide. *Human Rights Review, 19*(2), 211–228.

Busso, L., Combei, C. R., & Tordini, O. (2020). The mediatization of femicide: A corpus-based study on the representation of gendered violence in Italian media. *Analisi Linguistica e Letteraria, 2020*(3), 29–48.

Candelario, G. E. (2005). *Miradas desencadenantes: Los estudios de género en la República Dominicana al inicio del Tercer Milenio*. Intec.

Caridad Bueno, C., & Henderson, E. A. (2017). Bargaining or backlash? Evidence on intimate partner violence from the Dominican Republic. *Feminist Economics, 23*(4), 90–116.

Castillo, A. (2019). Reporting femicide: A failure of Latin American journalism. *Media Development, 65*(4), 25–29.

Comas-d'Argemir, D. (2015). News of partner femicides: The shift from private issue to public problem. *European Journal of Communication, 30*(2), 121–136.

Corradi, C., & Bandelli, D. (2019). Femicide. In *Handbook on gender and violence*. Edward Elgar Publishing.

Corradi, C., Marcuello-Servós, C., Boira, S., & Weil, S. (2016). Theories of femicide and their significance for social research. *Current Sociology, 64*(7), 975–995.

Djupe, P., McClurg, S., & Sokhey, A. E. (2018). The political consequences of gender in social networks. *British Journal of Political Science, 48*(3), 637–658.

Edwards, J. L. (Ed.). (2009). *Gender and political communication in America: Rhetoric, representation, and display*. Lexington Books.

Estrada, M. S. (2017). Feminist politics, drones and the fight against the 'Femicide State' in Mexico. *International Journal of Gender, Science and Technology, 9*(2), 99–117.

Flicker, E. (2013). Fashionable (dis-) order in politics: Gender, power and the dilemma of the suit. *International Journal of Media & Cultural Politics, 9*(2), 183–201.

Folgueiras, P., & Marín, M. Á. (2009). Evaluación del proyecto de "mejora de la calidad educativa mediante la incorporación del enfoque de género" en escuelas de República Dominicana: resultados de su impacto. *Revista de Investigación Educativa, 27*(2), 487–508.

García, H. B. (2014). La violencia conyugal en la República Dominicana. *Ciencia y sociedad, 39*(4), 573–600.

Gillespie, L. K., Richards, T. N., Givens, E. M., & Smith, M. D. (2013). Framing deadly domestic violence: Why the media's spin matters in newspaper coverage of femicide. *Violence Against Women, 19*(2), 222–245.

Gius, C., & Lalli, P. (2014). "I loved her so much, but I killed her" Romantic love as a representational frame for intimate partner femicide in three Italian newspapers. *ESSACHESS-Journal for Communication Studies, 7*(2(14)), 53–75.

Harrison, O. D. P. (2020). Injured and suffering bodies: The trafficking and femicide of Dominican immigrant women in Puerto Rico. *Perichoresis, 18*(2), 47–58.

Hurtado, V., & Fríes, L. (2010). *Estudio de la información sobre la violencia contra la mujer en América Latina y el Caribe*. Cepal.

Ince Yenilmez, M., & Demir, M. H. (2016). The challenge of femicide and violence against women in Turkey. *International Journal of Contemporary Economics & Administrative Sciences, 6.*

Joseph, J. (2017). Victims of femicide in Latin America: Legal and criminal justice responses. *Temida, 20*(1), 3–21.

Leguizamón, F. G. (2018). Medios de comunicación y educación: Reflexiones a propósito de la renovación curricular en la República Dominicana. *Ciencia y Educación, 2*(2), 29–40.

Luffy, S. M., Evans, D. P., & Rochat, R. W. (2015). "It is better if I kill her": Perceptions and opinions of violence against women and femicide in Ocotal, Nicaragua, after law 779. *Violence and Gender, 2*(2), 107–111.

Mahadeen, E. (2017). 'The martyr of dawn': Femicide in Jordanian media. *Crime, Media, Culture, 13*(1), 41–54.

Masciave, G. (2019). 'Til Death Do Us Part: Representations of men in the Italian mainstream press coverage of femicide.

Mencía-Ripley, A. (2020). Aceptación de la violencia de género en docentes de escuelas públicas. *RECIE. Revista Caribeña de Investigación Educativa, 4*(1), 81–91.

Meneghel, S. N., & Hirakata, V. N. (2011). Femicides: female homicide in Brazil. *Revista de saude publica, 45*, 564–574.

Montiel, F. C. (2019). Eliminar la violencia contra las mujeres en América Latina y el Caribe: objetivo imprescindible para el desarrollo sostenible, la igualdad y la paz. *Análisis Carolina, 19*, 1.

Munévar, D. I. (2012). Delito de feminicidio. Muerte violenta de mujeres por razones de género. *Estudios socio-jurídicos, 14*(1), 135–175.

Paiva, R. (2019). # MeToo, feminism and femicide in Brazil. *Interactions: Studies in Communication & Culture, 10*(3), 241–255.

Panadero, A. (2012). Feminicidios en República Dominicana: Por una vida sin violencia. *Cambio, 16*(2100), 40–43.

Pola, M. J. (2003). *La mujer dominicana en la relación de pareja: respuesta de la justicia a la violencia de género.* Intec.

Prieto-Carrón, M., Thomson, M., & Macdonald, M. (2007). No more killings! Women respond to femicides in Central America. *Gender and Development, 15*(1), 25–40.

Richards, T. N., Kirkland Gillespie, L., & Dwayne Smith, M. (2011). Exploring news coverage of femicide: Does reporting the news add insult to injury? *Feminist Criminology, 6*(3), 178–202.

Rodríguez, S. G. (2012). *The femicide machine* (Vol. 11). MIT Press.

Romero Nova, E. A. (2018). *Factores determinantes de violencia de género, Hospital Regional Taiwan 19 de Marzo, Azua República Dominicana Periodo julio 2016-junio 2017* (Doctoral dissertation). Universidad Nacional Pedro Henríquez Ureña.

Ross, K., & Comrie, M. (2012). The rules of the (leadership) game: Gender, politics and news. *Journalism, 13*(8), 969–984.
Saccomano, C. (2017). El feminicidio en América Latina:¿ vacío legal o déficit del Estado de derecho?/Feminicide in Latin America: Legal vacuum or deficit in the rule of law? *Revista CIDOB d'Afers Internacionals, 117*, 51–78.
Taylor, R. (2009). Slain and slandered: A content analysis of the portrayal of femicide in crime news. *Homicide Studies, 13*(1), 21–49.
Usher, N., Holcomb, J., & Littman, J. (2018). Twitter makes it worse: Political journalists, gendered echo chambers, and the amplification of gender bias. *The International Journal of Press/Politics, 23*(3), 324–344.
Wasuna, N. (2019). *Media framing of intimate partner femicide in mainstream print media in Kenya* (Doctoral dissertation). University of Nairobi.
Weil, S. (2016). Making femicide visible. *Current Sociology, 64*(7), 1124–1137.

CHAPTER 7

Contemporary Society, Crossroads Between Social Movements and Party Systems in México

Sandra Flores-Guevara and Laura Georgina Ortega-Luna

1 Introduction

Given the rapid changes that we have experienced over recent decades from diverse latitudes and in various sceneries where new social processes become tangibles, a new mode to understand us as a society and as individuals is made visible. Therefore, expression modes and communication are shown in constant change, always evolving, and in search of new symbolic attributes.

While we are facing impressive development models, there is also a counterpart to place us in front of a world that lives through serious processes of political, social and economic crisis that reveal the inefficacy of the institutions in responding to the consequences of those processes.

S. Flores-Guevara (✉) • L. G. Ortega-Luna
Autonomous University of the State of Hidalgo, Pachuca, Mexico
e-mail: sandra_flores@uaeh.edu.mx

B. García-Orosa (ed.), *Digital Political Communication Strategies*, The Palgrave Macmillan Series in International Political Communication, https://doi.org/10.1007/978-3-030-81568-4_7

Increasing global troubles are still presenting poverty, famine and inequality at high levels, and this shows a clear and persistent reality that modifies thinking in relation to dominant hegemonies, leading to a social conscience awakening. This is the way it has been throughout history, opening fields to acts of rebellion against institutions and democracy.

Our contemporaneity grants a new sense of permissibility as a lawful act typical of the human condition, the natural right to resistance, mobilization and activism, as well as to political organization in favor of generating new modes of organization in the absence of inefficacy and little credit from institutions, increasingly exhibiting a high degree of assertiveness to public requests.

Social distrust grows more and more, and disenchantment with the political scene wreaks more havoc with a party system that desperately seeks methods that go beyond the philosophies of its own essence.

Therefore, social movements raise the need to recover public space and to be present in sectors classified as minors in civil society, although not, they represent a high value on the prevailing needs for both social and individual stability, opening the way to the consolidation of new mechanisms of political expression and representation.

Facing a political scenario, worn out for obvious reasons, such as the one we are experiencing, and an ambiguous democracy that leaves a space of latent uncertainty for contemporary society, it is necessary to position ourselves from a point away from the synergies and inefficiencies of the ideological apparatuses of the state, of those that Althusser (2015) refers to as a certain number of realities that are presented in the form of different and specialized institutions.

From that position and from a vision far removed from the uncomfortable parameters of institutionality, we will visualize the ways in which social movements in Mexico have been temporarily modified, movements that give rise to a reconfirmation and interpretation of social activism in contemporary settings, and that exist in parallel with the symptomatic declines of the political party systems in Mexico.

2 A Case Study

To understand this reconfirmation, we have to mention one of the most important social movements in our country and the way in which it signified a new direction for Mexico: the Zapatista Army of National Liberation (EZLN), whose cultural projection at the international level and within the country completely changed the perception and symbolism with which to conceive indigenous multiculturalism. This movement is considered among those with the greatest claiming force and paradigm shifts that did not seek to take power in the State.

Bizberg (2015) says that with the EZLN the claim to indigenous identity was erected, as well as their own identity and the right to be different. He even refers to its cultural, political and economic autonomy without rejecting the other, the others, pointing out that, in a fair measure, a movement like Zapatismo never sought to separate from the nation, but quite the opposite. In this sense, Bizberg takes up French sociologist Yvon Le Bot to specify that this kind of movement generated such a strong impact that it became linked to alter-globalizing movements such as Seattle and the Indignados, to name a few (Bizberg, 2015, p. 166).

Le Bot notes that the Zapatistas have occupied an important place in the Latin American movements of indigenous revolt that represented "modernization and emancipation," and that they put the issues of dignity, justice and democracy at the center of the struggle as a political communication strategy that impacted the globalized world (entrevista realizada por José Gil Olmos a Yvon Le Bot para Revista Proceso Año 37, Edición Especial 43, Enero de 2014).

Zapatismo is concretized as the antecedent of the new social movements that reorient their essence, but currently we find ourselves in the need to observe in what way and under what modality from the "collective action" a crossing of the structures and procedures, not only for the communicative horizons, but for the political processes whose meaning is different, since the actors, the same participation, the objectives of both and the way of intervening, affect the way in which they are reoriented and restructured.

In the line of contemporary social movements in Mexico we find the Movimiento por la Paz con Justicia y Dignidad, which arose in March 2011 with the death of the son of the poet Javier Sicilia and being in a situation of severe insecurity in the country that places it in the midst of a so-called national emergency due to the serious conflicts of insecurity that marked the course of the country-, a movement that raised, through a report, three issues that interrelate the obvious problems of the nation.

The report referred to the tearing of the social fabric during those years due to the presence of organized crime, questioned the official strategy focusing mainly on combat by armed means, and was severe in pointing out the impunity and corruption of government institutions and some political actors. In the end, the movement did not seek to fill public places or take center stage, but actually focused on showing its strength through its speeches based on building hope to face an overwhelming reality.

Another mobilization that shows a clear demarcation in the face of the conjunctures of obtaining political lines is the #YoSoy132 movement, which arose from the visit of a presidential candidate to a private university in Mexico City due to the discomfort of young people with the Mexican political system and, of course, the situation of the country. The malaise of the youth multiplied and spread rapidly since digital social networks were their main axis of action, an element that adds to the scope of contemporaneity to give a certain identity and positioning to the mobilization action.

#YoSoy132 transcended borders, integrating thousands of students from other universities and countries, and then it was not only about proclaiming their discontent with the candidate and his power relationship with some media companies in the country, but they also joined other mobilizations that, as we have already mentioned, reoriented and vindicated the mobilization:

> Movement 132 is us; we are the demonstration of the indignation and rage of the dead children in the guardería abc, we are Wirikuta, we are Cherán in Michoacán, we are Copala, we are the dead Rarámuris, we are the outrage at the brutal force of the State, we are the outrage at the war against drug trafficking and its more than seventy thousand deaths. This whole story is us, we ask for justice! We ask for justice! Because this is our movement and we are going to fight for it until justice is done, justice! Justice! All this history today we vindicate and relive it, we relive it in the gale of this movement, today we decide and say to be 132, to be history and to be the Mexican conscience, we do not forget, and we will shout from our conscience, today and always: we are 132 (Bizberg, 2015).

3 Trends

Based on the analysis carried out on social movements, which are also inserted in different contexts, the idea that citizen participation organizations can have an impact on the formation of specific organizations that are directly involved in the democratic contexts of a country can be established. Clear examples are political parties, non-governmental organizations and groups of subjects that begin to meet specific demands of the people.

Each of these structures serves vulnerable sectors of society that spearhead or trigger social movements simply by being located in spaces that the government cannot cover, and they represent the materialization of democracy that sometimes ends up being understood only as the exercise of the vote, and yet they represent much more in terms of how citizens can drive far-reaching changes.

Nohlen (2006) understands citizen participation as an act in which the instrumental contributions of collective action and the regulations of each particular site come together to allow individuals belonging to a community to act to generate pressure. It should also be clarified that digital spaces allow a different method of organization by uniting individuals who share common characteristics, fill gaps in space and time, and allow them to achieve greater reach with their social movements.

Thus, citizen participation becomes the possibility of generating equitable spaces to make all people belonging to a community or region an active part of the actions that are carried out to impact all sectors of society. It is through citizen participation that individuals can really exercise democracy by getting involved in decision-making hand in hand with the government or the different institutions that demand a responsible act be for the benefit of all.

Following this idea, Sánchez (2009) considers that citizen participation is promoted when an entire community understands the sense of the demand to cover their needs as a whole, that is, to form the organized group, it needs to be a set of common objectives and interests which are translated into the search for access to a possibility of politically representing the entire vulnerable sector.

Thus, when citizens form a group, the recognition of the rights of all the subjects involved in participation begins, since they are the ones who will directly ask the authorities to respect their rights through social activism that aims for the democratic systems to be counted at the same level of representation as the subjects before the State, thus trying to promote a participatory and non-representative democracy in the first order.

It is thus important to understand that democracy is not only a system that the government decides to use to become "representative," but also encompasses the creation of sufficient spaces for citizens to become the voice that determines actions in favor of themselves, where the government representatives are vigilant that the corresponding actions be carried out correctly for the benefit of the people who live in a certain region, and are not figures of power who neglect what the citizen demands.

Accordingly, Touraine (1995) points out the existence of three dimensions of democracy that are associated with social movements: respect for the basic rights of the subjects, the conformation of citizenship and the way in which the leaders exercise representation. In addition, however, he recognizes that the "ideal" theory of democracy is not in fact reflected in government systems, and that it varies according to the context in which it is being lived, which, of course, is associated with specific sociocultural elements.

Thus, he makes mention of three types of democracy that must be taken into account: respect for fundamental rights, citizenship and representativeness of leaders. However, it distinguishes that there is no ideal democracy such as the one that is theoretically stipulated, it ensures that democracy is different according to the experiences in place, time and space on which this process is carried out and that is how it also recognizes three types of democracy:

The first type gives central importance to the limitation of the power of the State through the law and the recognition of fundamental rights [...] the second type gives the greatest importance to citizenship, the Constitution or the moral or religious ideas that ensure the integration of society and give a solid foundation to the laws [...] a third type insists more on the social representativeness of the rulers and opposes democracy, which defends the interests of the popular categories, to the oligarchy, whether it is associated with a monarchy defined by the possession of privileges or the ownership of capital (Touraine, 1995, pp. 46–47 [own translation]).

Returning to the topic referring to how democracy materializes from the existence of social movements, we can refer to Woldenberg (2006), who assures us that part of the quality of the exercise of representation and participation of subjects in government depends on the fact that the structure of political parties directly involves citizens, but also has an important link with the media and communication supports in charge of maintaining direct communication between members of society, since this is how the proposals and government actions that meet the demands pursued by different movements can be adapted.

A complement to this view of democracy is provided by Sartori (2003), who clarifies that this exercise is not carried out as it is ideally defined, and that is why social movements emerge. Also, Toussaint (1995) adds that it is necessary to blur the idea that the only way to make democracy visible is the exercise of the vote, since even this is determined by the hegemonic discourses of power that determine the real intention of the citizens' vote since the political parties, which should be made up mainly of people from the people, end up involving in their structure certain subjects of the political class themselves who block social demands.

In accordance with the foregoing, it is observed that freedom of expression plays an important role because when it is restricted, citizens find in the social movement the way for their voice to be heard if it has been censored in other ways. In this regard, Peñate (2017) states that for there to be a true democracy there would have to be a full and equitable policy that recognizes the constant struggle of citizens, which looks not only at the statistical plane of citizen participation in figures, but at the qualitative impact reflected in public policies that cover social demands.

The qualitative translation with respect to which mention is made is concretized in the creation of truly inclusive political parties, which transform the government system from the base (Núñez, 2011), since this is necessary to work based on respect for human rights but also in the attention of social sectors in which the traditional capitalist vision does not reach to observe basic requirements, for example young people, women, people with disabilities, people from marginalized communities, care of the environment and rights of animals, and social movements are in charge of generating representatives from these sectors in the structure of political parties to restructure proposals and influence the organic structure of the party itself.

The restructuring in reference to the party implies joint work with citizens through the analysis of specific contexts generating proposals aimed at solving latent problems through the reinforcement of values such as honesty, solidarity and transparency, which will be constantly renewed to provide solutions in the medium and long term. Thus, it can be observed that participation has an impact on transparency in the management of public affairs, in establishing true freedom of expression, association and press, and in ensuring that citizens have the real right to participate and influence the political life of their own territory.

The advantage of current democracies is the diversification of scenarios in which citizens can participate, with digital spaces being a concrete opportunity for them to raise their voices together and seek to generate a more direct criticism of government systems, since through traditional media like the press, radio and television information is provided to people, but social-digital media allow people to respond to such information and consider themselves participants in political activity. This exercise is known as cyberpolitics (Fernández, 2008).

According to Castillo (2014), currently the existence of the Internet as a factor involved in democratic systems favors the inclusion of those who use it, mainly the young population, becoming an alternative space for the expression of social demands, where they can take advantage of a myriad of resources such as Web pages, blogs, wikis, chats, forums and digital social networks (the main ones because they are the most used), which together make up an ecosystem that promotes contents and spreads it where citizens are involved in a more direct way.

In this way, it is possible to say that the Internet has become a tool that allows citizens to express themselves differently in the face of politics, and to find in cyberspace the way to criticize their governments or to make themselves heard by politicians as well as by other citizens. The Internet, through digital social networks, has built scenarios to open dialogues during electoral processes or mandates, and makes it possible to share information, so that social movements will have a greater influence on the exercise of democracy.

Thus, following Fernández (2008), it can be established that all constitutions of citizen representation, such as political parties, need to generate messages in cyberspace that speak intelligently to voters, with good aim and directly impacting those social movements that have emerged. The Internet promotes mass communication but at the same time allows one to have more customized communication, allowing specific messages to be directed to specific sectors, messages that in turn allow them to regain interest in the political sphere.

Notwithstanding the foregoing, it is also convenient to understand that when a specific structure, such as that of a political party, loses sight of the relevance of the impact on the interests of social movements, structures such as non-governmental organizations (NGOs) can be generated, and can impact those citizen sectors that are still deserted or without specific attention to their demands.

NGOs function as private entities, which have humanitarian and social goals and objectives determined by their members, created independently from local, regional and national governments, as well as international organizations, which are often promoted by the citizens themselves as another form of materialization of social movements. Generally, NGOs are involved through social movements that obviously include the participation of volunteers who serve different social causes. They can have a broad organization that is strengthened over time, and they obtain financing for their activities from different sources such as individuals, voluntary donations, State resources targeted to them, international organizations, companies and other NGOs.

Thus, observing the ways in which movements are integrated into parties or other types of organizations serves to help understand that citizen participation represents, through social movements, new ways of establishing relationships, links and, therefore, understanding to reach agreements between the individuals that make up societies and government systems.

In this way, and returning to Ziccardi (1998), it can be concluded that citizen participation materialized in political parties or NGOs implies recognition by the State to be able to get more actively involved within a true system of democracy, generating a response through public affairs that allows citizen—government collaborative work in the restructuring of institutions, decision-making and construction of more equitable public spaces that converge in the understanding of the requests made by the different social movements formed both in physical space and in cyberspace.

References

Althusser, L. (2015). *La reproducción como desvío. A propósito de Sobre la Reproducción*. Akal. México.

Bizberg, I. (2015). Los nuevos movimientos sociales en México: el Movimiento por la Paz con Justicia y Dignidad y #YoSoy132. *Foro Internacional, LV, 1*(219) Enero-Marzo, 2015 El Colegio del México.

Castillo, L. (2014). Medios y elecciones 2012: viejos y nuevos desafíos para la comunicación política en México. *Noésis. Revista de Ciencias Sociales y Humanidades*, 22–48.

Fernández, C. B. (2008). *Ciberpolítica: ¿Cómo usamos las tecnologías digitales en la política latinoamericana?* Konrad Adenauer Stiftung.

Le Bot, Y. (2014). En J. Gil, *Una antiguerrilla por la dignidad. Revista Proceso* Año 37, Edición Especial 43, enero de 2014.

Nohlen, D. (2006). *Diccionario de ciencia política*. Porrúa.

Núñez, O. (2011). Movimientos sociales y partidos políticos. *Cultura de Paz*, 40–45.

Peñate, K. K. (2017). Mujeres y democracia: en busca de una política plena y equitativa. *Hechos y Derechos*, 1–38.

Sánchez, M. Á. (2009). La participación ciudadana en la esfera de lo público. *Espacios Públicos*, 85–102.

Sartori, G. (2003). *¿Qué es la democracia?* Santillana Ediciones Generales.

Touraine, A. (1995). *¿Qué es la democracia?* Fondo de Cultura Económica.

Toussaint, F. (1995). Inequidad y democracia: realidad en los medios. En F. Toussaint, *Democracia y medios de comunicación: un binomio inexplorado.* Centro de investigaciones interdiscilpinarias en ciencias y humanidades UNAM.

Woldenberg, J. (2006). *Después de la transición. Gobernabilidad, espacio público y derechos.* Ediciones Cal y Arena.

Ziccardi, A. (1998). *Gobernabilidad y participación ciudadana en la ciudad capital.* Porrúa.

PART II

CHAPTER 8

VR and 360-Degree Video Storytelling in Political Communication: Threats and Opportunities

Sara Pérez-Seijo, Pavel Sidorenko Bautista, and María José Benítez de Gracia

1 Virtual Reality in the Mass Market

The virtual reality (VR) industry has risen again in the second decade of the twenty-first century. The first attempts at popularizing the technology occurred in the late 1980s and early 1990s, but that attempt to bring VR to the mass market failed, mainly due to technological limitations (Sherman

S. Pérez-Seijo (✉)
University of Santiago de Compostela, Santiago de Compostela, Spain
e-mail: s.perez.seijo@usc.es

P. Sidorenko Bautista
Francisco de Vitoria University, Madrid, Spain
e-mail: pavel.sidorenko@ufv.es

M. J. Benítez de Gracia
Universidad Isabel I de Castilla, Burgos, Spain
e-mail: mariajose.benitez@ui1.es

B. García-Orosa (ed.), *Digital Political Communication Strategies*, The Palgrave Macmillan Series in International Political Communication, https://doi.org/10.1007/978-3-030-81568-4_8

& Craig, 2003). Thus began the oft-labeled "VR Winter" (Furness, 2014), roughly spanning the years 2000–2010, and in which production is fundamentally replaced by research (Jerald, 2015).

In 2012, the industry shook off the VR Winter, and confidence and commercial interest in VR began to resurface following a Kickstarter crowdfunding campaign, which served as catalyst.

The company behind the campaign was Oculus VR, which sought to finance development of the prototype of its Oculus Rift visor. Two years later, Facebook announced it would purchase Oculus VR (Facebook, 2014), thus marking the beginning of a new stage in the VR industry (Sirkkunen et al., 2016), in which VR glasses, from low-cost models, such as Google Cardboard, to more sophisticated alternatives, such as Daydream View or Samsung Gear, have been gradually commercialized at more affordable prices.

This time, VR not only has burst into the video game sector, but has also created new opportunities in education, medicine, tourism, military training, engineering, marketing, journalism, and communication in general. VR is incorporated in communication as part of a set of high technologies, which in the 2010s, redefined how stories are told and disseminated and offered new ways to experience and consume them (Pérez-Seijo et al., 2020). Cue the arrival of VR/360 storytelling, or immersive storytelling, based on computer-generated experiences and 360-degree video.

In particular, 360-degree video is presented as "a gateway to true VR" (Watson, 2017) because, although spherical video is less interactive than what is often referred to as true virtual reality (Damiani, 2016; Watson, 2017), given the user's agency is limited to controlling the point of view in an immersive scene (Dolan & Parets, 2016; Dominguez, 2017), it is less expensive and requires less labor-intensive production compared with computer-generated experiences (Mabrook & Singer, 2019; Pérez-Seijo & López-García, 2018).

Regarding its application in communication, the impact of 360-degree video and VR experiences on public relations (e.g., Fraustino et al., 2018; García-Orosa & Pérez-Seijo, 2020; Herranz de la Casa et al., 2019), tourism (e.g., Pasanen et al., 2019; Wagler & Hanus, 2018), and journalism (e.g., Doyle et al., 2016; Owen et al., 2015; Watson, 2017) has stood out, the latter being the most studied field to date.

In the field of journalism, several studies have explored the impact of VR and 360-degree video on news consumption, which is now understood as an experience: "the goal is not so much the presentation of 'what happened' but to give people experiential, non-analytic insight into the events, to give them the illusion of being present in them" (Slater & Sánchez-Vives, 2016: 32). Thus, because of immersive storytelling, consumption is no longer confined to the traditional passive reception of information:

> A significant formal shift from traditional storytelling mediums to VR is that "telling" is less central to a VR experience. The audience learns through engagement and embodiment, by entering into a scene, inhabiting a digital entity, experiencing what it knows. Viewers experience the story as though they lived it. This is consistent with an understanding of VR as storyliving. (Maschio, 2017: 9)

However, the sense of presence referred to by the authors will be greater the more immersive the system used to view these contents (Hendriks et al., 2019; Van Damme et al., 2019), limited today to VR glasses. In addition, several studies suggest that, compared with conventional formats, immersive content leads to higher levels of audience engagement (Suh et al., 2018), enjoyment (Hendriks et al., 2019; Van Damme et al., 2019), story-sharing intention (Sundar et al., 2017), credibility, and even trust in the narrator (Archer & Finger, 2018; Kang et al., 2019; Sundar et al., 2017), as well as "a higher likelihood of participants to take 'political or social action'" (Archer & Finger, 2018: 3) after viewing the content.

While this immersive storytelling has been widely studied in journalism, both analytically and theoretically, this has not been the case with institutional communication in general and political communication in particular. For this reason, this chapter aims to explore the possibilities VR and 360-degree video presents for political communication and to review the immersive initiatives, projects and content created to date, and paying special attention to American election campaigns—including rallies, debates, and media coverage—as a paradigmatic example of narrative experimentation.

2 VR and 360-Degree Video Opportunities in Institutional and Political Communication

The coverage and presentation of political issues through immersive multimedia formats has arisen because such formats can create a more empathetic nexus between content and audience (Pressgrove & Bowman, 2020; Van Loon et al., 2018) as well as the "sounding board" principle

(Habermas, 1996) on which civil society acts in relation to this type of issues.

Various government institutions have promoted publications and initiatives based on immersive storytelling for awareness-building and educational and cultural purposes, sometimes with ideological underpinnings (Herranz de la Casa et al., 2019; Sidorenko Bautista et al., 2020). It has also been used in journalism, as a proselytizing tool and as an educational alternative for new audience segments.

As such, three large categories of immersive political multimedia content can be identified: media coverage (with national, regional, and/or local scope); content prepared by politicians, political parties, or political organizations; and projects and experiments carried out by universities, producers, NGOs, or individuals. All of the following content appears in the annexes.

During the 2016 U.S. presidential election, *The New York Times* used the immersive format to cover some of the candidates' events, while Bloomberg, NBC News, ABC News, and *The Washington Post* did so with the town halls, partisan pre-event meetings, debates, and interviews with Republican and Democratic spokesmen. Conventional television shows such as Showtime's *The Circus* also created immersive content, highlighting supporters' statements and the atmosphere at different campaign events. Regional and local media and outlets with less reach, such as *PBS NewsHour*, WTAE-TV Pittsburgh, KGW News, *The Atlantic*, and the *Des Moines Register*, also produced immersive content to show the mood and size of the crowds, giving a more complete and transparent picture of the Republicans' and Democrats' events.

On the same day as the U.S. presidential election in 2016, NBC used the AltspaceVR social network's VR technology to emulate its traditional "election center" in Rockefeller Center Complex Square (NYC). ABC News also broadcasted its special election coverage live in 360 degrees from Times Square. In each case, the medium aimed to extend the reach of their programming to new user segments. On inauguration day, ABC News, *TIME*, and *USA Today* used the 360-degree format to give a sense of the environment and show the preparation for and execution of the event.

In Spain, in the heat of the 2015 presidential campaign, the native-digital newspaper *El Español* organized a meeting of their newsroom journalists with the candidates Pedro Sánchez, Albert Rivera, and Pablo

Iglesias, where the camera placed the viewer at the center of a round table where the interview took place.

As such, viewers have been able to see the media in their on-site work or as organizers of specific events, so as to develop alternative and innovative narratives that could enhance and energize political communication. However, the parties and politicians themselves have also made use of this resource with similar intentions, because today they see how the "square", understood as a public space for disseminating slogans and interacting with voters, has been redefined in increasingly digital environments, with their own messaging and with increasingly segmented audiences.

In 2016, the U.S. Republican Party covered its National Convention (Cleveland, Ohio) in 360-degree video, while, in Spain, the Podemos party filmed in 360 degrees one of its events in Catalonia. Another example can be found in 2020, when the *Trump 360°* channel was created on YouTube, with content reflecting popular support for presidential candidate Donald Trump.

At the beginning of 2019, in Armenia, then Minister of High-tech Industry Hakob Arshakyan set up street stands with Oculus Go VR headsets where it was possible to have a closer look at the development of various infrastructure works, aimed to be accountable to the public.

Multilateral organizations, such as the United Nations, have also developed content on social and political issues, as well as on their work in conflict-affected areas, such as *Iraq 360* or *Clouds over Sidra*, a UNICEF-produced piece on the challenges faced by displaced people in Syria. In addition, the international tour of then UN Secretary General Ban Ki-moon was documented in 2016, so as to demonstrate the political, social, economic, and environmental problems on the UN's agenda.

From the State institutions, it has been possible to see the Executive, for example, leveraging immersive storytelling to improve communication and bring citizens closer to restricted areas such as the White House. With the help of Facebook and Felix & Paul Studios, the Obama administration created a tour of the White House, which included a conversation with the President in an intimate setting. Produced in the final two weeks of Obama's presidency, it was the former president's second appearance in a 360° production, following his participation in a 360° National Geographic short to celebrate the centennial of the National Park Services. For her part, then First Lady Michelle Obama also collaborated on an immersive production with The Verge, not only to grant a closer interview from a distinct perspective, but also to lay out her goals and plans.

South of the U.S. border, Mexico's Ministry of Tourism used the immersive format between 2017 and 2019 to showcase Mexico's vast cultural heritage. In Spain, the regional government of the Comunidad de Madrid created the *Madrid 360°* YouTube channel with a similar purpose.

Among productions that use immersive storytelling for educational-political purposes, *Project Empathy* stands out in its attempt to reduce social polarization through personal testimonies and social experiments. Also worthy of note is a piece by the NGO Mencap, which aims to help people with disabilities overcome election anxiety.

There are also highly political immersive documentaries, such as: *Meeting a Monster* (the story and testimony of a former white supremacist in the United States), *The Day the World Changed* (on the danger of nuclear arsenals), *1000 Cut Journey* (about a Stanford University experiment that seeks users' empathy through the first-person experience of a black man subjected to racism), or *This Is Climate Change* (the problem of global warming and its causes, many political).

In each case, the image of the candidates, their message, and that of their organizations, the institutional image and, in short, political communication, are reinforced and developed through narratives that seek to create a stronger connection between audience and content by bringing the two closers together.

A 60-Degree Video Coverage of the 2016 U.S. Presidential Election

As indicated in previous sections, American elections have been the main proving ground for immersive storytelling with 360-degree video and VR in political communication. Political parties and media have mainly taken advantage of 360-degree video storytelling to bring campaigns closer to citizens and allow them to have a first-person experience from afar. In this section, we will discuss the immersive projects created during the 2016 U.S. presidential election campaign.

In mid-2015, just as media outlets, such as *The New York Times*, *The Wall Street Journal*, *Al Jazeera*, *BBC*, *RTVE*, or *Vice News*, among others, began experimenting with spherical video, the Virtuality Lab studio presented Bernie Sanders with the idea of filming one of his campaign fundraising events. The video, released at the end of June 2015 on the studio's Los Angeles-based YouTube channel, not only represented a total innovation in campaign coverage, but also introduced a new strategy to bring politicians and campaign events closer to their voters and people generally.

In the video, we see an approachable Bernie Sanders, in a garden, accompanied by assistants who will surely support him in his upcoming primary election campaign. The camera is eye-height and no more than 50 cm away, such that VR glasses wearers can feel like they are right next to the candidate while he speaks about income inequality and wealth in the United States. 360-degree video, especially if viewed with a VR headset, thus becomes a great ally of political strategy since it creates a certain degree of proximity with the candidate and generates the first-person feeling of being at an official campaign event.

A few months later, Virtuality Lab filmed another Sanders campaign event, this time before a huge crowd: the speech he gave to more than 27,000 people on August 10, 2015, at the Los Angeles Memorial Sports Arena. The user's perspective changes relative to the previous video: it becomes a front-row seat with thousands of people behind him, applauding, and reacting to the candidate's words. Once again, the video seeks to convey proximity, this time with the candidate's followers.

A few months later, at the end of January 2016, *The New York Times* released four 360-degree videos dedicated to four candidates for the presidency (one for each politician): Hillary Clinton, Bernie Sanders, Ted Cruz, and Donald Trump. In each video, we see the respective candidate cheered by his or her followers and potential voters. We see them up close, in the middle of crowds, giving autographs, taking pictures, or chatting with ordinary people. But, we also see them giving their speeches on the stages that each has chosen depending on the audience he or she is addressing (a basketball stadium, a restaurant, an auditorium, etc.).

With this pioneering strategy in campaign coverage, *The New York Times* sought to allow any citizen, regardless of their state of residence or ideology, to experience, albeit virtually and simulated, a rally held by their favorite candidate. VR technology and 360-degree video have democratized and opened up these types of experiences for a large part of the citizenry, as explained in a *New York Times* article:

> Being alongside voters as they react to their favorite candidate is a privilege that watching such moments on television just does not afford. Through virtual reality, Republicans can get a taste of Democratic campaign events, and Democrats can soak up Republican ones, without having to wait in long

lines or listen to partisan speeches in their entirety. Democracy is alive and well when as many people as possible see it in action. (Healy et al., 2016)

3 Ethical Challenges in Election Campaigns with 360-Degree Video

Showing the viewer candidates' speeches or bringing them closer to different campaign events in these immersive narratives requires adherence to the same ethical standards that undergird journalistic practice. However, the innovative characteristics of immersive journalism add several unique details in order to ensure truthful, objective, and complete work (Benítez & Herrera, 2019; Pérez-Seijo & López-García, 2019).

Combining 360° video and a VR glasses system generates a certain amount of "brain deception", such that the viewer has "the feeling of being in the place where a believable action is occurring and thinks it's really happening" (De la Peña et al., 2010: 299). To achieve this result, some images have to be manipulated.

One of the first debates to arise on ethics in immersive journalism revolves around the use of film crews during filming. At the start of the U.S. election campaign in October 2015, *The Washington Post* published "The Democratic Debate Spin Room", in which the viewer can walk backstage right before a Democratic Party debate. The cameraman remains in the scene and even addresses the viewer on several occasions. The same option is taken by the *El Español* newspaper's interviews of three candidates during Spain's 2015 election campaign and *The Verge*'s "Michelle Obama 360", in which the former first lady is interviewed sitting in a White House office.

On the contrary, sometimes the film crew and their equipment are deleted from the image. For example, in "Drive Down the Vegas Strip", another of *The Washington Post's* first immersive narratives, the camera perched atop the vehicle driving down Las Vegas is edited out. In February 2016, The Verge used the same technique in "360° video takes the viewer around New Hampshire before the primary".

One of the major ethical debates on immersive journalism has revolved around the aforementioned practices. Whereas some theorists consider that deleting these elements from the scenes alters reality, others maintain that failing to do so can distract viewers and disrupt the feeling of presence (Benítez & Herrera, 2020: 173). The Associated Press has chosen to expressly "forbids manipulating photographs and the camera stays in" (Kent, 2015).

Moreover, deleting these items without previously advising the viewer can leave him or her in a vulnerable position upon interacting with the environment depicted. Sarah Jones warns of the discomfort that this experience with proximity can generate. An experiment featuring 12 immersive narratives revealed a sense of discomfort in participants when they found themselves virtually surrounded by other people (Jones, 2017). An example of this proximity can be found in "*Inside Trump's America*", *published by RYOT in 2016*, which focuses on Donald Trump's election campaign in Janesville, Wisconsin. The viewer can walk in first person among several groups of people who demonstrate for and against the candidate. However, the viewers' over-proximity to them means they sometimes find themselves in the middle of clashes, which can be discomforting.

According to Chouliaraki (2006: 221), "proper distance" requires a mix of proximity and distance. Proximity should be sufficient to appreciate the reality of the other's situation, and it is also necessary to establish a "sufficient distance for the viewer to move from a focus to their own affective response".

This need for distance can arise in face-to-face encounters with victims and their testimonies, all while this kind of reporting invites the viewer to explore the new environment. Such is the case with "*A rooster touring to support Bernie Sanders*", published by BBC News in February 2016. In the experience, the camera stands opposite Makk Buckey, a Bernie Sanders supporter who includes the viewer on his journey as he drives a themed bus across the United States to support candidate Sanders.

Finally, in keeping with Kool (2016), any medium capable of turning viewers into participants can make them emotionally vulnerable:

> Under the realism of VR experiences, it is easy to forget as the viewer that the story is being told and constructed with intention. As the viewer develops a personal stake within another reality through an empathy engendering machine, the viewer becomes emotionally vulnerable. (p. 7)

Thus, this type of immersive content can be highly persuasive and, taken to the extreme, "could very well become an incubator for propaganda and exploitation" (Kool, 2016: 7). Kool describes several tools of persuasion, including music, directional sound, or abbreviating an event by incorporating only the most shocking moments. The political underpinnings of such productions can often conceal a certain attempt to influence voter intent. In addition to the tools Kool describes, having celebrities deliver a message can also be persuasive, as seen in several episodes of "*Iowa Caucus in 360°*", published by RYOT in 2016. For example, in "*Gaby Hoffmann takes you to breakfast*", the actress questions the suitability of then-presidential candidate Hillary Clinton. In these cases, the journalist's responsibility and good faith are fundamental in maintaining credibility and rigor in such narratives.

4 Conclusions

Virtual reality technologies and 360-degree video recording systems broke into the mass market as potential tools for general communication and storytelling. At the same time as the news media was beginning to produce their first 360-degree video reports, the political media sector (parties, politicians, and government institutions) began to take an interest in this form of immersive storytelling.

Throughout this chapter, we have seen some of immersive storytelling's main uses as a tool for institutional communication and as a communication strategy for political parties, especially during election campaigns and cycles. Compared to other ways of producing content and broadcasting events, immersive storytelling presents the following benefits and opportunities for political communication: it can bring events ever-closer to the viewer, turning the viewing into a first-person experience; it democratizes "attendance" of events that people would not otherwise be able to attend; when showing the entire scene in 360 degrees, it is more transparent; it offers an innovative alternative for education and orientation on electoral or sociopolitical issues; it connects with new audiences, especially young people; and in some cases it provides a privileged view of places or events.

However, in addition to the myriad possibilities that immersive storytelling has opened up for political communication, ethical dilemmas have arisen around image manipulation, content's emotional impact, subliminal propaganda, and among other issues, the potential influence on voter intent.

Annexes

Table 8.1 National, regional, and/or local media videos

Broadcaster	*Topic/title*	*Type*	*Link*
The New York Times	Hillary Clinton, Bernie Sanders, Ted Cruz and Donald Trump rallies (2016)	360° video	https://bit.ly/3acJzeX https://bit.ly/3aeYHJ1 https://bit.ly/2OxIGFD https://bit.ly/3qXen9t
	President Trump's Plan Could Erase This After School Program		https://bit.ly/3uJR7hQ
	Jimmy Carter: From Peanuts to Solar Panels		https://bit.ly/3dV9r1b
	Lincoln in the Bardo		https://bit.ly/3dZMMAX
	Inside President-elect Donald Trump's Cabinet Room		https://bit.ly/2NNntaE
	Tour Trump's Childhood Home		https://bit.ly/37XUbNj
	Donald Trump Cheered On By Ohioans On "Thank You" Tour		https://bit.ly/3kzdcLd
	On Fidel Castro's Old Campus, Students Pay Tribute		https://bit.ly/2NGfGLX
	French Election: The Moment Emmanuel Macron Won		https://bit.ly/3sGcte7
	Inside the Trump Victory Party		https://bit.ly/2PmRaQk
	Snap a Selfie with Hillary Clinton		https://bit.ly/3q1wxWj
Bloomberg	Interview with Ben Carson (2016)	360° video	https://bit.ly/3bhijeX
	Dance with Delegates (National Democrats Convention, 2016)	360° video	https://bit.ly/2NlmKNi
NBC News	Preparations for the National Democratic Convention in Philadelphia	360° video	https://bit.ly/3daQtmP
	Summary of the Democratic National Convention in Philadelphia (2016)	360° video	https://bit.ly/3jHOckw
	Exploring the National Republican Convention (2016)	360° video	https://bit.ly/3s2EvjJ
	Live Election Day Tracking 2016—Virtual Democracy Plaza	VR	https://altvr.com/nbcnews-2/

(*continued*)

Table 8.1 (continued)

Broadcaster	*Topic/title*	*Type*	*Link*
ABC News	David Muir Tour of the National Convention of Democrats in Philadelphia (2016)	360° video	https://bit.ly/379YxAF
	Republican Convention (Ohio, 2016)	360° video	https://bit.ly/3aZmPOZ
	Live Coverage of Election Day 2016	360° video	https://bit.ly/3tXHlrG
	360th View Inside the GOP Debate Spin Room	360° video	https://bit.ly/2PlHTbf
	Havana Streets During President Obama's Visit to Cuba	360° video	https://bit.ly/3bLRxve
BBC News	Iowa 2016: On the campaign trail	360° video	https://bit.ly/3q1DXco
	A rooster touring to support Bernie Sanders	360° video	https://bit.ly/3uFlrKg
	David Cameron calls EU referendum for June	360° video	https://bit.ly/3dWkuHq
	US Elections: Political tribes of Georgia	360° video	https://bit.ly/3kxTRtH
Washington Post	Democratic Party Debate (2015)	360° video	https://bit.ly/2LR3hUq
	Democratic Party Debate (2016)	360° video	https://bit.ly/2Zebjda
	The Democratic debate spin room, in 360°	360° video	https://bit.ly/3sCIWly
	360 video: Donald Trump's military fundraiser	360° video	https://bit.ly/3b7Vxax
	Watch a Donald Trump event in Iowa	360° video	https://bit.ly/2Od2UnH
	Thousands rally for Sanders before Iowa caucuses	360° video	https://bit.ly/3q1yemD
	Take a peek inside a Republican Iowa caucus	360° video	https://bit.ly/3sCJcRy
	Watch a Democratic caucus in 360°	360° video	https://bit.ly/3sCGxHn
	Watch a Republicans caucus in 360°	360° video	https://bit.ly/2NM7TvO
	360° video takes you around New Hampshire before the primary	360° video	https://bit.ly/3b1SnVn
	Washington Post-Univision debate opening	360° video	https://bit.ly/3kyb1r5
	A view from Trump's podium at his future hotel, in 360°	360° video	https://bit.ly/3dWq9NG

(*continued*)

Table 8.1 (continued)

Broadcaster	*Topic/title*	*Type*	*Link*
	360° video takes you around New Hampshire before the primary	360° video	https://bit.ly/2NN0D2V
	Drive down the Vegas Strip in 360	360° video	https://bit.ly/3q81lVw
The Circus (Showtime)	Hillary Clinton Rally (Election 2016)	360° video	https://bit.ly/3qjxLgS
	Donald Trump Rally (Election 2016)	360° video	https://bit.ly/377DUoS
PBS NewsHour	National Convention of The Democrats (Philadelphia, 2016)	360° video	https://bit.ly/3769rHF
WTAE-TV Pittsburgh	National Convention of Republicans (Ohio, 2016)	360° video	https://bit.ly/3daCBcw
KGW News	Republican National Convention Tour (2016)	360° video	https://bit.ly/37axFka
The Atlantic	National Convention of Republicans (Ohio, 2016)	360° video	https://bit.ly/3tZ02ey
Des Moines Register	Iowa Caucus Victory by Ted Cruz (2016)	360° video	https://bit.ly/3qhQ0TN
TIME	Donald Trump's Oath as President of the United States (2017)	360° video	https://bit.ly/2OCv247
USA Today	Donald Trump's Oath as President of the United States (2017)	360° video	http://bit.ly/37eyWGJ
	360 degrees of Donald Trump	360° video	https://bit.ly/3dUuXTM
	Inside Donald Trump rally as Ted Cruz wins	360° video	https://bit.ly/3sCV99O
	Sarah Palin speaks in Cedar Rapids	360° video	https://bit.ly/3r4RL7e
	360 video: Cubans watch President Obama	360° video	https://bit.ly/3q5CIZs
	Cubans in Miami and Havana debate President Obama's trip to Cuba	360° video	https://bit.ly/3r5SeGj
El Español	Pedro Sánchez's meeting with journalists from the newspaper *El Español*	360° video	https://bit.ly/2TScHj3
	Debate with Albert Rivera in 360°	360° video	https://bit.ly/3bIrQvC
	Debate with Pablo Iglesias in 360°	360° video	https://bit.ly/3r6iTm7

Source: Created by authors

Table 8.2 Videos prepared by politicians, political parties, or political organizations

Broadcaster	*Topic/title*	*Type*	*Link*
US Republican Party	Donald Trump at the Republican National Convention (Ohio, 2016)	360° video	https://bit.ly/3aZVJan
Donald Trump's Campaign Commando	*Trump 360°* YouTube Channel (Election 2020)	360° video	http://bit.ly/3jQI89u
Podemos Party (Spain)	Event in Catalonia 2016	360° video	https://bit.ly/3tVBIui
Armenian Ministry of High-Tech Industry	Report by Armenian High-Tech Minister of Industry Hakob Arshakyan (2019)	360° video	https://bit.ly/3aSAO8Y
UN	*Iraq 360* (2019)	360° video	https://bit.ly/3d85G8g
	Clouds over Sidra (2015)	360° video	https://bit.ly/3qhSvFs
	2016 International Tour by UN Secretary Ban-Ki Moon	360° video	https://bit.ly/3tVtTof
Barack Obama—Facebook	White House Inside Tour	360° video	https://bit.ly/3b8bGvo
Barack Obama—National Geographic	Centenary of National Parks	360° video	http://bit.ly/3rPF8Nb
The Verge	*Michelle Obama*	360° video	https://bit.ly/3agUu7x
Mexican Ministry of Tourism	Promotion of Mexico's history and heritage	360° video	https://bit.ly/3d9BycT
Community of Madrid	YouTube Channel *Madrid 360*	360° video	http://bit.ly/3tU7bNf

Source: Created by authors

Table 8.3 Projects and experiments carried out by universities, producers, NGOs, or individuals

Broadcaster	*Topic/title*	*Type*	*Link*
Mencap	Helping people with disabilities reduce anxiety before an election event	VR	http://bbc.in/3b5STRh http://bit.ly/3rOCCqz
Benefit Studios	Fighting social polarization by creating empathy	VR and 360° video	http://bit.ly/3pgLQu5

(*continued*)

Table 8.3 (continued)

Broadcaster	*Topic/title*	*Type*	*Link*
Gabriela Arp, Oculus VR for Good and Life After Hate	*Meeting a Monster*	360° video	http://ocul.us/3dhQFAW
Gabo Arora, Saschka Unseld, Tomorrow Never Knows	*The Day the World Changed*	VR	http://bit.ly/3b3XcMS
RYOT	Bernie Sanders on Immigration and Inequality	360° video	https://bit.ly/2NHEd3c
	Bernie Sanders Behind the Scenes | Episode 1 of Iowa Caucus in 360°	360° video	https://bit.ly/2ZWxxRc
	Justin Long Volunteers | Episode 2 of Iowa Caucus in 360°	360° video	https://bit.ly/37WfKOy
	Gaby Hoffmann takes you to breakfast | Episode 3 of Iowa Caucus in 360°	360° video	https://bit.ly/39oUrWu
	Bernie Sanders At A Campaign Rally	360° video	https://bit.ly/37VIAhT
	Bernie Sanders' Campaign Headquarters in Iowa	360° video	https://bit.ly/3bLwdpL
	Iowa Caucus in 360°	360° video	https://bit.ly/3kzfji7
	Red Hot Chili Peppers perform for Bernie Sanders	360° video	https://bit.ly/3bOt6NJ
	Inside Trump's America—Donald Trump Rally in 360	360° video	https://bit.ly/3sHVlER
Stanford University	*1000 Cut Journey*	VR	https://stanford.io/3d80gZe
Danfung Dennis and Eric Strauss	*This is Climate Change*	360° video	http://bit.ly/37gm9Un

Source: Created by authors

References

Archer, D., & Finger, K. (2018). *Walking in another's virtual shoes: Do 360-degree video news stories generate empathy in viewers?* Columbia Journalism School: Tow Center for Digital Journalism. https://www.cjr.org/tow_center_reports/virtual-reality-news-empathy.php

Benítez, M. J., & Herrera, S. (2019). Good ethical practices in immersive reporting with 360° video. *Telos, 111*, 22–25. https://telos.fundaciontelefonica.

com/telos-111-asuntos-de-comunicacion-maria-jose-benitez-susana-herrera-periodismo-inmersivo-360o-practicas-eticas

Benítez, M. J., & Herrera, S. (2020). *How to produce immersive reports with 360° video*. UOC.

Chouliaraki, L. (2006). *The spectatorship of suffering*. Sage.

Damiani, J. (2016). The great semantic divides: Virtual reality vs. 360-degree video. *UploadVR*. https://uploadvr.com/virtual-reality-vs-360-degree-videosemantic-divide/

De la Peña, N., Weil, P., Llobera, J., Spanlang, B., Friedman, D., Sánchez-Vives, M.-V., & Slater, M. (2010). Immersive journalism: Immersive virtual reality for the first-person experience of news. *Presence: Teleoperators and Virtual Environments, 19*(4), 291–301.

Dolan, D., & Parets, M. (2016). Redefining the axiom of story: The VR and 360 video complex. *TechCrunch*. https://techcrunch.com/2016/01/14/redefining-the-axiom-of-story-the-vr-and-360-video-complex/

Dominguez, E. (2017). Going beyond the classic news narrative convention: The background to and challenges of immersion in journalism. *Frontiers in Digital Humanities, 4*, 1–11.

Doyle, P., Gelman, M., & Gill, S. (2016). Viewing the future? Virtual reality in journalism. *Knight Foundation*. http://www.knightfoundation.org/media/uploads/publication_pdfs/VR_report_web.pdf

Facebook. (2014). Facebook to acquire Oculus. *About.fb*. https://about.fb.com/news/2014/03/facebook-to-acquire-oculus/

Fraustino, J. D., Lee, J. Y., Lee, S. Y., & Ahn, H. (2018). Effects of 360 video on attitudes toward disaster communication: Mediating and moderating roles of spatial presence and prior disaster media involvement. *Public Relations Review, 44*(3), 331–341.

Furness, T. A. (2014). Introduction. In B. Delaney (Ed.), *Sex, drugs, and tessellation: The truth about virtual reality as revealed in the pages of Cyberedge Journal* (pp. 7–10). CyberEdge Information Services.

García-Orosa, B., & Pérez-Seijo, S. (2020). The use of 360 video by international humanitarian aid organizations to spread social messages and increase engagement. *VOLUNTAS: International Journal of Voluntary and Nonprofit Organizations, 31*(6), 1311–1329.

Habermas, J. (1996). *Between facts and norms: Contributions to a discourse theory of law and democracy*. MIT Press.

Healy, O., Roberts, G., Schmid, C., & Parshina-Kottas, Y. (2016). Experiencing the presidential campaign: A virtual reality film. *The New York Times*. https://www.nytimes.com/2016/01/30/us/politics/election-2016-virtual-reality-vr-video.html

Hendriks, P., Wiltink, D., Huiskamp, M., Schaap, G., & Ketelaar, P. (2019). Taking the full view: How viewers respond to 360-degree video news. *Computers in Human Behavior, 91*, 24–32.

Herranz de la Casa, J. M., Caerols Mateo, R., & Sidorenko Bautista, P. (2019). Virtual reality and 360° video in business and institutional communication. *Journal of Communication, 18*(2), 177–199.

Jerald, J. (2015). *The VR book: Human-centered design for virtual reality*. Morgan & Claypool Publishers-ACM.

Jones, S. (2017). Disrupting the narrative: Immersive journalism in virtual reality. *Journal of Media Practice, 18*(2–3), 171–185.

Kang, S., O'Brien, E., Villarreal, A., Lee, W., & Mahood, C. (2019). Immersive Journalism and Telepresence: Does virtual reality news use affect news credibility? *Digital Journalism, 7*(2), 294–313.

Kent, T. (2015). An ethical reality check for virtual reality journalism. *Medium*. https://medium.com/@tjrkent/an-ethical-reality-check-for-virtual-reality-journalism-8e5230673507

Kool, H. (2016). The ethics of immersive journalism: A rhetorical analysis of news storytelling with virtual reality technology. *Intersect, 9*, 1–11.

Mabrook, R., & Singer, J. B. (2019). Virtual reality, 360 video, and journalism studies: Conceptual approaches to immersive technologies. *Journalism Studies, 20*(14), 2096–2112.

Maschio, T. (2017). Storyliving: An ethnographic study of how audiences experience VR and what that means for journalists. *Google News Lab*. https://newslab.withgoogle.com/assets/docs/storyliving-a-study-of-vr-in-journalism.pdf

Owen, T., Pitt, F., Aronson-Rath, R., & Milward, J. (2015). Virtual reality journalism. *Columbia Journalism Review*. https://www.cjr.org/tow_center_reports/virtual_reality_journalism.php

Pasanen, K., Pesonen, J., Murphy, J., Heinonen, J., & Mikkonen, J. (2019). Comparing tablet and virtual reality glasses for watching nature tourism videos. In J. Pesonen & J. Neidhardt (Eds.), *Information and communication technologies in tourism*. Springer.

Pérez-Seijo, S., & López-García, X. (2018). The two sides of immersive journalism: The challenge of participation and ethical problems. In M. López Paredes (Ed.), *New communication scenarios: Challenges and convergences* (pp. 279–305). PUCE Publication Center.

Pérez-Seijo, S., & López-García, X. (2019). The ethics of journalism immersive to debate. *Hipertext.net, 18*, 1–13.

Pérez-Seijo, S., Gutiérrez-Caneda, B., & López-García, X. (2020). Digital and high-tech journalism: From consolidation to renewed challenges. *Index Communication, 10*(3), 129–151.

Pressgrove, G., & Bowman, N. D. (2020). From immersion to intention? Exploring advances in prosocial storytelling. *International Journal of Nonprofit and Voluntary Sector Marketing, e1689*, 1–12.

Sherman, W. R., & Craig, A. B. (2003). *Understanding virtual reality*. Morgan Kauffman.

Sidorenko Bautista, P., Herranz, J. M., & Cantero, J. I. (2020). 360° multimedia content as tools in public institution awareness campaigns. *Sphera Publica, 1*(20), 95–118.

Sirkkunen, E., Väätäjä, H., Uskali, T., & Rezaei, P. P. (2016). Journalism in virtual reality: Opportunities and future research challenges. In *Proceedings of the 20th international academic mindtrek conference* (pp. 297–303).

Slater, M., & Sánchez-Vives, M. V. (2016). Enhancing our lives with immersive virtual reality. *Frontiers in Robotics and AI, 3*(74), 1–47.

Suh, A., Wang, G., Gu, W., & Wagner, C. (2018). Enhancing audience engagement through immersive 360-degree videos: An experimental study. In D. Schmorrow & C. Fidopiastis (Eds.), *Augmented cognition: Intelligent technologies. AC 2018*. Springer.

Sundar, S. S., Kang, J., & Oprean, D. (2017). Being there in the midst of the story: How immersive journalism affects our perceptions and cognitions. *Cyberpsychology, Behavior and Social Networking, 20*(11), 672–682.

Van Damme, K., All, A., De Marez, L., & Van Leuven, S. (2019). 360 video journalism: Experimental study on the effect of immersion on news experience and distant suffering. *Journalism Studies, 20*(14), 2053–2076.

Van Loon, A., Bailenson, J., Zaki, J., Bostick, J., & Willer, R. (2018). Virtual reality perspective-taking increases cognitive empathy for specific others. *PLoS One, 13*(8), e0202442.

Wagler, A., & Hanus, M. D. (2018). Comparing virtual reality tourism to real-life experience: Effects of presence and engagement on attitude and enjoyment. *Communication Research Reports, 35*(5), 456–464.

Watson, Z. (2017). *VR for news? The new reality*. Reuters Institute for the Study of Journalism.

CHAPTER 9

Emotions, Engagement and Social Media

Nieves Lagares Diez, Erika Jaráiz Gulías, and Gina Sibaja Quesada

1 Introduction

For some years now, political participation and political engagement have gone hand in hand, being sometimes treated as the same thing, especially in the digital spaces, where the constant emergence of new platforms of social communication, such as Instagram or the mobile instant messaging services (MIMS) have rendered the connection between the two more explicit as well as more analysable. The emergence of this new space of analysis also entailed the addition of new techniques and methods, which compel us to give special attention not only to the form of communication, but also to the content generating said communication and to the impact it has.

N. Lagares Diez • E. Jaráiz Gulías (✉)
University of Santiago de Compostela, Santiago de Compostela, Spain
e-mail: mnieves.lagares@usc.es; erika.jaraiz@usc.es

G. Sibaja Quesada
University of Costa Rica, San José, Costa Rica
e-mail: gina.sibaja@ucr.ac.cr

B. García-Orosa (ed.), *Digital Political Communication Strategies*, The Palgrave Macmillan Series in International Political Communication, https://doi.org/10.1007/978-3-030-81568-4_9

The researchers' attention focused on many different things, from the limited expression of the presence of political engagement or its connection to political participation to the role of emotions and the effects thereof, to the so-called emotional framing, to the engagement in political campaigns and even its impact on electoral participation.

However, the idea of political engagement was not always clear, nor was it used in the same sense (Dahlgren, 2009). Political engagement is a vast notion which, generally, encompasses behaviours, cognitive processes and attitudes referring to politics and its activities, but which has to be distinguished from civic engagement, which is defined as the organisation of a volunteer activity meant to help, and solve problems of third parties (Zukin et al., 2006). Political engagement may be considered a specific kind of civic engagement, and thus, while the latter is a means of participating in and influencing the life of a community, political engagement seeks to influence political issues, systems and structures.

2 The Political Engagement

Interest in political engagement was initially linked to the studies concerning political participation and to the research trying to explain changes in the patterns of participation, as well as to the measurement of the effects that the media and political communication itself have on the citizens' actions within the political arena. If the interpretation of the Virtuous Circle was used by Pippa Norris to respond to the theories on negative mass media effects emerging in the 1990s (Norris, 2011), the Civic Engagement Thesis was pivotal in the formulation of her concept of an "active" public exposed to the influence of information coming from the media; a public which not only selects the message it consumes, but which also, at the same time, learns about the political system, reinforcing its positive attitudes towards it. This positive interpretation, which Norris tries to construct, will be the very Gordian knot of the relationship between the presence on digital media and the positive attitudes regarding the system.

The extent of the use of new technologies led very quickly to studies on online engagement, as an expansion of the repertoire of ways and channels of political participation, communication and information (Anduiza et al., 2012), assuming that digital media reduce the cost of acquiring information (Brundidge & Rice, 2009; Tolbert & McNeal, 2003), are a source of learning (Lupia & Philpot, 2005; Norris, 2011) and have an impact on our perception of the political world and on our capacity of dealing with its intricacies (Kallinikos, 2004).

The notion of engagement entails a twofold significance, in matters of mobilisation (participation) and of cognitive processes (learning, interests, search for information, etc.) respectively; whereas the former (active engagement) makes us contact the politicians, attend and participate in political meetings and urges our electoral participation, the latter (cognitive engagement) alludes to a psychological attachment to politics, manifesting itself through attitudes (Eckstein et al., 2012) such as interest in politics, search for political information (attitude and behaviour) or identifying oneself with a political party (feeling) (Carreras, 2016).

Finally, there is a third and broader significance of political engagement in which, without overlooking the behaviours, there is a twofold psychological dimension, involving knowledge and emotions (Barrett & Zani, 2014), thereby making engagement a prerequisite of participation, a precondition for it (Dahlgren, 2009). In this interpretation, it is possible to speak of a cognitive engagement (political knowledge, attention to the media, conversations on political topics) or of an emotional engagement (intensity of feelings regarding political or civic issues) without any need of having an engaged behaviour.

The motivational interpretation of engagement also had different trains of thought. Whereas Emler (2011), following Barrett, speaks of two motivational conductors of political engagement, namely, the interest in politics and the sense of civic duty, which can occur simultaneously or as alternatives, other approaches focused on the perceptions of injustice and on the feelings towards injustice as the motivational origin of engagement and generators of collective action. Within this motivational sequence, interest and civic duty arouse attention for politics, which generates knowledge and it is this knowledge which provides the basis for the formation of opinions on political issues and topics and these, in turn, make up the ideological identity of the political actors. For Emler, these are the contents but not the determinants (reasons) of engagement; each of these contents is necessary, but not sufficient for generating engagement, because there are other factors which must be taken into account and which can influence the process, such as the individual features and the environmental factors associated with socialisation, education, and so on. These personal and environmental elements Emler refers to indicate motivations which are outside the contents themselves and mark some objectives which, sometimes, go beyond the impact on political life, like in the case of "slacktivism", referring to online political participation and engagement, aiming not at the impact on political outcomes, but serves the only purpose of increasing the "feel-good-factor" of those participating (Christensen, 2011). Moreover, even if we have to admit that some degree of engagement is necessary for participation, not all the forms of engagement facilitate democracy; some are directed towards non-political areas or may trigger non-democratic behaviours, such as ethnic (Dahlgren, 2009) or gender discrimination. The problem, as pointed out by Dahlgren, consists in the fact that, in the present-day vision of democratic theory, political participation is generally understood as deliberation and, in this sense, as a generator of democratic quality, which is not necessarily guaranteed. This may be due to the fact that there is no reason to consider the lack of engagement as the absence of something, but rather it can be interpreted as a political act: the choice not to commit.

In this perspective, engagement refers to subjective states, focusing one's attention on certain objects, and it is in this psychological dimension that some connection with practical activities must occur, in order to make citizens feel empowered and to turn towards political participation. By contrast, the lack of commitment and participation may have different expressions, such as resignation, or alternative attitudes, such as lack of trust, ambivalence and indifference (Bennulf & Hedberg, 1999). The latter will be the psychological condition which better describes the majority of those who are disconnected (disengaged).

In any case, both connection and disconnection must have a motivational basis (Dahlgren, 2009) in which the emotional engagement will be rooted. Therefore, when democratic theory argues in favour of the citizens' political engagement solely on the basis of rationality, forgetting the existence of the affective, emotional, passional factors, it ends up ignoring, as pointed out by Hall (2005) that motivation without affection is impossible to understand and explain.

3 Engagement and Social Media

The relationship between mobilisation and political participation is clear and was widely studied (Rosenstone & Hansen, 1993; Verba et al., 1995); the contact between the political leaders and parties and the voters, particularly the direct contact plays an important role in the voting decision

(Rosenstone & Hansen, 1993). This mobilisation basically occurs in electoral periods, during campaigns, when both the parties and the leaders focus their efforts on the activation, reinforcing and conversion of voters, as once defined by Lazarsfeld et al. (1968). In the function of activating and establishing political engagement, a fundamental role is played both by the information the voters receive from the media (McLeod et al., 1999) and by personal influences received by the citizens from their most immediate surroundings (Katz & Lazarsfeld, 1979). In this regard, social media gain a particular prominence over other traditional communication channels, given that they allow for personalised and direct contact with voters, by building digital communities and social networks (Lilleker, 2013) which stimulate citizens' exposure to political information with a mobilising character (Tang & Lee, 2013). The increasingly habitual use of social media for information purposes is furthermore associated to an increase in the citizens' political engagement (Gil de Zúñiga et al., 2012). The new technologies brought about an important source of innovation in the instruments available to politicians in order to carry out mobilisation—which, in turn, becomes a relevant element in the construction of political engagement, even to the extent of the effects of digital mobilisation becoming more prominent in the construction of political engagement than in the individual's electoral participation (Vaccari, 2016).

In order to understand this idea, one has to take into account the twofold dimension of the facilitating role of digital media in the access to information: first of all through encountering information, often accidentally (Gil de Zúñiga et al., 2012; Tang & Lee, 2013), without actively seeking it; and secondly, by rendering the mobilisation of voters by politicians, party members and other citizens more straightforward and accessible, primarily in the case of younger voters (Aldrich et al., 2016), many of whom would not have been invited to participate through the traditional means of mobilisation (Verba et al., 1995). This leads to the interpretation of Internet access in terms of its capacity to attract new, previously inactive participants to political and civic life (Vaccari, 2016); it also triggers opposing views, with some contending that the mobilising capacity of the new technologies is limited, for they will only contribute to reinforcing the engagement of those who had already been involved (Bimber, 1999; Norris, 2003).

The debate on the political function of social media is therefore still open, with many arguing that digital tools are rarely used in order to engage with political parties or electoral candidates and that their main role is focused on the contribution to learning and to the building of communities, facilitating the participation and the engagement (Koc-Michalska & Lilleker, 2017), and even if we were to compare them with other types of participation such as protests and, above all, civic engagement (Boulianne, 2015), the relationship between the use of social media and participation in electoral campaigns is much weaker. However, social media have become an important arena of action, especially for organisations belonging to civil society, so that, besides mobilising efforts during electoral campaigns, mobilisation also occurs in other moments (Rosenstone & Hansen, 1993), resulting in a political participation more oriented towards civic engagement (Koc-Michalska & Lilleker, 2017).

But, beyond this debate, the increasing use of digital media has led to a growing interest in the research of their mobilising function and their capacity to generate political engagement. In the beginning, research focused on the use of emails as a form of contact during election campaigns (Krueger, 2010); subsequently, and most of all following Obama's victory in the 2008 elections (Bimber, 2014), they focused on the role played by text messages (SMS) (Kenski et al., 2010; Malhotra et al., 2011) and, finally, due to the problems regarding access to email and phone data which caused political parties and leaders to focus on social networks as tools of digital communication, researchers also turned their attention to the analysis of the role played by social networks, primarily Facebook and Twitter, in the communication with voters (Gerodimos & Justinussen, 2015; Bond et al., 2012). Both social networks offered a platform for political participation and election campaigns, with Twitter being more polarised than Facebook (Yarchi et al., 2020). Moreover, over the recent years, the use of MIMS, especially of WhatsApp, has been growing exponentially and this fact had important effects, both in the way we as citizens obtain our information (or disinformation) and in the political engagement we acquire through the Internet. These applications allow the sharing of multimedia messages and facilitate dialogue and discussion within the network (Valenzuela et al., 2019) offering, unlike Twitter and Facebook, a relatively private and controlled environment for political conversations (Valeriani & Vaccari, 2017). Indeed, notwithstanding the early stage of the research, there is already evidence that WhatsApp and especially the dialogic construction generated through this application, was successfully used to increase political and electoral participation (Moura & Michelson, 2017), though one has to be very careful with the marketing of the companies which sell these services and give weight to their importance.

Boulianne's (2015) meta-analyses show that the use of social networks as well as of the Internet in general (Boulianne, 2009), positively associates with higher levels of political participation, though not exactly within the framework of election campaigns. On the other hand, Aldrich et al. (2016), in their comparative analysis of the relationship between online mobilisation and political engagement in the 2010 British and the 2012 US elections, conclude that, despite the fact that offline mobilisation shows signs of having a bigger impact, the role of digital media is not negligible; the authors establish a strong connection between this kind of online mobilisation and political engagement, especially regarding the voters' involvement in the political campaign. Following a similar path, Cantijoch et al. (2015), single out low-intensity political activities on the Internet, especially the search for information, as the first step towards higher levels of political and electoral participation.

In short, the use of social media plays, at present, a relevant role in the construction of the citizens' political engagement towards political parties and leaders, by facilitating the interaction and access to information; however, there is no agreement as yet on whether this role is greater than that of other, more traditional activities; nor is it clear which are the mediating factors in this process. Moreover, it is for this reason that, from an angle of interpretation which addresses constructivist contextual factors and cognitive factors, we point out the importance of emotions as a catalyser of the development of the political engagement in the case of those citizens who participate in the social networks.

4 The Use of Emotions on Social Networks During Election Campaigns

Regardless of the debate on the reasons, the impact or the effects thereof, the generalisation of the use of social media in election campaigns over the last few years has been playing an increasingly decisive role in the marketing strategies of parties and candidates alike: whoever is not there on the networks does not exist in politics. Social media allow for a larger professionalisation of electoral strategies while facilitating the direct contact of the leaders with the voters, creating the possibility for a larger degree of personalisation of political campaigning. The research on the use of social networks in campaigns taking place in different countries are numerous (Bond et al., 2012; Gerodimos & Justinussen, 2015), ranging from those focusing on the fundraising function, on the integration of social media tools with core campaign activities or the use of data analytics in order to generate personalised messages to voters (Bimber, 2014), to those who cover the flows of information and disinformation (Valenzuela et al., 2019), fake news, the role of social media in the setting of the political agenda or in audience engagement,[1] or the use of message framing and its effects on voters' behaviour (Sahly et al., 2019). This last focal point is especially relevant for our approach, for it includes the so-called 'emotional framing', which generally refers to the use of affective language with the aim of mobilising the electorate (Nabi, 2003), which further underscores the role emotions play in politics and especially in the voting decision.

5 Emotions, Social Media and Engagement

The rationalism that dominates Social Sciences has given way, in some sectors of the political analysis, to an increasing acknowledgement of the importance of emotions in explaining political and electoral behaviour. The impact of emotions is being analysed with a more and more multidisciplinary focus and with numerous methodological approaches, especially in the field of Political Communication, where identifying the importance of affective elements and emotions in processing information (Neuman et al., 2018) has resulted in the proliferation of studies concerning sentiment analysis, especially when it comes to social networks. This approach was furthermore encouraged by the wide range of sentiment analysis techniques and software currently available which facilitate the conducting of such research.

The methodological approach to the analysis of emotions on social networks was basically carried out from two perspectives: that of valence categories (positive and negative emotions) and that of discrete categories, that is, the individual presence of emotions, such as anger, fear or enthusiasm among others (Sahly et al., 2019). Regarding the latter, some studies pointed out the role of emotions in the citizens' information-seeking

[1] Twitter defines engagement as the number of times a user interacted with a tweet, including clicks, retweets, replies, follows, likes, links, cards, hashtags, embedded media, username, profile photo or tweet expansion.

process, identifying anxiety as a generator and anger as an inhibitor of information seeking and of the need for learning (Valentino et al., 2008), whereas enthusiasm would increase the interest in election campaigns (Vasilopoulos et al., 2018). The use of emotional language in social media messages increases their dissemination capacity across various digital communities (Brady et al., 2017), thereby stimulating Emotional Social Sharing (Bazarova et al., 2015). This constructivist vision of emotions, as being socially shared (Gordon, 1981), led us to identify, in one of our previous studies on emotions expressed on Twitter during national elections in Bolivia and Spain, a certain process of emotional convergence, a 'constructed state of mind' as the end of the election campaign was drawing closer (Jaráiz-Gulías et al., 2021).

The US presidential campaigns in 2008 and 2016, bringing to power Barack H. Obama and Donald Trump respectively, were two archetypal cases of both intensive use of the new ICTs and recourse to emotions. Both used similar technological tools and resorted to emotions in order to strengthen the connection between citizens and the respective candidate, both enjoyed electoral success, but with the background of different ideologies, parties, policy proposals and emotions.

From the legendary "Yes, we can!" to the insistence on positioning Obama as a candidate in favour of equality, on the *www.glee.com* portal belonging to the LGBT community in the U.S., the uploading of whole speeches to YouTube, with the option of Spanish subtitles, so as to bring the candidate closer to the Hispanic community, to creating a profile on the *www.migente.com* platform or to having recourse to such platforms as AsianAve (of the Asian community) or to *www.BlackPlanet.com* (of the Afro-American one), the whole Obama campaign consisted of a hitherto unseen effort to generate engagement by associating emotions to targets.

This same objective was also targeted by publicity in video games, used as yet another strategy for segmenting the population, but also for triggering the political and affective engagement among younger people (Hendricks & Denton, 2010), or the constant attempt to break, by means of dialogue, the traditional one-way character of the process of communication through the media, giving special importance to actions initiated by the citizens, such as the Hope poster, created by street artist Shepard Fairey, which became one of the most iconic images of the electoral clash, or the video clip of Will.i.am, the lead singer of the Black Eyed Peas band, with the 'Yes, we can!' slogan, in which the singer is joined by other artists, including actress Scarlett Johansson. The song, accompanied by Spanish and Sign Language translations was posted together with an Obama speech (https://www.youtube.com/watch?v=Q8boC4tMK_g), thereby ensuring the emotional engagement which paid off so much during the said campaign.

Similar elements appear in Trump's 2016 campaign, under the slogan "Make America Great Again" (MAGA). The Republican candidate based his campaign upon stimulating the "fear of the other" as the core focus of his narrative, staged with the help of social networks, especially Twitter. MAGA speaks of the emotional link between the idea of a nation in decline and an irreverent and powerful "saviour" figure, as it was projected.

With Trump, we see the emergence of "data mining"—the identification of patterns or profiles within a great volume of data—thanks to AI tools furnished by the Cambridge Analytica consulting firm; this allows the microsegmentation of the population, identifying what was termed as "the persuadables", who were then bombarded with messages likely to be accepted, according to each target. However, this high level of analytical precision, so extensively talked about, would have been to no avail, had there not been, in its background, a certain emotional semantics focused on each target. With Trump, the presence of an emotional framing in which only one semantics—that of Trumpism—found a place, became apparent.

It is certain that using emotional messages in election campaigns by candidates and the effect these messages have on voters' behaviour, became generalised and, at present, there already is a body of research focused on emotionally rooted political engagement (Gerbaudo et al., 2019); this research mainly deals with negative emotions in the campaigns' digital communication (Savoy, 2017), up to the point of attributing a larger amount of success to communication strategies having a strong negative emotional charge (Ceron & d'Adda, 2015; Liu & Lei, 2018). However, not even on this point are the researchers unanimous; some, in fact, state that campaign strategies focused on triggering positive emotional reactions (positive posting) are capable of generating motivation and higher engagement levels among social network users (Gerbaudo et al., 2019) and show that positive news contents are more likely to go viral on social media (Berger & Milkman, 2012). Some even found a positive correlation between the emotional charge of the emitted messages and the number of retweets elicited (Stieglitz & Dang-Xuan, 2013). This happens because in politics there are no fixed recipes and every race, every campaign, has a different scenario.

The aim of this chapter is to approach these analyses, as an example, in a way which would allow us to test, in a concrete case, some of these statements. To this end, we used the lexicon-based approach for the sentimental analysis of the reactions (*replies*) posted by Twitter followers of the main presidential candidates in the 2018 Mexican elections. Using the text mining technique, we analysed the emotional content of the citizens' response to contents emitted by politicians during the election campaign period (2 April–1 July 2018).[2] There were a total of 891,089 tweets belonging to the accounts of: Ricardo Anaya (@RicardoAnayaC, 260,953 replies), Andrés Manuel López Obrador (@lopezobrador_, 194,380 replies), Jaime Rodríguez El Bronco (@JaimeRdzNL, 104,611 replies), José Antonio Meade (@JoseAMeadeK, 331,145 replies). We correlated the results obtained regarding sentiment analysis with the level of engagement[3] of their Twitter accounts over the same period (Graph 9.1).

In the first graph we show the number of Twitter followers of each one of the four main candidates in the 2018 Mexican presidential election, as

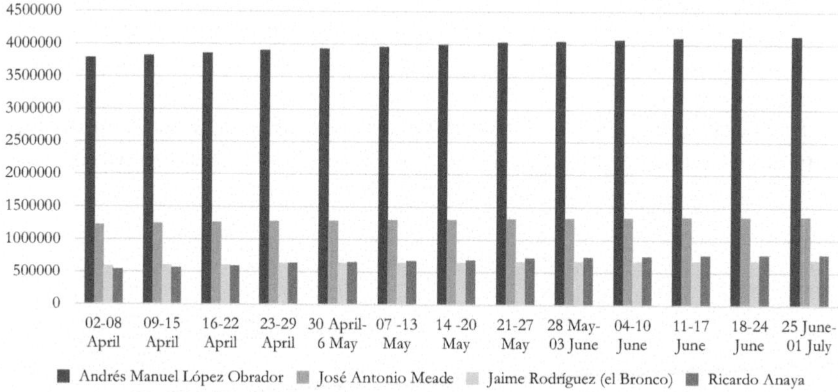

Graph 9.1 Number of followers of the accounts belonging to the main candidates during the campaign for the Mexican presidential election in 2018. (Source: Elaborated by the authors using Twitter data)

[2] In our analysis, we used the 2015 version of the Linguistic Inquiry and Word Count (LIWC) software and the Spanish dictionary from the year 2007, containing 7515 entries. All information included in our analysis is secondary data obtained from publicly available Twitter data.

[3] The engagement indicator refers to the average number of interactions per day on tweets of a day in relation to the number of followers of the same day in the selected time period.

well as their evolution along the 13 weeks of the election campaign. One can clearly notice the enormous difference between Andrés Manuel López Obrador, the most popular of the candidates and the eventual landslide winner, and the rest of the candidates.

However, Graph 9.2 shows how the most competitive candidates are not necessarily those who have a higher level of audience engagement. During the whole campaign, Meade and Anaya were the leaders with the highest levels of audience engagement, whilst Obrador actually had the lowest. The increase in the numbers of followers during the campaign, which is a characteristic common to all candidates, is not reflected in a higher engagement level of those same followers. Moreover, the engagement level is highly variable over the weeks of the campaign, which leads us to the conclusion that said level is very dependent on the agenda, especially in the case of the more competitive candidates.

If we take a look at Table 9.1, we will see that there is a positive correlation between audience engagement and negative emotions in the case of the real contenders, Obrador and Anaya, and not in the case of the other candidates. That is to say, the agenda would indeed generate the spaces in which emotions are generated in the network, but does not affect all the candidates to the same extent; it is the competition which emotionalises the engagement.

In short, our analysis shows the existence of a positive relationship between the engagement level and the presence of negative emotions in

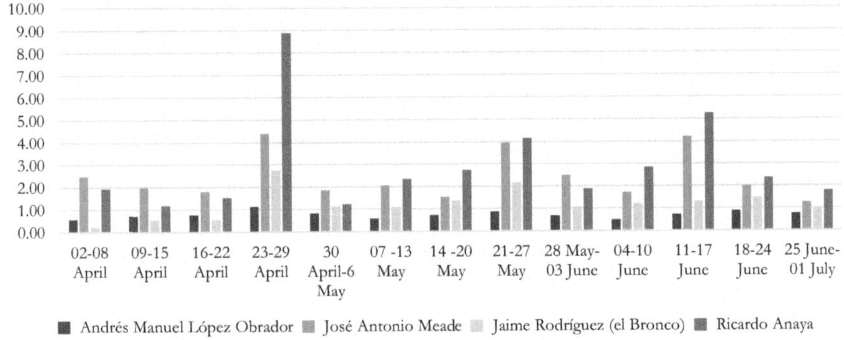

Graph 9.2 Engagement level of the accounts belonging to the main candidates during the campaign for the Mexican presidential election in 2018. (Source: Elaborated by the authors using Twitter data)

Table 9.1 Correlation between the engagement level and the emotional content of the replies posted by followers of the main candidates during the campaign for the Mexican presidential election in 2018

	PosEmotion Anaya	NegEmotion Anaya	Engagement Anaya	PosEmotion El Bronco	NegEmotion El Bronco	Engagement El Bronco	PosEmotion Obrador	NegEmotion Obrador	Engagement Obrador	PosEmotion Meade	NegEmotion Meade	Engagement Meade
PosEmotion Anaya	1	-0.150	-0.441	0.184	-0.152	-0.468	0.540	-0.327	-0.209	0.494	0.171	-0.410
NegEmotion Anaya	-0.150	1	.745**	0.261	-0.493	.727**	0.267	0.007	0.473	0.093	0.162	.641*
Engagement Anaya	-0.441	**.745****	1	-0.072	-0.259	.824**	0.045	0.312	.600*	-0.085	0.171	.830**
PosEmotion El Bronco	0.184	0.261	-0.072	1	-.619*	0.156	0.547	-.681*	-0.252	0.540	-0.321	-0.181
NegEmotion El Bronco	-0.152	-0.493	-0.259	**-.619***	1	-0.383	-.681*	0.221	-0.329	-0.501	0.314	-0.160
Engagement El Bronco	-0.468	**.727****	**.824****	0.156	-0.383	1	0.170	0.295	.716**	-0.115	0.353	.642*
PosEmotion Obrador	0.540	0.267	0.045	0.547	**-.681***	0.170	1	-0.211	0.165	.741**	0.023	-0.017
NegEmotion Obrador	-0.327	0.007	0.312	**-.681***	0.221	0.295	-0.211	1	.714**	-0.135	0.528	0.192
Engagement Obrador	-0.209	0.473	**.600***	-0.252	-0.329	**.716****	0.165	**.714****	1	-0.025	.572*	0.488
PosEmotion Meade	0.494	0.093	-0.085	0.540	-0.501	-0.115	**.741****	-0.135	-0.025	1	-0.100	-0.334
NegEmotion Meade	0.171	0.162	0.171	-0.321	0.314	0.353	0.023	0.528	**.572***	-0.100	1	0.082
Engagement Meade	-0.410	**.641***	**.830****	-0.181	-0.160	**.642***	-0.017	0.192	0.488	-0.334	0.082	1

Source: Elaborated by the authors

the replies of the candidates' followers, but only for some of them, especially those who are the real contenders of the election campaign.

6 Conclusions

The notion of engagement is a diffuse and general one, encompassing both political and civic spaces and in which the debate on the motives generating it and the effect it produces still offers largely contradictory interpretations. It is certain, however, that the majority of the approaches to political engagement started from the study of cases which concern different political actors as well as different situational contexts.

Social media have become instruments in the construction of political engagement, generating a new space for analysis, providing a vast amount of data, which can hardly be approached in the offline spaces. This fact has led to the emergence of numerous studies correlating the participation and mobilisation on social media with the production of political engagement. Despite the early stage of these studies, the analyses showing a connection between dialogical production of negative elements in the social networks and political engagement are, at this point in time, the majority. Adding emotions to the analysis of this relationship has allowed proving that political engagement does not need to be limited to the area of behaviours, but rather can also be included in cognitive and emotional areas. However, even in such areas, the current tendency leads one to think, as shown by our example, that negative emotions weigh more than positive ones when it comes to the production of political engagement, an approach which may be the result of the polarising moment that world politics is going through, which has a clearly centrifugal character. The fact is that, only a few years ago, campaigns such as Obama's made us think that the creation of a positive emotional framing would be electorally invincible.

References

Aldrich, J. H., Gibson, R. K., Cantijoch, M., & Konitzer, T. (2016). Getting out the vote in the social media era: Are digital tools changing the extent, nature and impact of party contacting in elections? *Party Politics, 22*(2), 165–178.

Anduiza, E., Jensen, M. J., & Jorba, L. (2012). *Digital media and political engagement worldwide. A comparative study.* Cambridge University Press.

Barrett, M., & Zani, B. (2014). *Political and civic engagement: Multidisciplinary perspectives.* Routledge.

Bazarova, N. N., Choi, Y. H., Schwanda Sosik, V., Cosley, D., & Whitlock, J. (2015). Social sharing of emotions on Facebook: Channel differences, satisfaction, and replies. In *Proceedings of the 18th ACM conference on computer supported cooperative work & social computing* (pp. 154–164). ACM.

Bennulf, M., & Hedberg, P. (1999). Outside of democracy: On the social and political roots of declining electoral participation. In E. Amná (Ed.), *Changes in electoral participation*. SOU.

Berger, J., & Milkman, K. L. (2012). What makes online content viral? *Journal of Marketing Research, 49*, 192–205.

Bimber, B. (1999). The internet and citizen communication with government: Does the medium matter. *Political Communication, 16*, 409–428.

Bimber, B. (2014). Digital media in the Obama campaigns of 2008 and 2012: Adaptation to the personalized political communication environment. *Journal of Information Technology & Politics, 11*(2), 130–150.

Bond, R. M., Fariss, C. J., Jones, J. J., Kramer, A. D., Marlow, C., Settle, J. E., & Fowler, J. H. (2012). A 61-million-person experiment in social influence and political mobilization. *Nature, 489*(7415), 295–298.

Boulianne, S. (2009). Does internet use affect engagement? A meta-analysis of research. *Political Communication, 26*(2), 193–211.

Boulianne, S. (2015). Social media use and participation: A meta-analysis of current research. *Information, Communication & Society, 18*(5), 524–538.

Brady, W. J., Wills, J. A., Jost, J. T., Tucker, J. A., & Van Bavel, J. J. (2017). Emotion shapes the diffusion of moralized content in social networks. *Proceedings of the National Academy of Sciences, 114*(28), 7313–7318.

Brundidge, J., & Rice, R. E. (2009). Political engagement online: Do the information rich get richer and the like-minded more similar. In A. Chadwick & P. N. Howard (Eds.), *The handbook of internet politics* (pp. 144–156). Routledge.

Cantijoch, M., Cutts, D., & Gibson, R. (2015). Moving slowly up the ladder of political engagement: A "spill-over" model of internet participation. *The British Journal of Politics and International Relations, 18*(1), 26–48.

Carreras, M. (2016). Compulsory voting and political engagement (beyond the ballot box): A multilevel analysis. *Electoral Studies, 43*, 158–168.

Ceron, A., & d'Adda, G. (2015). E-campaigning on Twitter: The effectiveness of distributive promises and negative campaign in the 2013 Italian election. *New Media & Society*, 1–21.

Christensen, H. S. (2011). Political activities on the internet: Slacktivism or political participation by other means? *First Monday, 16*, 1–10.

Dahlgren, P. (2009). *Media and political engagement: Citizens, communication, and democracy*. Cambridge University Press.

Eckstein, K., Noack, P., & Gniewosz, B. (2012). Attitudes toward political engagement and willingness to participate in politics: Trajectories throughout adolescence. *Journal of Adolescence, 35*, 485–495.

Emler, N. (2011). What does it take to be a political actor in a multicultural society? In M. Barrett, C. Flood, & J. Eade (Eds.), *Nationalism, ethnicity, citizenship: Multidisciplinary perspectives*. Cambridge Scholars Publishing.

Gerbaudo, P., Marogna, F., & Alzetta, C. (2019). When "positive posting" attracts voters: User engagement and emotions in the 2017 UK election campaign on Facebook. *Social media + Society*, 1–11.

Gerodimos, R., & Justinussen, J. (2015). Obama's 2012 Facebook campaign: Political communication in the age of the like button. *Journal of Information Technology & Politics, 12*(2), 113–132.

Gil de Zúñiga, H., Jung, N., & Valenzuela, S. (2012). Social media use for news and individuals' social capital, civic engagement and political participation. *Journal of Computer-Mediated Communication, 17*, 319–336.

Gordon, S. L. (1981). The sociology of sentiments and emotions. In M. Rosenberg & R. Turner (Eds.), *Social psychology: Sociological perspectives* (pp. 551–575). Routledge.

Hall, C. (2005). *The trouble with passion: Political theory beyond the reign of reason*. Routledge.

Hendricks, J. A., & Denton, R. E., Jr. (2010). *Communicator-in-Chief: How Barack Obama used new media technology to win the White House*. Lexington Studies in Political Communication.

Jaráiz-Gulías, E., Pereira-López, M., & Rivera Otero, J. M. (2021). Análisis de emociones originadas por las publicaciones Twitter de los candidatos en las elecciones generales de Bolivia y España en 2019. *Journal of Iberian and Latin American Research*, 1–18.

Kallinikos, J. (2004). Farewell to constructivism: Technology and context-embedded action. In C. Avgerou, C. Ciborra, & F. Land (Eds.), *The social study of information and communication technology: Innovation, actors, and contexts* (pp. 140–161). Oxford University Press.

Katz, E., & Lazarsfeld, P. (1979). *La influencia personal. El individuo en el proceso de comunicación de masas*. Editorial Hispano Europea.

Kenski, K., Hardy, B. W., & Jamieson, K. H. (2010). *The Obama victory: How media, money, and messages shaped the 2008 election*. Oxford University Press.

Koc-Michalska, K., & Lilleker, D. G. (2017). Digital politics: Mobilization, engagement, and participation. *Political Communication, 34*(1), 1–5.

Krueger, B. S. (2010). Opt in or tune out: Email mobilization and political participation. *International Journal of E-Politics, 1*(4), 55–76.

Lazarsfeld, P., Berelson, B., & Gaudet, H. (1968). *The People's choice. How the voter makes up his mind in a presidential campaign* (3rd ed.). Columbia University Press.

Lilleker, D. G. (2013). Empowering the citizens? Political communication, co-production and the harnessed crowd. In R. Scullion, R. Gerodimos, D. Jackson, & D. Lilleker (Eds.), *The media, political participation and empowerment* (pp. 24–38). Routledge.

Liu, D., & Lei, L. (2018). The appeal to political sentiment: An analysis of Donald Trump's and Hillary Clinton's speech themes and discourse strategies in the 2016 US presidential election. *Discourse Context & Media, 25*, 143–152.

Lupia, A., & Philpot, T. S. (2005). Views from inside the net: How websites affect young adults' political interest. *The Journal of Politics, 67*(4), 1122–1142.

Malhotra, N., Michelson, M. R., Rogers, T., et al. (2011). Text messages as mobilization tools: The conditional effect of habitual voting and election salience. *American Politics Research, 39*, 664–681.

McLeod, J. M., Scheufele, D. A., & Moy, P. (1999). Community, communication, and participation: The role of mass media and interpersonal discussion in local political participation. *Political Communication, 16*(3), 315–336.

Moura, M., & Michelson, M. (2017). WhatsApp in Brazil: Mobilising voters through door-to-door and personal messages. *Internet Policy Review, 6*(4).

Nabi, R. L. (2003). Exploring the framing effects of emotion: Do discrete emotions differentially influence information accessibility, information seeking, and policy preference? *Communication Research, 30*(2), 224–247.

Neuman, W. R., Marcus, G., & Mackuen, M. B. (2018). Hardwired for news: Affective intelligence and political attention. *Journal of Broadcasting & Electronic Media, 62*(4), 614–635.

Norris, P. (2003). Preaching to the converted? Pluralism, participation and party websites. *Party Politics, 9*(1), 21–45.

Norris, P. (2011). *Democratic deficit: Critical citizens revisited*. Cambridge University Press.

Rosenstone, S., & Hansen, J. M. (1993). *Mobilization, participation and democracy in America*. Longman.

Sahly, A., Chao, S., & Kwon, H. (2019). Social media for political campaigns: An examination of Trump's and Clinton's frame building and its effect on audience engagement. *Social Media & Society*, 1–13.

Savoy, J. (2017). Trump's and Clinton's style and rhetoric during the 2016 presidential election. *Journal of Quantitative Linguistics*, 1–22.

Stieglitz, S., & Dang-Xuan, L. (2013). Emotions and information diffusion in social media—Sentiment of microblogs and sharing behavior. *Journal of Management Information Systems, 29*, 217–248.

Tang, G., & Lee, F. L. F. (2013). Facebook use and political participation: The impact of exposure to shared political information, connections with public political actors, and network structural heterogeneity. *Social Science Computer Review, 31*(6), 763–773.

Tolbert, C. J., & Mcneal, R. S. (2003). Unraveling the effects of the internet on political participation? *Political Research Quarterly, 56*(2), 175–185.

Vaccari, C. (2016). Online mobilization in comparative perspective: Digital appeals and political engagement in Germany, Italy, and the United Kingdom. *Political Communication, 34*(1), 69–88.

Valentino N. A., Hutchings V. L., Banks, A. J., & Davis, A.K. (2008). Is a Worried citizen a Good citizen? Emotions, political information seeking, and learning via the internet. *Political Psichology, 29*(2), 247–273.

Valenzuela, S., Halpern, D., Katz, J. E., & Miranda, J. P. (2019). The paradox of participation versus misinformation: Social media, political engagement, and the spread of misinformation. *Digital Journalism, 7*(6), 802–823.

Valeriani, A., & Vaccari, C. (2017). Political talk on mobile instant messaging services: A comparative analysis of Germany, Italy, and the UK. *Information Communication and Society, 21*(11), 1715–1731.

Vasilopoulos, P., Marcus, G. E., Valentino, N., & Foucault, M. (2018). Fear, anger, and voting for the far right: Evidence from the November 13, 2015 Paris terror attacks. *Political Psychology, 40*(4), 679–704.

Verba, S., Schlozman, K. L., & Brady, H. E. (1995). *Voice and equality: Civic voluntarism in American politics.* Harvard University Press.

Yarchi, M., Baden, C., & Kligler-Vilenchik, N. (2020). Political polarization on the digital sphere: A cross-platform, over-time analysis of interactional, positional, and affective polarization on social media. *Political Communication*, 1–42.

Zukin, C., Scott, K., Molly, A., Krista, J., & Delli Carpini, M. X. (2006). *A new engagement?: Political participation, civic life, and the changing American citizen.* Oxford University Press.

CHAPTER 10

Television Debates, Live-Tweeting and Social Audience

José Sixto-García, Ana-Isabel Rodríguez-Vázquez, and Alba Silva-Rodríguez

1 Cross-Platform Consumption and Modeled Audiences

The dizzying transformation that the media have undergone over the last 21 years is the result of the impact of technology (López-García, 2010) and various multidimensional convergence processes (Salaverría & García-Avilés, 2008), as well as an ever-evolving economic and cultural environment. With the advent of digital technologies, journalism has undergone significant changes with respect to the production, distribution and reception of content (Jensen et al., 2016; Neira, 2015). Difficulties in finding sustainable business models and the struggle to capture the attention of an increasingly dispersed audience are some of the current concerns of the media. In addition, hyper-multimedia content has emerged (Canavilhas,

J. Sixto-García (✉) • A.-I. Rodríguez-Vázquez • A. Silva-Rodríguez
University of Santiago de Compostela, Santiago de Compostela, Spain
e-mail: jose.sixto@usc.es; anaisabel.rodriguez.vazquez@usc.es; alba.silva@usc.es

B. García-Orosa (ed.), *Digital Political Communication Strategies*, The Palgrave Macmillan Series in International Political Communication, https://doi.org/10.1007/978-3-030-81568-4_10

2012) and created new narratives deployed in different media and supports (Jenkins, 2008).

With the advent of digital devices and the emergence of social media, the concept of the audience itself has taken on a new dimension (Bengtsson & Johansson, 2020). Social media transcends traditional media models (Campos, 2008) and helps to reconsider the role of the audience to the point that the audience can occasionally control the media agenda by establishing the most important topics of the day (de Aguilera & Casero-Ripollés, 2018; Hawthorne et al., 2013). Citizens even have the power to redefine the interpretive frameworks proposed by the media and/or political figures (Bentivegna & Marchetti, 2015). In addition, users' expectations vary depending on the platform on which they consume media (Chyi & Chadha, 2012; Molyneux, 2017). The theory of uses and gratifications (Katz et al., 1974), which discusses the active role of consumers, has become more valuable than ever before (Doyle, 2010), as it is these consumers who choose which media they consume to meet their own needs. The ubiquitous computing model of mobile communication, which allows users to connect and interact even if on the move (Moloney, 2012), has created a new sense of identity in the audience (Farman, 2012; Nelson, 2019). Thus, audience experiences are transformed and new concepts emerge to define audience behavior. So it is with the help of multitasking, a term used to explain the simultaneous use of television and digital technologies such as mobile devices (Ha, 2021), various perks for users such as emotional, social and contextual interactions are generated (Su & Chen, 2019).

2 The Social Audience

To refer to the phenomenon that occurs when social platforms serve as a conversational channel around what happens in a program, Castelló (2013) coined the term *social television* (Castelló, 2013). In this sense, the social audience is that which combines communication with watching TV and gives the viewer company (Boertjes et al., 2009) because it uses technologies, services and practices that allow it to interact with the television product directly on the screen or through other auxiliary devices (Gallego, 2012), usually mobile, and whose options for participation are the result of the popularization of the web 2.0 (Aroldi & Vittadini, 2015). It is, therefore, a two-way and personalized communicative model in which the user goes from linear to experimental, such that the viewer's attitude takes the form of engagement with the medium, which, for its part, still fulfills the need for entertainment, information, communication and transaction (León & García-Avilés, 2012; Saavedra et al., 2015).

This change in the viewers' role not only affects reception and the way they consume; it has also forced network managers to change the way they make television (Buschow et al., 2014). Co-viewing (Ducheneaut et al., 2008) has allowed audiences to gain visibility (Walvaart et al., 2018), to the point that the media consider them a strategic management resource (Malmelin & Villi, 2016). Journalistic companies are committed to forging long-lasting, mutually beneficial relationships with their audiences (Belair-Gagnon et al., 2019), even in the most alternative journalism (Harcup, 2016).

Social audiences bring new meanings, values and experiences (Lee & Kim, 2016) to the communicative process. The variety of connected media and the user-generated flow created by the viewer public actions on various devices has allowed the viewer to take the lead in the communication relationship (Marinelli, 2015). The audience has a high emotional component when discussing with other social network users the content they are watching, which adds value to the audiovisual experience (Iñesta, 2015). However, social television is more than just interaction on social networks (Quintas-Froufe & González-Neira, 2015), since interpersonal communication also takes place on instant messaging applications, mainly WhatsApp and Telegram. As far back as 2015, Van der Schuur and his research partners identified two models of multitasking, one in which two types of media are used simultaneously, and another in which the user consumes media while performing unrelated activities. Thus, everything points to the eventual evolution of the social audience as new technologies are incorporated into the public daily life.

Despite today's myriad messaging networks and apps, many of which boast millions of users, Twitter is the social network of reference for traditional media. Consequently, it is still the best network to learn about what is happening at a specific time in a particular place (Sixto, 2018) and therefore where most journalism is still practiced (Lasorsa et al., 2012). Twitter is the leading platform for journalists to offer news and to gain followers, but also to interact with the public (Gil et al., 2018).

The relevance of social audiences is such that audiences themselves condition not only programming but also the agenda. Indeed, a recent study (Zheng & Shahin, 2020) has revealed that the agendas of Twitter posts during presidential debates in the United States were established long before the televised debates themselves. Another paper concluded that Twitter exerts more influence on the media than vice versa (Su et al., 2020) and, with respect to users, in other previous studies, researchers discovered that people who used two screens during a debate about parliamentary elections in the United Kingdom were often more educated and showed great political commitment, especially when they developed a productive and active attitude on that social network (Vaccari et al., 2015).

Watching television while *second-screening* on Twitter changes the nature of the media experience (Miranda & Fernández, 2020), because the media mix favors the establishment of open space for various opinions, dialogue and debate (Williams & Gonlin, 2017). Discussing media content with others, even if they are strangers from a distant place, helps to improve the media experience and acquire new knowledge (Pires, 2015), although perhaps the media should recognize more explicitly these research ideas and the source of such knowledge, as McGeeney (2015) pointed out in a paper on the relationship between live-tweeting and building the digital archive.

3 Political Debates on Television

The first political debates were the seven public contests between Stephen Douglas and Abraham Lincoln in 1848, followed by the first radio debate in the 1948 race for the US presidency between Thomas Dewey and Harold Stassen. Ten years later, the famous debate between Nixon and Kennedy during the 1960 US presidential election took place, a watershed moment in the history of political communication on television, given the large audiences garnered in these and subsequent debates. Since then, TV has become politicians' medium of choice for making themselves known and presenting their ideas to the public.

Politics on television attracts audiences like no other medium and serves as the foundation of political information upon which aspiring politicians rely to be seen on the screens of myriad households (Rúas & Quintas-Froufe, 2020; Berrocal-Gonzalo et al., 2005. For these reasons, these formats have become the mainstay in election campaigns throughout the world.

Researchers have focused on various features of televised debates (Luengo, 2011): they allow people to hear the politicians' opinions directly, they reach a large audience and generate a lot of media information, indirectly spurring the dissemination of political information throughout society. Some of these features are also reflected in the Pew Research Center's analysis (Desilver, 2020) of the last US presidential election between Donald Trump and Joe Biden. In its study, the American *fact tank* lays out five important aspects of televised election debates: they attract a very large audience (in 2016 the first debate between Trump and Clinton garnered 84 million viewers); citizens consider them useful but not decisive; vice-presidential debates are eclipsed by the presidential ones; today's debates differ significantly from those of past eras and debate commentary has become particularly relevant; and finally, the moderators are often renowned TV journalists.

In this context, it is worth noting that research on political communication in general, and televised debates in particular, is based on the work of American academia, which means that conclusions of many studies are based on Hallin and Mancini's Liberal model (2004). However, researchers in other political contexts have taken on this object of study and presented interesting work on televised debates in several countries, as is the case in Spain.

Spain's first televised debates took place in the 1993 prime ministerial election between Felipe González and José María Aznar and were broadcast by Antena 3 and Telecinco, two private networks which only in 1990 had entered the Spanish television market, in which the State-run *Radio y Televisión Española* (RTVE) and several regional public broadcasters had enjoyed a monopoly. Following those debates, the country had to wait until 2008 for another "face-to-face" between then-candidates José Luis Rodríguez Zapatero and Mariano Rajoy. Since then, television debates have become a key part of election campaigns. In addition, political debates in other modern television formats also warrant discussion.

4 Audience Participation in Television Debates

Televised political debates maintain their strength as informative reference points and as one of the engines of audience participation with the debates themselves. This force increases during elections and in times of political upheaval, as seen in Donald Trump's coming to power, the Brexit debate, Spain's two general elections in 2019 or the vote of no confidence against the then-prime minister Mariano Rajoy. Political communication on television has evolved into a hybrid system (Chadwick, 2013; Shah et al.,

2015; García-Orosa & López-García, 2019) in which the main actors (parties, media and audiences) interact through different platforms.

Livingstone and Lunt (1994) had already begun work on the effects of active audience participation on television and wondered how the media managed the audiences of debate programs open to citizen participation. More than 20 years later, the value and importance of public discussion and television debate have grown in an environment dominated by two programming standards: that which features real events or events arising from media-created shows, where consumption is immediate and its impact is reflected in traditional audience data (audiometry) and social audience data (immediate conversation on social networks); and the deferred model, based on personalized, à la carte consumption, the impact of which is reflected in the new online metrics. Political debates, and especially special coverage during election cycles, contribute to the strength of the first model, that of immediacy and the "noise" of public conversation around television content (Rodríguez-Vázquez et al., 2020). In this context, a sense of political efficacy and the involvement of society's youngest members can lead to greater participation, thereby confirming the connections between citizen empowerment, political engagement and what Spyridou (2018) called participatory journalism.

The new challenges of communication and audiovisual journalism on television require a reworking of the traditional schema of televised political debates (Casado-Ruiz, 2012). Programming strategies and content need structural reforms. During this transformation, social networks, which accelerate audience participation revolving around television programs, generate new perspectives for political communication on television. There have been changes both in debates and in other contemporary formats, from breakfast television to debate shows, which the viewer can consume in a multiscreen environment, beyond the traditional TV set.

In today's media ecosystem, the political debate does not stick strictly to linear television broadcasting; rather, other media and channels can now distribute such content to new audiences (Rúas & Quintas-Froufe, 2020). The social audience, though political parties' social media channels or the TV channels themselves, can easily and directly access the public sphere to create new discourse on particular topics based on sociological aspects such as education or social status (Casero-Ripollés, 2017). In Spain, this strength manifested in the social audience data collected in the Kantar Media yearbook (2020), which showed that political issues still topped the Social TV rankings in a year (2019) in which election debates were the most talked-about television programming and inspired some of the hashtags mostly used by Twitter users in Spain.

The combination of television with *multitasking* on various devices (tablets, computers, mobile phones, etc.), and, especially, the use of social networks, is considered an explosive cocktail that networks and politicians leverage by placing the audience at the epicenter of their strategies.

5 Mobile Phones as a Second Screen: Social Television and the Phenomenon of Live-Tweeting

In a context dominated by ubiquitous, cross-platform, social consumption (Aguado, 2020) and multi-screening (Neira, 2015), mobile technology stands out. Mobile devices are consumers' first choice for consuming digital content and open new avenues to access personalized information from anywhere at any time (Westlund, 2015). They become the second screen (Van Cauwenberge et al., 2014; Blake, 2017; Guo, 2020) which amplifies the social role of journalism (Ha, 2021). This concept alludes to a unique blend of social, interactive and mass media (Auverset & Billings, 2016) which creates opportunities and challenges for the media industry (Guo, 2020). Although its presence and linkage with television content has been increasing in recent years, efforts are not always joined to promote two-way conversation and communication between television media and internet users (Fontenla-Pedreira et al., 2020; Ji & Danyang, 2015).

In an era conditioned by audience segmentation, social television (Auverset & Billings, 2016; Giglietto & Selva, 2014; Salomaa, 2020) helps to create imaginary communities out of users who can tweet live streams, communicating with each other from a dispersed secondary channel (Stewart, 2019). Therefore, It is not surprising that there is an incipient interest in the study of social networks, especially Twitter, within journalism (Bentivegna & Marchetti, 2015; Rodríguez-Vázquez et al., 2020). Twitter incorporates traditional media components, builds on them (Harrington et al., 2013) and adds features related to computer-mediated interpersonal communication (Hawthorne et al., 2013).

The literature on the use of social television has focused mainly on the phenomenon of live-tweeting (Ji & Danyang, 2015), during which consumers use Twitter as a communication platform to share their thoughts about the content while watching live TV. In other words, the ability to spur conversation stems from tweets while a show is broadcast on linear television. This practice turns out to be a good strategy to promote user traffic on social media (Direito-Rebollal et al., 2017), spaces that become the new agora of communication. These are the channels through which one can share content, discuss topics and participate in social discussions that are important to the community. Twitter further promotes such conversation, which happens to take place simultaneously. Users can participate in various ways and varying degrees. They can be mere observers (e.g., by *liking* something), disseminators (e.g., by *retweeting*) or commentators (e.g., creating content by *replying*). Then there are hashtags, which allow for the ad hoc eliciting of similar feelings independent of the conversation.

In short, Twitter has proven itself a powerful platform for the media, especially for television. Experience shows that increased use of this social network while consuming television (either as secondary support or integrated into transmedia contexts) adds a new dimension to the audience experience. Moreover, it can play an important role in anticipating and monitoring issues and even keeping attention on a particular program (Harrington et al., 2013). The challenge for television producers, therefore, is to implement effective strategies that facilitate interactions with the audience in a ubiquitous and eminently social context.

References

Aguado, J. M. (2020). *Mediaciones ubicuas. Ecosistema móvil, gestión de identidad y nuevo espacio público.* Gedisa.

Aroldi, P., & Vittadini, N. (2015). Audiences as socio-technical actors: The "styles" of social network site users. In F. Zeller, C. Ponte, & B. O'Neill (Eds.), *Revitalising audience research: Innovations in European audience research* (pp. 195–214). Taylor & Francis.

Auverset, L. A., & Billings, A. C. (2016). Relationships between social TV and enjoyment: A content analysis of the walking dead's story sync experience. *Social Media + Society, 2*(3), 1–12. https://doi.org/10.1177/2056305116662170

Belair-Gagnon, V., Nelson, J., & Lewis, S. (2019). Audience engagement, reciprocity, and the pursuit of community connectedness in public media journalism. *Journalism Practice, 13*(5), 558–575. https://doi.org/10.1080/17512786.2018.1542975

Bengtsson, S., & Johansson, S. (2020). A phenomenology of news: Understanding news in digital culture. *Journalism*. https://doi.org/10.1177/1464884919901194

Bentivegna, S., & Marchetti, R. (2015). Live tweeting a political debate: The case of the 'Italia bene comune'. *European Journal of Communication, 6*(30), 631–647. https://doi.org/10.1177/0267323115595526

Berrocal-Gonzalo, S., Campos-Domínguez, E., & Redondo-García, M. (2005). La información política en televisión: ¿apatía o interés entre los telespectadores? *Comunicar, 25*(5). https://doi.org/10.3916/C25-2005-047

Blake, J. (2017). *Television and the second screen: Interactive TV in the age of social participation*. Routledge.

Boertjes, E., Klok, J., Naimut, O., & Staal, M. (2009). ConnectTV: Share the experience. In P. Cesar, D. Geerts, & K. Chorianopoluds (Eds.), *Social interactive television: Immersive shared experiences and perspectives* (pp. 187–201). IGI Global.

Buschow, C., Schneider, B., & Ueberheide, S. (2014). Tweeting television: Exploring communication activities on Twitter while watching TV. *Communications-The European Journal of Communication Research, 39*(2), 129–149.

Campos, F. (2008). Las redes sociales trastocan los modelos de los medios de comunicación tradicionales. *Revista Latina de Comunicación Social, 63*, 287–293. https://doi.org/10.4185/RLCS-63-2008-767-287-293

Canavilhas, J. (2012). *Jornalismo para dispositivos móveis: informação hipermultimediática e personalizada*. Actas del IV CILCS – Congreso Internacional Latina de Comunicación.

Casado-Ruiz, A. (2012). *Debates electorales en televisión. Nuevos contenidos para nuevos formatos.* Comunicació i risc: III Congrés Internacional Associació Espanyola d'Investigación de la Comunicació (AE-IC). http://ae-ic.org/Tarragona/contents/comunicacions_cd/ok/350.pdf

Casero-Ripollés, A. (2017). Producing political content for web 2.0: Empowering citizens and vulnerable populations. *El profesional de la información, 26*(1), 13–19. https://doi.org/10.3145/epi.2017.ene.02

Castelló, A. (2013). El uso del hashtags en Twitter por parte de los programas de televisión españoles. I Congreso Internacional de Comunicación y Sociedad Digital. 17, 18 y 19 de abril de 2013, Universidad Internacional de La Rioja.

Chadwick, A. (2013). *The hybrid media system: Politics and power.* Oxford University Press.

Chyi, H. I., & Chadha, M. (2012). News on new devices. Is multiplatform news consumption a reality? *Journalism Practice, 6*(2), 431–449. https://doi.org/10.1080/17512786.2011.629125

de Aguilera, M., & Casero-Ripollés, A. (2018). ¿Tecnologías para la transformación? Los medios sociales ante el cambio político y social. Presentación. *Icono 14, 16*(1), 1–21. https://doi.org/10.7195/ri14.v16i1.1162

Desilver, D. (2020, August 28). 5 facts about presidential and vice presidential debates. *Pew Research Center.*

Direito-Rebollal, S., Lago-Vázquez, D., & Rodríguez-Vázquez, A. I. (2017). Television and social networks: An analysis of the influence of live-tweeting in the social audiences. In Á. Rocha, A. Correia, H. Adeli, L. Reis, & S. Costanzo (Eds.), *Recent advances in information systems and technologies* (WorldCIST 2017. Advances in intelligent systems and computing) (Vol. 571). Springer. https://doi.org/10.1007/978-3-319-56541-5_13

Doyle, G. (2010). From television to multi-platform: Less from more or more for less? *Convergence: The International Journal of Research into New Media Technologies, 16*(4), 431–449. https://doi.org/10.1177/1354856510375145

Ducheneaut, N., Moore, R. J., Oehlberg, L., Thornton, J. D., & Nickell, E. (2008). Social TV: Designing for distributed, sociable television viewing. *International Journal of Human-Computer Interaction, 24*(2), 136–154. https://doi.org/10.1080/10447310701821426

Farman, J. (2012). *Mobile interface theory: Embodied space and locative media.* Routledge.

Fontenla-Pedreira, J., Rúas-Araújo, X., & Puentes-Rivera, I. (2020). El debate electoral de las elecciones generales del 10N de 2019 en las redes sociales de RTVE. *El Profesional de la Información, 29*(6), 1699–2407. https://doi.org/10.3145/epi.2020.nov.03

Gallego, F. (2012). La medición de la televisión social en España: concepto, evolución y posibilidades presentes y futuras. III Congreso Internacional Comunicación 3.0, Salamanca, 10 y 11 octubre de 2012, p.1.

García-Orosa, B., & López-García, X. (2019). Language in social networks as a communication strategy: Public administration, political parties and civil society. *Communications Society, 32*(1). https://doi.org/10.15581/003.32.1.107-125

Giglietto, F., & Selva, D. (2014). Second screen and participation: A content analysis on a full season dataset of tweets. *Journal of Communication, 2*(64), 260–277. https://doi.org/10.1111/jcom.12085

Gil, H., Diehl, T., & Ardèvol-Abreu, A. (2018). When citizens and journalists interact on Twitter. *Journalism Studies, 19*(2), 227–246. https://doi.org/10.1080/1461670X.2016.1178593

Guo, M. (2020). Second screening: Measuring second screen user behavior in a social television viewing environment. *International Journal on Media Management, 2*(22), 97–116. https://doi.org/10.1080/14241277.2020.1803326

Ha, L. (2021). The changing audience. In M. Mahoney & T. Tang (Eds.), *The Rowman & Littlefield Handbook of media management and business.* The Rowman & Littlefield.

Hallin, D., & Mancini, P. (2004). *Comparing media systems: Three models of media and politics.* Cambridge University Press.

Harcup, T. (2016). Asking the readers. *Journalism Practice, 10*(6), 680–696. https://doi.org/10.1080/17512786.2015.1054416

Harrington, S., Highfield, T., & Bruns, A. (2013). More than a backchannel: Twitter and television. *Journal of Audience and Reception Studies, 1*(10), 405–409. https://www.participations.org/Volume%2010/Issue%201/30%20 Harrington%20et%20al%2010.1.pdf

Hawthorne, J., Houston, J. B., & McKinney, M. (2013). Live-tweeting a presidential primary debate: Exploring new political conversations. *Social Science Computer Review, 31*(5), 552–562. https://doi.org/10.1177/0894439313490643

Iñesta, N. (2015). Espectador social y convergencia televisiva. *Ámbitos: Revista internacional de comunicación, 28*, 50–62.

Jenkins, H. (2008). *Convergence culture. La cultura de la convergencia de los medios de comunicación*. Paidós.

Jensen, J.-L., Mortensen, M., & Ørmen, J. (2016). *News across media. Production, distribution and consumption*. Routledge.

Ji, Q., & Danyang, Z. (2015). Tweeting live shows: A content analysis of live-tweets from three entertainment programs. *Proceedings of the 2015 International Conference on Social Media & Society (SMSociety'15)*. https://doi.org/10.1145/2789187.2789195

Kantar Media. (2020). *Anuario Social TV 2019*. Kantar Media. https://www.kantarmedia.com/es/blog-y-recursos/data-lab/anuario-social-tv-2019

Katz, E., Blumler, J. G., & Gurevitch, M. (1974). Utilization of mass communication by the individual. In E. Katz, J. G. Blumler, & M. Gurevitch (Eds.), *The uses of mass communications: Current perspectives on gratifications research* (pp. 19–32). Sage.

Lasorsa, D. L., Lewis, S., & Holton, A. (2012). Normalizing Twitter. *Journalism Studies, 13*(1), 19–36. https://doi.org/10.1080/1461670X.2011.571825

Lee, H. J., & Kim, J. H. (2016). After Felix Gonzalez-Torres. *Third Text, 30*(5–6), 474–489. https://doi.org/10.1080/09528822.2017.1355149

León, B., & García-Avilés, J. A. (2012). Los retos de la implantación de la televisión interactiva a la luz de su propia historia. *Zer-Revista de Estudios de Comunicación, 7*(13).

Livingstone, S., & Lunt, P. (1994). *Talk on television. Audience participation and public debate*. Routledge.

López-García, X. (2010). *La metamorfosis del periodismo. Historia de lo que permanece y de lo que cambia en el ciberperiodismo del tercer milenio*. Comunicación Social.

Luengo, Ó. (2011). Debates electorales en televisión: una aproximación preliminar a sus efectos inmediatos. *Revista Española de Ciencia Política, 25*, 81–96. https://www.researchgate.net/publication/324216503_Debates_electorales_en_television_una_aproximacion_preliminar_a_sus_efectos_inmediatos

Malmelin, N., & Villi, M. (2016). Audience community as a strategic resource in media work. *Journalism Practice, 10*(5), 589–607. https://doi.org/10.1080/17512786.2015.1036903

Marinelli, A. (2015). L'interattività della televisione. Da innovazione mai realizzata a pratica quotidiana nel networked media space. In Sarcagni (Ed.), *I media digitali e l'interazione uomomacchina* (pp. 275–304). Aracne.

McGeeney, E. (2015). Live tweeting and building the digital archive; #NFQLR – Who and what is it for? *International Journal of Social Research Methodology, 18*(3), 307–319. https://doi.org/10.1080/13645579.2015.1017898

Miranda, M. A., & Fernández, F. J. (2020). Adaptándose a la convergencia: Evolución del second screening en Twitter y en programas políticos de TV. *Cuadernos.info, 46*, 24–46. https://doi.org/10.7764/cdi.46.1708

Moloney, K. (2012). Transmedia journalism: A new storytelling strategy and a blog to go with it. *Transmedia Journalism*. https://transmediajournalism.org/author/cariocakev/

Molyneux, L. (2017). Multiplatform news consumption and its connections to civic engagement. *Journalism, 20*(6), 788–806. https://doi.org/10.1177/1464884917730216

Neira, E. (2015). *La otra pantalla. Redes sociales, móviles y la nueva televisión*. UOC.

Nelson, J. (2019). The persistence of the popular in mobile news consumption. *Digital Journalism, 1*(8), 87–102. https://doi.org/10.1080/21670811.2019.1612766

Pires, F. (2015). The co-viewing 2.0: Detaching from history and applying in the new media age. *Кyrmypa/Culture, 5*(11), 55–64.

Quintas-Froufe, N., & González-Neira, A. (2015). Revisión del concepto de televisión social. In N. Quintas-Froufe & A. González Neira (Coord.), *La participación de la audiencia en la televisión: de la audiencia activa a la social* (pp. 13–26). Asociación para la Investigación de Medios de Comunicación.

Rodríguez-Vázquez, A. I., Silva-Rodríguez, A., Direito-Rebollal, S., & García-Orosa, B. (2020). Convenciones y disrupciones en la cobertura de los eventos políticos en la TV lineal y social. Análisis de la noche de las elecciones del 26M de 2019. *Profesional De La Información, 29*(2). https://doi.org/10.3145/epi.2020.mar.05

Rúas, J., & Quintas-Froufe, N. (2020). Televisión, audiencias y debates electorales: hacia la multipantalla. *El profesional de la información, 29*(2), e290201. https://doi.org/10.3145/epi.2020.mar.01

Saavedra, M., Rodríguez, F., & Perlado, M. (2015). Audiencia social. In M. V. Carrillo, A. Castillo, P. Fernández, & J. L. Parada (Coord.), *La gestión de intangibles para la excelencia empresarial: nuevas oportunidades para la comunicación y sus profesionales* (pp. 60–69). Campgràfic.

Salaverría, R., & García-Avilés, J. A. (2008). La convergencia tecnológica en los medios de comunicación: retos para el periodismo. *Trípodos, 23*. https://www.raco.cat/index.php/Tripodos/article/view/118910

Salomaa, E. (2020). Dissertation: "In the intersection of television and Twitter: Social television as a tool for interaction and participation in a media event". *Fachsprache, 42*(1–2), 72–75. https://doi.org/10.24989/fs.v42i1-2.1840

Shah, D. V., Culver, K. B., Hanna, A., Macafee, T., & Yang, J. H. (2015). Computational approaches to online political expression: Rediscovering a 'science of the social'. In S. Coleman & D. Freelon (Eds.), *Handbook of digital politics* (pp. 281–305). Edward Elgar.

Sixto, J. (2018). *Gestión profesional de redes sociales. Rutinas y estrategias de community management*. Comunicación Social.

Spyridou, L. P. (2018). Analyzing the active audience: Reluctant, reactive, fearful or lazy? Forms and motives of participation in mainstream journalism. *Journalism, 20*(6), 827–847. https://doi.org/10.1177/1464884918784733

Stewart, M. (2019). Live tweeting, reality TV and the nation. *International Journal of Cultural Studies, 3*(23), 352–367. https://doi.org/10.1177/1367877919887757

Su, L., & Chen, S.-C. (2019). Exploring the typology and impacts of audience gratifications gained from TV–smartphone multitasking. *International Journal of Human–Computer Interaction, 36*(8), 725–735. https://doi.org/10.1080/10447318.2019.1683312

Su, Y., Hu, J., & Lee, D. K. L. (2020). Delineating the transnational network agenda-setting model of mainstream newspapers and Twitter: A machine-learning approach. *Journalism Studies, 21*(15), 2113–2134. https://doi.org/10.1080/1461670X.2020.1812421

Vaccari, C., Chadwick, A., & O'Loughlin, B. (2015). Dual screening the political: Media events, social media, and citizen engagement. *Journal of Communication, 65*(6), 1041–1061. https://doi.org/10.1111/jcom.12187

Van Cauwenberge, A., Schaap, G., & van Roy, R. (2014). TV no longer commands our full attention: Effects of second-screen viewing and task relevance on cognitive load and learning from news. *Computers in Human Behavior, 38*, 100–109. https://doi.org/10.1016/j.chb.2014.05.021

Van der Schuur, W. A., Baumgartner, S. E., Sumter, S. R., & Valkenburg, P. M. (2015). The consequences of media multitasking for youth: A review. *Computers in Human Behavior, 53*, 204–215.

Walvaart, M., Van den Bulck, H., & Dhoest, A. (2018). Engaging the audience in a digitised television production process. *Journalism Practice, 12*(7), 901–917. https://doi.org/10.1080/17512786.2017.1343093

Westlund, O. (2015). News consumption in an age of mobile media: Patterns, people, place, and participation. *Mobile Media & Communication, 3*(2), 151–159. https://doi.org/10.1177/2050157914563369

Williams, A., & Gonlin, V. (2017). I got all my sisters with me (on Black Twitter): Second screening of how to get away with murder as a discourse on black womanhood. *Information, Communication & Society, 20*(7), 984–1004. https://doi.org/10.1080/1369118x.2017.1303077

Zheng, P., & Shahin, S. (2020). Live tweeting live debates: How Twitter reflects and refracts the US political climate in a campaign season. *Information, Communication & Society, 23*(3), 337–357. https://doi.org/10.1080/1369118X.2018.1503697

CHAPTER 11

Platforms and Race: Exploring the Interpretation of *Dear White People*

Magomed-Emin Aliev and Deborah Castro

1 Introduction

Modern society is at odds with itself. Progress is observable in numerous shapes: the U.S. elected its first African American president; minorities have more means of expression than ever before; and the recent critical and commercial successes of majority-black movies like *Black Panther (2018)* and *Moonlight (2016)* and series such as *Dear White People (2017–)* seem to hint at an unprecedented era of diversity and equality (Carney, 2016). Simultaneously, black-led and female-led content is experiencing online trolling, hatred, and backlash from white, overwhelmingly male, groups (Salam, 2019). On top of that, the world is seeing a rise in authoritarianism, minority rights are getting endangered, and white nationalists and racists are again marching out in the open (Gusterson, 2017).

M.-E. Aliev • D. Castro (✉)
Erasmus University Rotterdam, Rotterdam, The Netherlands
e-mail: castromarino@eshcc.eur.nl

B. García-Orosa (ed.), *Digital Political Communication Strategies*, The Palgrave Macmillan Series in International Political Communication, https://doi.org/10.1007/978-3-030-81568-4_11

This context makes *Dear White People* a fascinating series to study. Originally a film, this Netflix-original show follows the lives of several university students as they attempt to fully realise their identities in a heavily politicised, divided, and white-dominant society. Politics of race, gender, sexuality, privilege, and power influence the lives of these predominantly African American students. The series not only presents a rare deviation in terms of representation but also tackles the current socio-cultural climate and developments with sharp satirical writing (Ray-Harris, 2017). Through these students, the series addresses and satirises modern-day race relations in the so-called post-racial America. As such, it provides smart commentary on the current state of affairs and sheds a light on underrepresented issues. The show thus adds to a more just public sphere by informing people on certain issues and triggering everyday political talk. Consequently, the show's messages, and others like it, may translate into real political action as implied by prior studies (Groshek & Krongard, 2016). In *Dear White People*'s case, by covering sensitive topics, it has placed itself in the centre of the current socio-political divide and has met strong reactions ranging from praise to hatred (Ugwu, 2018). To make further sense of the reactions and this divide, this study seeks to explore how young people living in the Netherlands value and interpret the representation of racial issues in *Dear White People*.

The empirical study was conducted in the Netherlands due to two main reasons. Firstly, this European country provides for a unique context due to its multi-cultural nature: almost one out of four persons has a migration background (Centraal Bureau voor de Statistiek, 2020). Secondly, there is the paucity of empirical academic work that explores how people living in the Netherlands interpret racial issues depicted in TV fiction. Finally, the initiatives that Netflix is implementing in the diversification of content[1] and in creating opportunities for the black creators[2] make the reception of this company's original content a good case study.

[1] Netflix acquired the distribution rights of several black sitcoms, in 2020. See: https://www.forbes.com/sites/alexandrasternlicht/2020/07/29/netflix-is-bringing-7-classic-black-sitcoms-to-platform/?sh=7d662a372156

[2] In 2020, Read Hasting announced that the company would give "$5 million to non-profits dedicated to creating direct opportunities for Black creators, Black youth and Black-owned businesses" such as Ghetto Film School. See: https://www.indiewire.com/2020/06/netflix-pledges-5-million-black-creators-1202237811/

2 Literature Review

This section is structured into two main parts. Firstly, we discuss the representation of black people on U.S. TV. This is followed by a reflection on the importance of mediated representations, particularly when it comes to race. Secondly, we present an overview of the theoretical concepts that help us understand people's TV preferences and their interpretation of a TV show.

TV Representation of Blackness

People of colour have traditionally been underrepresented on television (Hunt et al., 2019). A comparison of the number of the black populace in the U.S. with the number of actors and actresses that appear on U.S. TV productions shows that, during the 1970s, 6% of the characters in TV fiction were black in comparison to the 12% black populace of the U.S. The number increased to 8% in the 1980s and 11% in the early 1990s (Mastro & Greenberg, 2000). In the mid-1990s, black people were proportionally represented, with 13% characters played by black people. In 2016, this number increased to 16.1% (Hunt et al., 2019), slightly higher than their current ratio in the U.S. populace, which is about 15%.

Based on the above, one could argue that, technically, black people are no longer underrepresented in U.S. TV fiction. However, exploring the type of roles that black actors and actresses play remains crucial to understand the situation. In the 2016–2017 U.S. TV season, 31% of the cast belonged to black and other minorities groups. Nonetheless, non-white people are still frequently hired to play supporting characters with only 21% of the shows having a black or other minority lead. Placing white people in the leading roles and black people as supporting characters maintains the decades-long tradition of presenting the black character as a helper (Hughey, 2009).

The type of shows that black people are "permitted to inhabit" (Morley, 2001, p. 435) also shapes how they are represented. Black people are consistently underrepresented on dramas series on high viewership networks, where they frequently take on the role of criminals, gangsters, or rapists (Campbell, 2016). However, black people are overrepresented in situation comedies on lower viewership networks which, due to genre conventions, are less likely to present three-dimensional characters. Black actors and actresses' relegation to sitcoms leads to a perpetuation of stereotypes of black people as funny, loud, silly, lazy, and irrational (Park et al., 2006).

The creation of media products is deeply affected by the politics of the production process (Molina-Guzmán, 2016), which determines who narrates the stories and, consequently, which stories are told and how. In the U.S., between 9.4% and 16.5% of the show creators are non-white (Hunt et al., 2019). For example, behind a successful production such as *The Wire (2002–2008)* is a team of white people who, borrowing Hall's words (2001), end up writing about the cultures of others. In addition to this lies the fact that those who are most harmed by matters of media representation are usually the ones that do not have the means at their disposal to discredit negative meanings and discourses about themselves on a large scale (Campbell, 2016).

In this context, Netflix seems to deviate from these traditions by giving minorities the opportunity to create content. For instance, the focus of this chapter, *Dear White People*, is created by Justin Simien, who is a gay black man. Their brand strategy emphasises diversity and representation and moves the focus from the traditional white heterosexual male lead to a wider range of leads and representation (Jenner, 2018). As such, Netflix allows the creation of content by and for various minorities, such as *Master of None (2015–)*, *Patriot Act with Hasan Minhaj (2018–2020)*, and *Never Have I Ever (2020–)*. Moreover, their streaming platform emphasises content that resonates with audiences beyond the U.S. Diversity, whether that be in terms of race, gender, or language, fits into that strategy. In doing so, they are treading a delicate balance of content for the niches and the masses. As such, Netflix moves beyond the white heterosexual middle-class family that is the presumed audience for so many U.S. network television shows (Jenner, 2018). Producing a show like *Dear White People*, therefore, neatly fits into their ideals and brand strategy.

All in all, and looking at both quantity and quality of TV representation it is clear how, despite some improvements, the U.S. media tend to represent blackness in a limiting and rather negative fashion. These depictions have helped cement power structures by demeaning marginalised groups and, as such, have bolstered the privileged status of the ruling (white) class (Campbell, 2016).

Importance of Media Representations

Research has shown that the misrepresentation and the lack of diversity in media products have societal consequences for people who belong to both the out-group and the in-group (Ford, 1997; Ward, 2004). Concerning the members of the out-group, international researchers have argued that frequent exposure to *negative* discourses and stereotypes of minority groups increases negative person perception (Punyanunt-Carter, 2008), which can result in a real-world negative bias towards such minority groups (Ford, 1997). This effect is especially strong when there is a lack of direct contact with a minority group (Fujioka, 2005). Negative depictions also lead to a decrease in sympathy and extensive support for public policies aimed at controlling black bodies (Ramasubramanian, 2011; Tan et al., 2000). When it comes to the impact that these negative discourses have on the members of the minority group, Ward (2004) stated that extensive exposure to stereotypes can decrease the self-esteem of young members. Research also found that long-term exposure to negative depictions of black people in media leads to negative views on matters such as intelligence, work ethic, values, socioeconomic status, and criminality (Mastro & Kopacz, 2006; Tan et al., 2000).

Creators must, thus, reckon with the "myriad and diverse peoples" (Westwood & Williams, 1997, p. 10) who are part of a nation to make them feel at home within "the national symbolic space" that the media creates (Morley, 2001, p. 439). This idea becomes particularly relevant if we take into consideration two potential aspects of television stories. First, televisual stories can provide their audiences with "valuable material" to comprehend the world they live in "without faithfully mirroring reality" but "without actually distorting it" (Buonanno, 2008, p. 72). Television plays an important role in people's informal learning process, particularly when the content is perceived as realistic by the active viewer (Bandura, 1977; Bragg & Buckingham, 2004). Second, it has the potential to provoke debate about "the meaning of specific social objects" (Madill & Goldmeier, 2003, p. 474). In this chapter, we will explore how people from different racial/ethnic groups living in the Netherlands perceive and discuss the racial representations in *Dear White People*.

Audiences TV Preferences and Readings

One theoretical explanation to understand audiences' preferences lies in the concept of cultural proximity (Straubhaar, 1991). This suggests that viewers tend to prefer cultural productions that seem culturally closer to them and build on elements of attraction such as shared language, history, cultural symbols, religious traditions, and ethnic types (Straubhaar, 2007). Based on this, it is fair to expect that the black and other minority participants of this study preferred to consume TV fiction that represents them and with which they could relate. But how do people interpret these texts?

Classic authors such as Hall (2001) and Eco (1987[1979]) have emphasised that media texts, although structured, are relatively open to be read and interpreted in different ways based on people's backgrounds, experiences, and knowledge of the medium itself. The term "open text" coined by the Italian semiologist illustrates well this dynamic. On the one hand, the term acknowledges the cooperative activity a viewer engages with when consuming a TV programme and, on the other, the presence of the producer deciding how and when to exert some sort of surveillance and guidance on this cooperative activity (Eco, 1987[1979]).

When it comes to reception studies focused on racial, ethnic, or religious minorities, researchers suggest that Caucasian American audiences generally do not oppose negative depiction of these minorities (Punyanunt-Carter, 2008; Ramasubramanian, 2011) whilst in-group viewers tend to engage in the following two main types of reactions. Some viewers accept the meanings contained within media texts and subjugate to hegemonic notions prescribed to their race, ethnicity, or religion, whilst others resist the negative ideas and notions contained about them within media texts (Fujioka, 2005; Ward, 2004). These ideas of accepting or resisting meanings connect with the well-known encoding-decoding model proposed by Hall in the 1970s, which suggests that audiences can accept the meaning that the producers encode (preferred or dominant reading), take a more distant interpretation (negotiated reading) or, even, reverse the intended meaning (oppositional reading). Identification with a character seems to play an important role in the formulation of counterarguments (Moyer-Gusé & Nabi, 2010) which leads us to hypothesise that black and other minority viewers are more inclined to accept the preferred reading of *Dear White People* than white people.

3 Methods

This chapter seeks to understand how a diverse group of young people value and interpret the series *Dear White People*. To do so, this study used a qualitative mixed-methods approach to data collection that consisted of three focus groups and six interviews. Data collected were examined using thematic analysis.

Data Collection

A combination of non-random purposive sampling and snowball sampling was employed to find participants (Flick, 2007) who meet the following general criteria: (a) be between 18 and 25 years old, (b) live in the Netherlands, (c) must have (formerly[3]) enrolled at Erasmus University Rotterdam. Additionally, interviewees had to have seen at least one season of the show *Dear White People*. A delicate balance between gender, race, and ethnicity was sought to obtain an assortment of data and to prevent biased results (Brennen, 2017). The final sample consisted of 15 focus group participants (9 females and 6 males) and six interviewees (3 females and 3 males). Ages ranged from 20 to 25 years.

To allow all opinions to be stated on the sensitive topics, the three focus groups were divided into (i) white, (ii) black, and (iii) mixed groups. The former two included either white participants or black participants. The third one contained a combination of white, black, and other minority people such as those with a Chinese or Turkish background. As such, comparisons could be drawn not only between individuals but also between the focus groups. Seven of the participants were white, six were black, and two were from another minority background.[4] As for the six interviewees, two were white, two were black, and two were from another minority background.

In order to obtain a structured in-depth analysis, a comprehensive topic list for the focus group was constructed. Relevant questions were created, partially informed by concepts and ideas from existing literature. Six scenes were selected and shown during the focus groups to act as a stimulus and incentivise conversation about racial issues portrayed in this show. In turn,

[3] Only persons that graduated less than a year prior to the focus group session/interview were accepted.

[4] Persons that do not fit into the white or black category are referred to as other minority in this study.

discussions from the focus groups informed the topic list of the semi-structured in-depth interviews. This ensured that topics that were found to be more relevant and that needed more elaboration were given extra attention during the interviews.

Data Analysis

The focus groups and interviews were transcribed verbatim. Thereafter, the coding process and data analysis ensued. The data were analysed by the first author of the paper following the rigorous coding process suggested by Braun and Clarke (2006) with the use of data analysis software ATLAS.ti. This process was primarily data-driven and therefore followed an inductive approach to thematic analysis. The principle of reflexivity, i.e. by critically self-reflecting on the research process (Guba & Lincoln, 1982), was especially relevant due to the researcher's minority background and skin colour. Similarly to what Bucholtz (2011) experienced as a white professor in her study on gendered race talk among white Californian youth, the first author became complicit in the race talk that arose during the focus groups and interviews. The black people and the other minority people recognised the researcher as "one of their own", whilst white people felt comfortable expressing thoughts that, with a non-white researcher's presence, would most likely not have been expressed as comfortably. Regarding ethical issues, all participants signed an informed consent approved by the Ethics Committee of the Erasmus School of History, Culture and Communication and are referred through pseudonyms.

4 Analysis

In this section, we start by offering a brief portrayal of our participants' profiles in terms of, for instance, their awareness of black-led TV shows. We considered that this information allowed us to reach a better understanding of our participants' perceptions about and experiences with the show, as well as of the way they interpret some of the racial issues the series tackles.

Where Our Participants Stand At

To explore participants' level of awareness with black-led programmes, the focus group moderator started the meeting by asking them to name three black-led television shows they had seen. On average, black and other minority[5] people named 2.9 (e.g. *Atlanta (2016–)*, *Chewing Gum (2015–2017)*, and *Empire (2015–)*). They also explained that they tend to consciously search for diversity on screen and that they try to give new black-led shows a try.

Conversely, the white participants named, on average, 1.3 shows (e.g. *How to Get Away with Murder (2014–)*). The most recurring explanation given to justify this low number was that black-led shows are just rare. Interestingly, one of the white participants argued that black-led shows may get less visibility on Netflix than white-led shows due to the platforms' algorithm. This observation actually echoed an accusation that Netflix received in 2018 of targeting black subscribers with thumbnails featuring black cast members to make the person more likely to watch it. Flip this around, and one can see how this mechanism can achieve the effect of only targeting white-led content to white subscribers (Quico, 2019). This is particularly relevant considering 8 out of the 15 focus group participants explicitly mentioned Netflix recommendations as a source of new content. Although the majority clarified that characters' race does not influence their viewing decision-making, one white participant explained that she generally avoids these shows because they are not aimed at her.

To explore peoples' opinions about role distribution and stereotypes in films and series focus group, the moderator asked them to think of one white and one black actress/actor and write down three characteristics of the type of characters they typically play. The following table collects the main adjectives used by white people and people from minority groups, which coincide with previous findings (see Campbell, 2016; Ward, 2004) (Table 11.1).

As we will see in the next section, participants argued that this does not occur in *Dear White People*—a show that puts black people at the centre of attention and gives them the same care and importance as white leading characters typically get.

[5] The Turkish-Dutch person noted that she primarily watches programming from Turkey. Therefore, she could name none. As Turkey has a tiny portion of black residents, it is unlikely that they are extensively represented in Turkish programming. Therefore, this reply is to be expected (Lerner & Whitehouse, 2017). For that reason, she was excluded from this calculation.

Table 11.1 Defining black and white actors/actresses

Participants	*Black actors/actresses*	*White actors/actresses*
Minority groups	Crazy, funny, loud	Gentleman, smart, pretty
White participants	Subservient supporting roles, calm, wise, less versatile	Leading roles, versatile

Dear White People: *A Smart Show*

When researching what young people living in the Netherlands value of *Dear White People*, the discussions spun around the narrative of the show, particularly about its tone, characters, and informative nature.

The Smart and Realistic Tone Regardless of their background, every research subject was positive and receptive to the tone and understood how the show addresses racial themes. All focus group participants lauded the satirical, comedic, and smart writing of *Dear White People*, especially in its handling of (racially tinted) social issues (e.g. police brutality, white people touching black people's hair without permission). Although the show is focused on university experiences of black Americans and, therefore, may not entirely reflect and capture black people's experiences in the Netherlands, participants considered the show to be authentic and realistic in depicting not only racial problems, sexism, or homophobia, but also the impact of these social issues. For instance, Odette said that the show's approach to discussing social issues is not only smart and refreshing, but also provocative and, to some extent, unique: I think it's really smart.... The way it's written is pretty cool and, of course, when I watched the trailer, I already knew it was pretty provocative. And for some people, they are not gonna be happy with it. But I think it's nice... because people are afraid to say these things....They are walking on eggshells.... It's pretty rare to see someone say it in a TV show. (Odette, white female)

Well-Rounded Characters When compared to other shows and movies, *Dear White People* is considered to offer a complex and realistic portrayal of black people. For example, every interviewee celebrated that the show depicts black people not as a monolithic group, but as three-dimensional characters with their own feelings, problems, and desires. In other words, characters are not defined by their blackness, but they have their own individual traits and opinions. They are "dynamic", "make mistakes", and "feel like real persons" (Coen, white male). The series also does an excellent job at not engaging in colourism (i.e. the preference for light-skinned black actors/actresses over dark-skinned ones) contributing, this way, to the representation of African Americans as a diverse community. Furthermore, five out of six interviewees noted the lack of negative stereotypes in the show. Instead of overwhelmingly portraying black people as thugs, criminals, or as the comic relief with an exaggerated stereotypical character trait, *Dear White People* displays black people as smart and educated without removing black elements such as their culture (e.g. clothing and manner of speech). The stereotypical traits that some characters have are smartly implanted to subvert the viewers' expectations later in the show. Participants named such examples as Lionel, who is a nerdy gay person, or Troy, who is a popular athletic black guy who has mastered the art of respectability politics. Based on first impressions, those characters seem quite clichéd. During the series, however, they develop and show different sides of themselves.

The construction of realistic portrayals also applies to how white characters are constructed. Two of the interviewees noted that, before watching the show, they were worried that the white characters were going to be portrayed as bad people. Instead, they were surprised at the amount of care creators had put into them. According to Coen, even some people that could be deemed as bad get a fair and nuanced portrayal:

> It's more a misunderstanding because I feel that people are not bad inherently, but there's just a lot of misunderstanding and…a lack of knowledge. And that's why we need a series like *Dear White People* to give us different perspectives and see how this racial tension got so high and that we should all calm down a bit. (Coen, white male)

Two of the interviewees noted, however, that the black characters were frequently frustrated or trying to make the world a better place for black people. They worried that this might put off some viewers (primarily white) from watching the show as it could be seen as unpleasant or hostile. Nevertheless, they noted that this is inherent to the series itself given its focus on black identity and black issues.

All in all, the interviewees were positive and receptive to the representation of black people in the show which they considered pretty unique. In fact, interviewees had a hard time identifying similarities between *Dear White People* and other series. In some cases, this was due to the participants having trouble remembering other shows. In others, this was because the show is simply too different in both its representation of black people and the stories it tells.

Informal Learning Participants noted on various occasions how informative the series was about racism, and how it fostered some sort of self-reflection upon their own identity and race, and how the latter played a role in shaping their lives. Young people also acknowledged the importance of proper minority representation to create more understanding for one another and show different life perspectives: I think it's important for people to be represented. To show other people that you are capable of the same things, that we are the same kind of person with the same capabilities and hopefully options and chances one day, which we are not [getting]. Because people have prejudice. And I think once you can show that you are the same, [they] go away. And as soon as you don't have [them], you won't act racist or discriminate people. So, I think that [representation] is important to make this world a better place and to get people to make the most out of themselves, their talents and capacities, their own self-image, confidence. (Anjali, another minority female)

Participants stated that they became more aware and understanding of societal issues outside of their own scope after watching the show. Joanne gave the most elaborate answer to the series as a source of informal learning as she noted how she learned about minority issues in the U.S., which made her reflect on minority issues in the Netherlands. This made her more receptive to their struggles:

> Of course, I already knew a little bit [about] discrimination and violence against people with a different skin colour. Not only in America but just throughout the world...For me, it was a really new experience to place myself within their position and see how they felt instead of how I experienced the world... It made me understand their point of view better. Cause first... sometimes when you read something in the news about Muslims or people who feel discriminated I am like: 'Ah, well, don't. It's not such a big problem'. But when you put yourself in someone else's shoes and really see how they ... experience life and how they are treated. For me, [it] made me understand them better. (Joanne, white female)

The value of this American show within the Netherlands was a topic of discussion during the interviews. For instance, participants referred to implicit or subtle racism present in the Netherlands against problematised Dutch minorities such as the Moroccan community (de Koning, 2016). However, some interviewees also explained that the series is probably most effective in educating or attracting people that are receptive to its ideas. Both focus groups and interviewees noted that the show and its title might be too confrontational for prejudiced (white) audience members.

Dear White People: *Interpreting Racial Issues*

The second goal was to explore how young people, with different racial/ethnic backgrounds, interpret the way that the show portrays racial issues. For this purpose, six scenes were showcased or brought up during the interviews to stimulate the conversation. "Lack of awareness and political correctness", on the one hand, and "self-perception of threat and victim-blaming", on the other, were the two main sub-themes that emerged from the data.

Lack of Awareness and Political Correctness In multiple scenes, *Dear White People* refer to the lack of awareness or sensitivity that white people express towards black people. One of the best examples happens in episode 5, when a white guy raps the n-word[6] during a party. Reggie, a black male character, asks him not to use that word. The white guy does not understand why he cannot say it. An argument unfolds and others get involved. Multiple participants, particularly black and people from other minorities, celebrated this clip to be a clear example of white people not being aware of sensitive matters, such as the use of the n-word. However, this is only one of the readings. When listening to white viewers we identify resentment. White viewers complain about the difficulty to talk about minorities without being accused of being a racist. More precisely, five out of seven white participants expressed their concerns about political correctness, and three of the white participants implied that black people are

[6] The n-word refers to "nigger", which is a racial slur directed at black people. Over the years, it has become taboo to pronounce the word in modern (American) society as a non-black person. Since a few decades, the word has been re-appropriated and repurposed by black rappers in its modern variation "nigga". It is now used amongst black people with more positive meanings such as "friend" or "brother". The word has gone mainstream following the worldwide popularisation of hip hop and rap music.

just victimising themselves. According to those white participants, this fosters self-censoring practices. These comments align with previous findings that illustrate how white people, especially ones that live and move in overwhelmingly white spaces, think 'anti-white' racism is a larger problem than anti-black racism (Hammon, 2013). Moreover, it also hints at what is known as "white fragility", which is the tendency that white people have to escape discomfort with their whiteness and instead position themselves as the victims (Di Angelo, 2018).

Self-Perception of Threat and Victim-Blaming One of the most remarkable moments of the show is when a black man gets brutalised by a white cop. This scene relates to the fatal shooting of unarmed black teenager Trayvon Martin by a white cop in 2012 and who, as the character of the TV show, was wearing a hoodie. This clothing element was the main point of discussion during the focus groups. The initial complaint made by the white participants about the cop's actions turned into a sort of justification for the cop's behaviour. Five white focus group participants remarked that the black character could have avoided the situation if he had worn something different, something that presented him as less hostile. Once again, fitting into the concept of white fragility (Applebaum, 2017; Di Angelo, 2018). Unsurprisingly, black participants living in the Netherlands acknowledged the scene to be representative of their personal experiences and explained how they carefully consider the clothes they wear to accommodate to white people's expectations and to avoid being perceived as hostile and dangerous: I have kept, at night, my hoodie off just because me without a hoodie looks a bit more normal and less dangerous. (Boaz, black male)

As the results presented above suggest, black and other minority people related to the content of the show and engaged in what Hall (2001) conceptualises as the preferred reading of a text. This did not always happen with white participants who took oppositional or negotiated readings (Hall, 2001). Data from the focus group and the interviews suggests that race plays a role when relating to characters and the situations they are involved in. Due to self-experience and/or awareness, black participants and people from other minority groups easily identified to the characters and the situations depicted in the show. For instance, Boaz related to the fact that his university force coloured students to pose for pictures to present itself as diverse just like they do in the show. Zara, Memphis, Boaz, and

Ngoni noted how they related to how a black character felt about being black and being perceived as different and as a potential threat. Therefore, it seems like the show does an excellent job at portraying real-life experiences of black people, both female and male.

However, race is not the only component that affects the relatability to a show. The experiences the characters go through play an important role. For example, one black interviewee explained that she had a relatively hard time relating to the black characters in *Dear White People*. In this case, the interviewee had light skin, had a white parent, and was raised in a white environment. Consequently, she feels more at home in native Dutch crowds than in those with a different background. Therefore, she cares more about elements like "Dutch culture" than race when watching a show. As such, she argued that she could relate more to characters that share her upbringing and social surroundings than characters that share her skin colour. Such a worldview is not uncommon in persons of colour that are raised by white parents in a white environment (Twine, 1996). The role that experiences play in the identification process was further reaffirmed by Hoang, who related to how Coco was trying to fit into a group of white people by changing her personality to make herself appear "white". Although it is natural that some storylines resonate with people from certain backgrounds more so than others, the experiences characters go through seem to play a stronger role in the identification process than race.

In the case of the *white focus group*, the participants frequently focused on the white characters and related to those characters' experiences. According to the two white interviewees, race and culture can become an obstacle to relate to other people's problems. In this vein, the Asian respondent also said that he favours Asian characters.

5 Conclusion

Black people have been traditionally underrepresented, misrepresented, and relegated to supporting roles (Hunt et al., 2019) in the mass media created in U.S. The Netflix series *Dear White People* presents a visible deviation from that norm. In line with Netflix's brand strategy of creating diverse and inclusive content that foregoes centring around a traditional white heterosexual male lead (Jenner, 2018), the series boasts a majority black cast and tackles various racial issues head-on (Bavaro, 2018; Ray-Harris, 2017). In doing so, it presents both the joy and the pain that come with black life in the U.S. Given its universal themes, the show resonates with black and other minority viewers across the Western world. This study examined how white, black and other minority people living in the Netherlands, a multicultural country, perceive and value the show.

The tone, well-rounded characters, and storylines of *Dear White People* were all praised in some form by the participants. Several people remarked how subversive, stereotype disconfirming, and representative the show was regarding black people and the real world. Although the viewers were overall receptive and positive towards the show, their experiences varied significantly. Black people mostly hailed the fact that someone finally made a show that speaks about issues that matter to them (e.g. microaggressions, feelings of othering, and silencing black voices). White people acknowledged the learning potential of the show about social issues. As previously documented by Ramasubramanian (2007, 2011) and others (Ramasubramanian & Oliver, 2007; Scharrer & Ramasubramanian, 2015) in a news media setting, a combination of media literacy training and stereotype-disconfirming messages can help change people's views. The responses of the interviewees indicate that this approach also works in an entertainment TV setting, as *Dear White People* engages in both (Bavaro, 2018; Ray-Harris, 2017).

From the focus groups and interviews, it became evident that media representation matters a lot to black and other minority persons (de Koning, 2016; Fujioka, 2005), as the vast majority of them seek out non-white content that represents them. The white persons interviewed, however, did not display a clear desire for racial representation (Chávez & Guido-DiBrito, 1999; Fujioka, 2005).

Meaning-making processes also differed between white, black, and other minority people. The majority of black and other minority people interpreted the show in the preferred way (Hall, 2001). They recognised the racial themes and issues that the show addresses, even though the American racial context is quite different from the Dutch one. However, it is worth noting that several black persons also explained how they suffer from biases and prejudices in real life based on how American media portrays black people. As such, there seems to be a demand for black-led non--U.S. content. Concerning white people, some of them interpreted the show in the intended way whilst, those who were less knowledgeable or aware about racial issues, tended to engage in negotiated or oppositional readings (Hall, 2001). This supports the Marley hypothesis, which posits that awareness and understanding of modern racism are affected by one's knowledge, or lack thereof, of racial history (Bonam et al., 2019). Moreover, white people frequently displayed white fragility when confronted with the privilege that their whiteness gives them (Applebaum, 2017; Di Angelo, 2018).

Findings also suggest that shared racial identity plays a more relevant role in the identification process than shared nationality. Both black and other minority people identified (a lot) with what the black characters were going through (e.g. marginalisation, othering). This supports the Group Empathy Theory, which posits that marginalised groups of society are more likely to empathise, understand, and support other marginalised groups (Sirin et al., 2016). As for the white persons, they primarily identified with the white characters from the show, and they resonated with the black characters with which they have shared certain experiences—for example, something as universal as failing an exam.

This chapter provides new insights into meaning-making processes of various audience members in the Netherlands, a country with a significant non-white populace. The study highlights how minorities living and raised in this European country experience similar feelings of exclusion and discrimination as their American counterparts. Findings also indicate that the show might work as empowerment and as a comforting shoulder for individuals that are experiencing feelings of isolation due to their racial difference to the majority populace. These ideas could be explored in the future. Future research would also benefit from exploring how people from different generations, different cities, and different educational backgrounds interpret the same text. It is also of relevance to further explore the effects that viewing U.S.A. media can have on minorities living in other countries.

From the findings one can already see the effects that the show is already having on people's knowledge and awareness of certain topics. By continuing to facilitate such diverse and inclusive shows, Netflix can contribute to the creation of a more informed and democratic public sphere (Jenner, 2018). In turn, this can translate in real political action as awareness can translate in movement. However, exploring the algorithm's effects remains important. As indicated by some of the findings, some people do not get confronted with shows like *Dear White People* as the algorithm favours safer choices for viewers that might be less inclined to watch such shows. Future research could further explore Netflix's effect on the public sphere and the role that the algorithm plays in this effect.

References

Applebaum, B. (2017). Comforting discomfort as complicity: White fragility and the pursuit of invulnerability. *Hypatia, 32*(4), 862–875. https://doi.org/10.1111/hypa.12352

Bandura, A. (1977). *Social learning theory*. Prentice Hall. http://www.asecib.ase.ro/mps/Bandura_SocialLearningTheory.pdf

Bavaro, V. (2018). Taking back one's narrative: *Dear White People*, cultural appropriation, and the challenge of anti-essentialism. *RSA Journal, 29*, 19–38.

Bonam, C. M., Nair Das, V., Coleman, B. R., & Salter, P. (2019). Ignoring history, denying racism: Mounting evidence for the Marley hypothesis and epistemologies of ignorance. *Social Psychological and Personality Science, 10*(2), 257–265. https://doi.org/10.1177/1948550617751583

Bragg, S., & Buckingham, D. (2004). Embarrassment, education and erotics: The sexual politics of family viewing. *European Journal of Cultural Studies, 7*(4), 441–459. https://doi.org/10.1177/1367549404047145

Braun, V., & Clarke, V. (2006). Using thematic analysis in psychology. *Qualitative Research in Psychology, 3*(2), 77–101. https://doi.org/10.1191/1478088706qp063oa

Brennen, B. S. (2017). *Qualitative research methods for media studies*. Taylor & Francis Group. http://ebookcentral.proquest.com/lib/eur/detail.action?docID=4891115

Bucholtz, M. (2011). 'It's different for guys': Gendered narratives of racial conflict among white California youth. *Discourse & Society, 22*(4), 385–402. https://doi.org/10.1177/0957926510395832

Buonanno, M. (2008). *The age of television: Experiences and theories*. Intellect.

Campbell, C. (2016). *The Routledge companion to media and race*. Routledge Handbooks Online. https://doi.org/10.4324/9781315778228

Carney, N. (2016). All lives matter, but so does race: Black lives matter and the evolving role of social media. *Humanity and Society, 40*(2), 180–199. https://doi.org/10.1177/0160597616643868

Centraal Bureau voor de Statistiek. (2020). *Hoeveel mensen met een migratieachtergrond wonen in Nederland?* [Webpagina]. Centraal Bureau voor de Statistiek. https://www.cbs.nl/nl-nl/dossier/dossier-asiel-migratie-en-integratie/hoeveel-mensen-met-een-migratieachtergrond-wonen-in-nederland-

Chávez, A. F., & Guido-DiBrito, F. (1999). Racial and ethnic identity and development. *New Directions for Adult and Continuing Education, 84*, 39–47. https://doi.org/10.1002/ace.8405

de Koning, M. (2016). You need to present a counter-message. *Journal of Muslims in Europe, 5*(2), 170–189. https://doi.org/10.1163/22117954-12341325

Di Angelo, R. (2018). *White fragility: Why it's so hard for white people to talk about racism*. Beacon Press.

Eco, U. (1977). *Tratado de semiótica general* (1. ed). Lumen.

Flick, U. (2007). *Designing qualitative research*. SAGE Publications, Ltd. https://doi.org/10.4135/9781849208826

Ford, T. E. (1997). Effects of stereotypical television portrayals of African-Americans on person perception. *Social Psychology Quarterly, 60*(3), 266–278. https://doi.org/10.2307/2787086

Fujioka, Y. (2005). Black media images as a perceived threat to African American ethnic identity: Coping responses, perceived public perception, and attitudes towards affirmative action. *Journal of Broadcasting & Electronic Media, 49*(4), 450–467. https://doi.org/10.1207/s15506878jobem4904_6

Groshek, J., & Krongard, S. (2016). Netflix and engage? Implications for streaming television on political participation during the 2016 US presidential campaign. *Social Sciences, 5*(4), 65. https://doi.org/10.3390/socsci5040065

Guba, E. G., & Lincoln, Y. S. (1982). Epistemological and methodological bases of naturalistic inquiry. *Educational Communication & Technology Journal, 30*(4), 233–252. https://doi.org/10.1007/978-94-009-6669-7_18

Gusterson, H. (2017). From Brexit to Trump: Anthropology and the rise of nationalist populism. *American Ethnologist, 44*(2), 209–214. https://doi.org/10.1111/amet.12469

Hall, S. (2001). Encoding/decoding. In M. Gigi Durham & D. M. Kellner, *Media and Cultural Studies: Keyworks, 2*, 163–174. Blackwell: Oxford.

Hammon, B. (2013). Playing the race card: White Americans' sense of victimization in response to affirmative action. *Texas Hispanic Journal of Law and Policy, 19*, 95–120.

Hughey, M. W. (2009). Cinethetic racism: White redemption and black stereotypes in 'magical negro' films. *Social Problems, 56*(3), 543–577. https://doi.org/10.1525/sp.2009.56.3.543

Hunt, D., Ramón, A. C., & Tran, M. (2019). *Hollywood diversity report 2019: Old story, new beginning*. UCLA College of Social Sciences. https://socialsciences.ucla.edu/deans-initiatives/initiative-archive/hollywood-diversity-report

Jenner, M. (2018). *Netflix and the re-invention of television*. Springer International Publishing. https://doi.org/10.1007/978-3-319-94316-9

Lerner, D., & Whitehouse, E. (2017, October 26). *The Afro-Turks: Turkey's little-known black minority reclaims its past*. Haaretz. https://www.haaretz.com/middle-east-news/turkey/.premium-the-afro-turks-turkeys-little-known-black-minority-reclaims-its-past-1.5460354

Madill, A., & Goldmeier, R. (2003). EastEnders: Texts of female desire and of community. *International Journal of Cultural Studies, 6*(4), 471–494. https://doi.org/10.1177/136787790364005

Mastro, D., & Greenberg, B. (2000). The portrayal of racial minorities on prime time television. *Journal of Broadcasting & Electronic Media, 44*(4), 690–703. https://doi.org/10.1207/s15506878jobem4404_10

Mastro, D. E., & Kopacz, M. A. (2006). Media representations of race, prototypicality, and policy reasoning: An application of self-categorization theory. *Journal of Broadcasting & Electronic Media, 50*(2), 305–322. https://doi.org/10.1207/s15506878jobem5002_8

Molina-Guzmán, I. (2016). #OscarsSoWhite: How Stuart Hall explains why nothing changes in Hollywood and everything is changing. *Critical Studies in Media Communication, 33*(5), 438–454. https://doi.org/10.1080/15295036.2016.1227864

Morley, D. (2001). Belongings: Place, space and identity in a mediated world. *European Journal of Cultural Studies, 4*(4), 425–448. https://doi.org/10.1177/136754940100400404

Moyer-Gusé, E., & Nabi, R. L. (2010). Explaining the effects of narrative in an entertainment television program: Overcoming resistance to persuasion. *Human Communication Research, 36*(1), 26–52. https://doi.org/10.1111/j.1468-2958.2009.01367.x

Park, J. H., Gabbadon, N. G., & Chernin, A. R. (2006). Naturalizing racial differences through comedy: Asian, black, and white views on racial stereotypes in rush hour 2. *Journal of Communication, 56*(1), 157–177. https://doi.org/10.1111/j.1460-2466.2006.00008.x

Punyanunt-Carter, N. M. (2008). The perceived realism of African American portrayals on television. *Howard Journal of Communications, 19*(3), 241–257. https://doi.org/10.1080/10646170802218263

Quico, C. (2019). Television reshaped by big data: Impacts and implications for Netflix-like platforms in the age of dataism. *International Journal of Film and Media Arts, 4*(1), 48–55. https://doi.org/10.24140/ijfma.v4.n1.04

Ramasubramanian, S. (2007). Media-based strategies to reduce racial stereotypes activated by news stories. *Journalism & Mass Communication Quarterly, 84*(2), 249–264. https://doi.org/10.1177/107769900708400204

Ramasubramanian, S. (2011). The impact of stereotypical versus counterstereotypical media exemplars on racial attitudes, causal attributions, and support for affirmative action. *Communication Research, 38*(4), 497–516. https://doi.org/10.1177/0093650210384854

Ramasubramanian, S., & Oliver, M. B. (2007). Activating and suppressing hostile and benevolent racism: Evidence for comparative media stereotyping. *Media Psychology, 9*(3), 623–646. https://doi.org/10.1080/15213260701283244

Ray-Harris, A. (2017, April 19). *The excellent dear white people doesn't care about white people.* TV Club. https://tv.avclub.com/the-excellent-dear-white-people-doesn-t-care-about-whit-1798191060

Salam, M. (2019, March 15). Trolls tried to sink 'Captain Marvel.' She triumphed. *The New York Times.* https://www.nytimes.com/2019/03/15/arts/captain-marvel-trolls.html

Scharrer, E., & Ramasubramanian, S. (2015). Intervening in the media's influence on stereotypes of race and ethnicity: The role of media literacy education. *Journal of Social Issues, 71*(1), 171–185. https://doi.org/10.1111/josi.12103

Sirin, C. V., Valentino, N. A., & Villalobos, J. D. (2016). Group empathy theory: The effect of group empathy on US intergroup attitudes and behavior in the context of immigration threats. *The Journal of Politics, 78*(3), 893–908. https://doi.org/10.1086/685735

Straubhaar, J. (1991). Beyond media imperialism: Assymetrical interdependence and cultural proximity. *Critical Studies in Mass Communication, 8*(1), 39–59. https://doi.org/10.1080/15295039109366779

Straubhaar, J. (2007). *World television: From global to local.* https://doi.org/10.4135/9781452204147

Tan, A., Fujioka, Y., & Tan, G. (2000). Television use, stereotypes of African Americans and opinions on affirmative action: An affective model of policy reasoning. *Communication Monographs, 67*(4), 362–371. https://doi.org/10.1080/03637750009376517

Twine, F. W. (1996). Brown Skinned White Girls: Class, culture and the construction of white identity in suburban communities. *Gender, Place & Culture, 3*(2), 205–224. https://doi.org/10.1080/09663699650021891

Ugwu, R. (2018, May 2). Why the creator of 'Dear White People' is doubling down on identity politics. *The New York Times.* https://www.nytimes.com/2018/05/02/arts/television/dear-white-people-creator-doubles-down-on-identity-politics.html

Ward, L. M. (2004). Wading through the stereotypes: Positive and negative associations between media use and black adolescents' conceptions of self. *Developmental Psychology, 40*(2), 284–294. https://doi.org/10.1037/0012-1649.40.2.284

Westwood, S., & Williams, J. (1997). *Imagining cities: Scripts, signs, memory.* Routledge.

CHAPTER 12

Elections in Latin America and the Image of Their Candidates

Paulo Carlos López-López, Daniel Barredo Ibáñez, and María Pereira López

1 Introduction: What Is Public Image?

Political reality can be *neither seen nor touched*; hence, the image of the candidates—and, in general, of any person one is not close to—is a construction process in which many factors play a part. These factors include party identification, ideology, or the emotions aroused within or around ourselves. However, there are also other types of key factors which influence the "image" citizens have of their representatives (e.g., orienting and

P. C. López-López (✉) • M. Pereira López
University of Santiago de Compostela, Santiago de Compostela, Spain
e-mail: paulocarlos.lopez@usc.es; maria.pereira.lopez@usc.es

D. Barredo Ibáñez
Universidad del Rosario, Bogotá, Colombia

Fudan University, Shanghai, China
e-mail: daniel.barredo@urosario.edu.co

B. García-Orosa (ed.), *Digital Political Communication Strategies*, The Palgrave Macmillan Series in International Political Communication, https://doi.org/10.1007/978-3-030-81568-4_12

altering the perspective), such as the analogue and digital media, or social networks, seen as spaces of exchange and dissemination of information. In fact, within this digital context, it is the social networks that allow the strategical construction of the image of political actors (López-Rabadán et al., 2016) and that hence play a very important role in political communication (Schill, 2012).

As a result, the individually and socially constructed perception has a cumulative character—which may, of course, change, but is stable over time. This particular fact is not that different from the way in which the public opinion spoken of by Walter Lippmann (1929) was formed in the early twentieth century: we consume information (by news or tweets), we internalize it according to our pre-existing preferences or attitudes, and we add small realities or *pseudo-realities* of the world, leading to our forming, *within our own mind*, an image of that which lies beyond our reach. In this way, the farther we are from a certain topic or political actor, the stronger the influence some external factors have on our perception, as stated in the agenda-setting theory to the topics referred to as *unobtrusive issues* (Yagade & Dozier, 1990).

The digital society and the new mechanisms and platforms of communication have not brought about any substantial change in the way in which we define our political images. Quite on the contrary, we keep using heuristic shortcuts for making decisions that, a priori, are complex, such as our position concerning a certain candidate or public representative. Indeed, the Internet and social networks are yet another source which, added to the traditional means of communication, mediate, transmitting the information in a stereotypical fashion, thereby activating a process which "assigns to each one of the realities which we perceive in our environment, a certain reference, a mental image" (Rubio Ferreres, 2009, p. 4). It is upon this image that we build the attributes transmitted, either in a limited and unidirectional way (traditional media) or by means of a dialogue process, through so-called packages, which indicate what and how to associate in the social networks (Vu et al., 2014), in which the intervention of digital communities and the "agenda melting" process have a fundamental role to play (Shaw et al., 1999).

The present chapter provides a review of the research carried out on election campaigns that occurred in various Latin American countries, especially those which have taken place online over the past few years, with the aim of establishing, through mediation and cyber-politics, the most frequent attributes of Latin American candidates and how they influence the construction of their public image. In order to do so, we observe the main social network-based campaigning patterns, how media—especially the public and private TV channels—act within this space, and the emotional reactions of the citizens to this kind of message.

2 Cyber-Politics in Latin America: From the Election Campaigns to Digital Propaganda

Television continues to be the medium of choice for the Latin American public. This is due to some enduring problems, such as the technological gap, when it comes to informing oneself on an election campaign. In fact, there are several studies measuring the effect of TV coverage in the voting intention, for example, that in favor of Fernando Collor de Mello in Brazil in 1989 or in favor of Alberto Fujimori and Alejandro Toledo in Peru in the early twenty-first century (Boas, 2005, 2013). Nevertheless, social networks kept gaining in importance and transferring the participative practices of the Latin American social movements from the *offline* to the *online* sphere, so much so that the online platforms took center stage in the elections taking place in the last two decades, albeit with obvious limitations in matters of both consumption and impact. Such was the case of Rafael Correa in Ecuador: his first victory in the presidential election (2006) was due to an efficient management of social networks, particularly Twitter (Barredo Ibáñez et al., 2015).

Likewise, and as a paradigmatic example, in El Salvador, the strategic use of platforms such as Twitter, Facebook, and Instagram provided an enormous boost to Nayib Bukele in his quest to become president of the country, for, as described by Lupu et al. (2020), the former Mayor of San Salvador supplanted his lack of political platform—he had run as an independent—with direct interaction with the voters.

In Mexico, the lack of credibility from which traditional media are suffering and the concentration of the market in just two big TV channels—Televisa and TV Azteca—led to a progressive appropriation of social networks by some active social movements like #YoSoy132 (De la Garza et al., 2019). This social participation has been capitalized by several political factors. The most notorious case occurred during the 2018 presidential election, when the then-candidate Andrés Manuel López Obrador projected his campaign mainly on Facebook, with a promotional rather than deliberative style (Toxtle & González, 2020). The success of the

Movimiento Regeneración Nacional (Morena) in the same country cannot be explained exclusively by its strategic management of cyberspace; other factors, such as the disenchantment with traditional political parties, must also be taken into account (De la Garza et al., 2019). But, the interesting fact is that the *online* sphere allows one to escape the moderation and interpretation which had formerly been in the firm grasp of the big Mexican TV channels.

Direct interaction with voters does more than just help introduce a set of ideas without journalistic mediators. It can also trigger an irresponsible dissemination of non-verified facts or cause damage to the reputation of other candidates (thereby worsening their image) as was the case with the 2018 Brazilian presidential election. A crucial factor in this campaign was the dissemination of fake contents through WhatsApp, primarily by groups associated with Jair Bolsonaro—who, subsequently, was elected. The libelous content of those messages would have been difficult to convey through some conventional mass media (Lupu et al., 2020) which, within Brazil itself, generated a less assertive image in matters of characterizing and associating the candidate with right-wing populism, compared to the international press (Araújo & Prior, 2020). The same dissemination mechanism was used in the 2018 Colombian presidential election, in which Chenou et al. (2021) found WhatsApp messages used to reinforce the prestige and the image of the then-candidate Iván Duque within a certain community, with the additional aim to expand his reputation in other communities. Such repeated messages were meant to create "echo chambers" (p. 137), encouraging polarization and the propagation of *fake news* with a clear partisan character.

The previously mentioned cases mark a shift in Latin American electoral routines which affect the public image perceived by the citizens—a shift from video politics to cyber-politics. The two spheres are complementary and do not exclude each other (López-López & Oñate, 2019). However, as new repertoires and agendas are developing, one is witnessing, across Latin America, the increased presence of cybertroops, that is, groups hired by the governments or by private organizations with the task of promoting simulated participation, expanding the fictitious outreach of a campaign, advertising the contents belonging to an individual or group, and establishing a spiral of silence 2.0—by trying to silence critical voices—among other things. In this regard, in countries such as Argentina, Brazil, Mexico, or Venezuela, evidence was found of social network accounts fully oriented toward attempts to distort public opinion (Bradshaw & Howard, 2017) (Fig. 12.1):

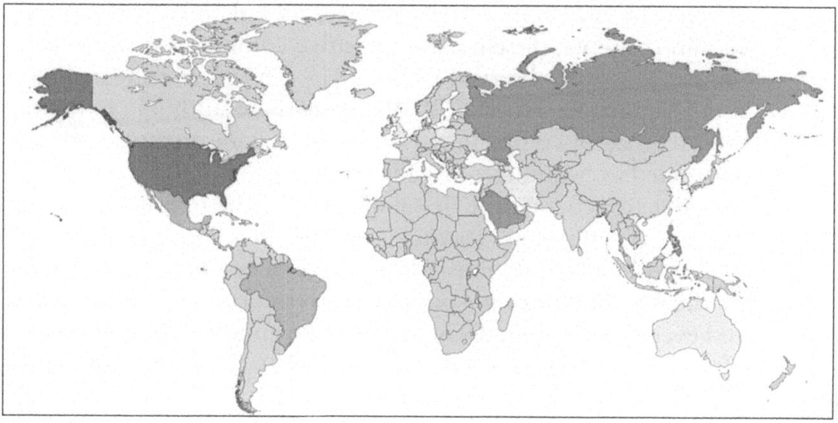

Fig. 12.1 Density of cybertroops in the world. (Source: Bradshaw & Howard, 2017, p. 22)

One of the most significant cases of this kind of movement that makes up organized participation occurred in Brazil, a country in which the use of bots has been proven at least since the 2014 presidential election (Arnaudo, 2017) won, in the second round, by Dilma Rousseff. Paradoxically, this very author explains that the social networks and the automated communication systems also contributed to the establishment of a narrative that was decisive in ousting Rousseff from office, which occurred two years after her election, in 2016.

The strategical interference of these automatic systems is by no means uniform. Its implementation seems to be associated with the more wide-ranging political exercises—such as presidential elections—rather than with local and regional ones, largely owing to the high management costs. The automated communication systems are primarily used for two specific purposes:

- In order to expand the outreach of the campaigns, this is one of the most frequent ways to do it: the programming of bots which would help make content viral. In the 2017 Ecuadorian election, one noted the automated publishing and re-publishing of contents associated with the image of various candidates (Puyosa, 2017). The orchestrated outreach expansion is, however, also performed manually, based upon affinity management, that is, effected by means of coordinating users tasked with promoting certain contents, disseminating positive comments, among other things. This was observed in the 2017 Chilean presidential election (Santana & Huerta, 2019), with these authors confirming the presence of commentators close to certain organizations and who acted as "volunteer brigade members" (p. 74).

- In order to generate the destabilization of the opponent's image within the campaigns, *trolling* is another procedure used. It consists of attempts to diminish the prestige of one or the other of the candidates, of blocking a positive conversation on a certain topic, and even of spreading defamations, in an approach not unlike that of war propaganda (Barredo Ibáñez, 2021). This cybertroops procedure—in which automated users or users aligned to the respective party or candidate are also used—can even reach the point of interfering with other international contexts (Bradshaw & Howard, 2017). Given the costs entailed by the activation of such transnational groups, this kind of international practice is available only to major powers. In the case of Latin America, accusations were leveled against China and Russia of having allegedly intervened by means of guerrilla tactics 2.0 (Morgus et al., 2019), with the aim of expanding their influence and protecting the economic and political interests of these respective nations. It is also not that farfetched to include the US in this relationship, given that the American electoral exercises are frequently attracted by digital propaganda, with the aim of "1) manufacturing consensus, and 2) democratizing online propaganda", as noted by Woolley and Guilbeault (2017, p. 8) about the 2016 presidential election.

However, beyond the expanse of the outreach or the destabilization of someone's image, in many of the cases of success in the Latin American elections, it is difficult to distinguish between a victory associated with a certain political agenda and one which would be due to the strategic management based upon the new repertoires of online participation (Barredo Ibáñez, 2021). It is true that the apparition of cybertroops is a global phenomenon (Bradshaw & Howard, 2017). But their use is particularly effective in the Latin American context, for, as noted by Baker et al. (2020), the strategic use of social networks is, to a larger extent, focused on generating a collective influence, rather than on encouraging the individual aspects of the voter. As a result, viralization may be paramount in a region that is essentially structured upon the basis of the interaction of collective factors such as the family, the social environment, or the religious centers, to mention but a few. We could cite as an example the Evangelical organizations that had a decisive contribution to the victories of Andrés Manuel López Obrador in Mexico or Jair Bolsonaro in Brazil (these are just the most striking examples). In order to propagate their agendas, these groups used online platforms like Facebook and WhatsApp. Thus, the strategic use of digital tools and platforms is common within these organized groups, who transfer to the cybersphere their expectations and ideas, thereby managing to introduce a type of discourse which, in earlier decades, would have been excluded by the editorial filters of the *offline* media.

3 The Campaigns and the Digital Image of Candidates in Latin America: Political Agenda, TV Channels, and Citizens' Reaction

The design of the social network-based political campaign in Latin America (López-López et al., 2018) tends to generate a self-referential model[1] showing the candidates in their everyday life (greeting people, going for a stroll, eating, presenting their families, etc.), from up close and with excessive use of the *horse-race campaign* model, very much in tune with the characteristic features of the respective political systems (populism and a presidentialist, direct election model). This results in the construction of a "soft" image or of a framework of an ideal candidate in terms of image (Lego Muñoz & Towner, 2017). We can note some differences: conservative candidates (e.g., Mauricio Macri in Argentina or Guillermo Lasso in Ecuador) use such resources to a larger extent than progressive candidates (Daniel Scioli in Argentina or Alejandro Guillier in Chile), within contexts in which ideologies and public policy proposals carry more weight (notably in the case of twenty-first-century Socialist candidates). In the case of the former, one generates the construction of templates that a citizen understands and can relate to, such as home and family, well-known elements which automatically assign attributes, without any need for further explanation or context. In the case of the latter, the image construction is

[1] We selected a sample of 2517 tweets by presidential candidates from Argentina, Peru, Ecuador, Honduras and Chile, published on the Twitter social network between 2015 and 2017.

much more effective in their militant rank and is activated through more elaborated messages from a political point of view.

The handling of issues within digital campaigns is another important aspect that has a bearing on the construction of candidates' images. It tends to reinforce the classical issues with progressive candidates generating social matters and, at the same time, more conservative candidates insisting on aspects like security and economic freedom (López-López & Vásquez-González, 2018). That is to say, there are no major specifics, and the *online* space mirrors some analogue types of logic, cultural remnants in a region which is identified with the technological gap.

Nevertheless, this model of constructing the political agenda in the digital environment does exhibit some differences which can be grouped geographically and which can affect the concept of political image. As can be observed in Table 12.1, the highest thematic correlations between candidates (i.e., the relationship between thematic agendas, ordered by frequency and intensity) are found in the political systems having the greatest stability (e.g., in Argentina and Chile) and with more centripetal competitive models, particularly in the case of Chile (Sebastián Piñera and Alejandro Guillier). This apparent relationship between the degree of institutionality and the construction of the agenda would generate more converging "images" among the candidates. On the other hand, the lowest correlations between the agendas of candidates from the same country (Pedro Pablo Kuczynski and Keiko Fujimori in Peru; Juan Orlando Hernández and Salvador Nasralla in Honduras; Lenín Moreno and Guillermo Lasso in Ecuador) would generate more contrasting images at the level of perception.

Likewise, television, by its penetration and coverage rate, also plays a prominent role in the configuration of the electoral scenarios and in the collective projections by means of the *spectacularization* and personalization of politics (Martínez-Pandiani, 2006). In the case of Latin America, an aspect which is crucial in the political construction of the image consists of the multiple features which connect it to the political system (Becerra, 2014): the private media are lacking the concept of public service and the public ones are used in a partisan fashion; media conglomerates which are closely connected with political actors; a center-periphery configuration inside a certain country which affects the contents and the presence of the candidates who find themselves outside this circuit; different regulations in each country, without any clear parameters, not even at a regional level.

Table 12.1 Correlation of thematic agenda of presidential candidates on Twitter 2015–2017

	MC	*SC*	*KU*	*FU*	*LE*	*LA*	*OR*	*NA*	*GU*	*PÑ*
MACRI	1.000	**0.723****	-0.126	**0.881****	0.354	**0.781****	0.471	**0.486***	**0.725****	**0.629***
SCIOLI	**0.723****	1.000	-0.071	**0.738***	**0.476***	**0.575***	0.475	0.440	**0.615***	0.354
KUCZY	-0.126	-0.071	1.000	0.371	-0.099	0.236	0.200	0.203	-0.103	0.064
FUJIMOR	**0.881****	**0.738***	0.371	1.000	0.333	**0.738***	0.500	0.619	0.700	**0.929****
MORENO	0.354	**0.476***	-0.099	0.333	1.000	0.439	0.032	0.386	**0.918****	0.293
LASSO	**0.781****	**0.575***	0.236	**0.738***	0.439	1.000	0.339	0.455	**0.846****	**0.521***
ORLAN	0.471	0.475	0.200	0.500	0.032	0.339	1.000	**0.582***	0.027	0.178
NASRAL	**0.486***	0.440	0.203	0.619	0.386	0.455	**0.582***	1.000	0.501	0.504
GUILL	**0.725****	**0.615***	-0.103	0.700	**0.918****	**0.846****	0.027	0.501	1.000	**0.755****
PIÑE	**0.629***	0.354	0.064	0.929**	0.293	**0.521***	0.178	0.504	**0.755****	1.000

Spearman's Rho**. * The correlation is significant at the 0.01 (bilateral) level

*. * The correlation is significant at the 0.05 (bilateral) level

Source: López-López and Vásquez-González (2018, p. 1210) and elaborated by the authors

The data[2] show that, in the electoral processes, the construction of the political image on the TV channels (and appearing on the Internet) follows an established pattern: the public TV channels tend to privilege common models of agenda construction ("agenda coalitions") and settings favorable to governing-party candidates; the same thing happens with private TV channels and the opposition, provided that the said opposition is conservative; with the exception—within the scope of our study—of Honduras. An example of this is the Argentinian Telefe (Televisión Federal) with Mauricio Macri (2015), Ecuador TV with Lenín Moreno (2017), and Televicentro de Honduras with Salvador Nasralla (2017), as well as in the case of the candidates and TV channels in Chile (2017). Among the TV channels themselves, as shown in Table 12.2, the correlations show a greater thematic convergence within the same country in Argentina, Chile, or Peru and a higher correspondence across the private Latin American TV channels, regardless of the country, generating more common "images".

This fact reveals, on a general basis, the existence of a model of information production characterized by political control starting from the content itself, the circulation of the message, and hence the orientation in the construction of the image.

Finally,[3] from the information posted by the public on social networks, in reply to the messages of their candidates (which would show a sort of "reaction" depending on the image perceived), one can draw some conclusions (López-López et al., 2020) which are continued in other studies (Jaráiz Gulías et al., 2021). In the first instance, the positive emotions outweighed the negative ones (in matters of both frequency and intensity) which suggests a congruence between the image projected by the candidate and the one expected by their followers, bearing in mind, at all times, the consumption patterns specific to the communities present in the social networks, as well as the existence of very much "noise" (cyber-activism,

[2] The research, carried out on the Twitter social network, analyzes the messages transmitted by a total of ten TV channels during the electoral processes which took place in Argentina, Peru, Ecuador, Honduras, and Chile for a duration of 28 days, corresponding to the electoral processes in Latin America between 2015 and 2017. A total of 16,359 TV programs were analyzed.

[3] Analysis of over a quarter of a million tweets in reply to messages by Mauricio Macri, Daniel Scioli, Pedro Pablo Kuczynski, Keiko Fujimori, Lenín Moreno, Guillermo Lasso, Juan Orlando Hernández, Salvador Nasralla, Sebastián Piñera and Alejandro Guillier on the Twitter social network.

Table 12.2 Correlation of the thematic agenda on Twitter of the TV channels during presidential elections 2015–2017

	TVP	*TLF*	*PTV*	*LAT*	*ETV*	*ECU*	*TNH*	*TEL*	*TVN*	*C13*
Public Television (ARG)	1.000	0.671**	0.378	0.441	0.490	0.853**	0.671**	0.713**	0.531*	0.531*
Telefe (ARG)	0.671**	1.000	0.266	0.427	0.434	0.629*	0.483	0.608*	0.671**	0.685**
TV Perú (PER)	0.378	0.266	1.000	0.776**	0.238	0.434	0.462	0.636*	0.189	0.336
Latina Televisión (PER)	0.441	0.427	0.776**	1.000	0.147	0.545*	0.476	0.818**	0.084	0.273
Ecuador TV (ECU)	0.490	0.434	0.238	0.147	1.000	0.629*	0.028	0.252	0.552*	0.315
Ecuavisa (ECU)	0.853**	0.629*	0.434	0.545*	0.629*	1.000	0.392	0.755**	0.538*	0.392
Televisión Nacional (HO)	0.671**	0.483	0.462	0.476	0.028	0.392	1.000	0.510*	0.455	0.545*
Televicentro (HO)	0.713**	0.608*	0.636*	0.818**	0.252	0.755**	0.510*	1.000	0.420	0.615*
TV Nacional Chile (CH)	0.531*	0.671**	0.189	0.084	0.552*	0.538*	0.455	0.420	1.000	0.846**
Canal 13 (CH)	0.531*	0.685**	0.336	0.273	0.315	0.392	0.545*	0.615*	0.846**	1.000

Spearman's Rho**. * The correlation is significant at the 0.01 (bilateral) level

*. * The correlation is significant at the 0.05 (bilateral) level

Source: López-López and Oñate (2019, p. 10) and elaborated by the authors

bots, etc.). At the same time, there is, generally speaking, a difference between progressive and conservative candidates, the latter being the ones who obtain the highest approval rates in the messages posted. This generates a stronger commitment and a better response rate: the amount of time that it takes a follower to share their candidate's message depends on the adequacy between the expressed image and the real image they have of him. This is called "latency" and is defined as "the time an individual takes in retweeting a message to which they are exposed on Twitter" (Calvo & Aruguete, 2018, p. 196). Hence, a greater latency denotes a greater dissociation between both images.

4 The Digital "CNN Effect"

The way in which the image of Latin American political actors is formed has many layers: besides the immediate effects, the fruit of the media/electoral confrontation within the same country, there is also a regional, Latin American, and continental dimension, which acts on the long-term, on the symbolic level. This corroborates the studies of the flow of information between the North (United States of America) and the Global South (Latin America), insofar as (cultural or political) ideology plays a very important, paramount role (Ramonet, 1998). The news flow through the major TV networks, as well as through digital media and the social networks, results in a clash between the local Latin American political identities (Parker, 2016) and the hegemonic vision of liberal democracy, with obvious consequences in the electoral processes as well as in the perception (image) of the candidates.

Within this context, the development of information technologies and knowledge, in general, favored the emergence of new digital spaces for political communication, as well as an enormous academic debate. On the one hand, some argue that vertical information flows continue to be dominant, be it from the North-Global South perspective (the capital of the major digital tools, such as Google, Facebook, or Twitter is located in the North) or in the Center-Periphery dimension within the communication circuits of each country. The transmitted content, especially the political one in an electoral period, is disseminated through social networks in the Global South, a sort of informational periphery (Vaquerizo Domínguez, 2020), thereby generating Western forms of interpretation and frameworks which interfere in the formation of the image of political actors, with a tendency toward "osmosis" or "copying". On the other hand, others assume, in a more positive vein, that social networks are capable of generating political, economic, and social changes, by means of various functions (Gordon, 2017; Shirky, 2011): raising the awareness of the digital community, defining its problems, generating a dialogue process with the media, organizing protests and raising funds. In this perspective, in Latin America, social networks and the digital society demonstrate new forms of collective action, giving a certain margin of autonomy to the media actors when it comes to conveying their content to the public, offering their own spaces for the interpretation (image) of their political reality.

This political and media reaction in a broad sense, beyond the electoral aspect, was called "the CNN effect" (Strobel, 1996) and in Latin America it has functioned as a "soft power" (Garrido, 2015), with said TV channel becoming itself a political actor influencing the construction of the above-mentioned identities, supporting the candidates more inclined to share its own opinions on economic and social relationships or its own "image" of the world. There are numerous studies on CNN's coverage (Hyun & Moon, 2016; Robinson, 2011; Stromer-Galley & Bryant, 2011), demonstrating the influence of news originating from the US on the worldwide media market, not only in matters of topic selection but also in matters of how the news is "framed" (Groshek, 2008). In response to this interpretation and "framing", some strong reactions emerged in the region, such as the integrationist and anti-hegemonic vision of Telesur, originating from Hugo Chávez's Venezuela (Cañizález & Lugo, 2007).

In 2018 and 2019 a survey[4] was conducted on Twitter, in which, three months prior to the elections, one analyzed the news broadcast by CNN in Spanish (@CNNEE) regarding Colombia, Costa Rica, Mexico, Paraguay, Bolivia, El Salvador, Argentina, Guatemala, Panama, and Uruguay. The results can be grouped into three sets of factors that influence, in the perspective of the US-based channel, the candidates' image:

(a) *Geography*: Latin America is a vast territory, having very diverse problems and with some topics on the agenda which vary according to the region. Violence (lack of safety and criminality) is a paramount concern primarily in Central America and in some

[4] The Political Research Team of the University of Santiago de Compostela analyzed more than 20,000 news items from the years 2018 and 2019, in a study which helped ascertain CNN's journalistic agenda and ways of presenting presidential candidates.

South American countries, such as Brazil and Colombia; the image of the candidates is therefore formed around their capacity to ensure social peace and security (Juan Orlando Hernández or Iván Duque, for instance). On the other hand, most Andean Community countries must tackle problems relating to the government institutions and the great cultural diversity; from their position, the candidates have to demonstrate the capacity to conjugate identity with institutional character ("legal security"/democracy) and progress (Carlos Mesa and Luis Arce in Bolivia). Finally, the Cono Sur region, especially Argentina, has an agenda dominated by "hard topics" (mainly economic) in which efficacy, control, and solvency themselves manifest as the candidates', presidents', or ex-presidents' main attributes (Sebastián Piñera and Mauricio Macri).

(b) *Ideology*: The candidates which show a more or less explicit closeness to positions pertaining to the so-called twenty-first-century socialism globally receive a more negative image on CNN and generally speaking, in the private media, primarily TV channels. With some nuances, it is the case of Andrés Manuel López Obrador (Mexico), Luis Arce (Bolivia), Alberto Fernández (Argentina), or Gustavo Petro (Colombia). The opinion sections are used to indicate these candidates' inability to address "security", to improve "institutions" (insisting on corruption issues), and to "manage the economy" (indicating that the model is inoperable, citing Venezuela as an example).

(c) *Regional issues and international politics*: over the last few years, Donald Trump's presidency in the US has changed the models of the relationships existing between the media companies from the Global North (most of them opposed to the President) with regard to the Latin American candidates and presidents; this has also influenced the national media systems. In fact, the interest of the great corporations has not always coincided with Trump's, an issue which had an impact on aspects such as the Central American migration and the evolution of Andrés Manuel López Obrador's image in Mexico. That was not the case for another type of migration, the Venezuelan one, which has always been presented as a "problem yet to be solved", with very serious social and coexistence problems, possibly attributable to the left-wing candidates. Finally, the regional political and economic integration through bodies like MERCOSUR, UNASUR, ALBA, Pacific Alliance, or

NAFTA has rarely been a prominent feature on the US channel, despite the fact that the candidates are more inclined toward liberalization and free trade received positive treatment.

The image is, therefore, affected by a news production framework created by this TV channel on a basis largely lacking any context and tending toward polarization among competitors (with a campaign model reinforcing the "horse race") and with some simplistic sets of topics which may be grouped even geographically. At the same time, there is a large number of reports "selectively" defending human rights, as a result of economic interests and ideological imperatives (Moyo, 2011).

5 Conclusions: An Image Constructed in Social and Media Terms

The image of presidential candidates in the elections may be classified as follows: the one projected by the political actors themselves, the one mediated by the means of communication, and the one received/perceived by the citizens. The matching rate between these three vectors of message circulation (projection, mediation, and reception/perception) generates both more outreach and more effectiveness in terms of electoral dividends. In the concrete case of Latin America, this drive is very much conditioned by the position taken by media actors, especially by private national and international TV channels. At the same time, Latin American politics largely transferred to the cybersphere, given that the online environment helps articulate strategies which are more social than individual (Baker et al., 2020) and with which one seeks to render the electorate more permeable using the voters' own affective environments. Even though social networks are not linked to any changes in the voting intentions, these platforms are relevant, because they allow personal groupings to become active influencers in election campaigns.

We may, therefore, conclude that there is an image which is constructed and stereotyped around socially accepted, or shall we say, consensual, reinforced by the candidates' campaign and with the following behavioral patterns: (a) assignation of counterposed or antagonistic attributes building on journalistic frameworks prevalent in the region and reproduced in social networks—as shown by several previous studies—such as security/lack of security, strong institutions/corruption or economic effectiveness/

squandering and with a particular emphasis on conflict (Gronemeyer & Porath, 2017; Muñiz et al., 2018); (b) regional differences between Latin American countries, even though the ideological variant "21st century socialism" can be singled out as a "unitary image" or "label" for certain candidates; (c) faced with an incentive of greater transparency or more reflected upon (Toxtle & González, 2020), we find that populism and polarization are the majority response of the technopolitics in the region. These adverse effects are due to causes having to do with the very narrative of the social networks: the filter bubbles, which prevent a stronger mainstreaming of the conversation; digital propaganda (Arnaudo, 2017; Bradshaw & Howard, 2017), which promotes a transfer of the logic belonging to the electoral machinery and former mass media, for example, better resources mean better possibilities of electoral victory; or the echo chambers which strengthen the identity and the affective connection around certain groups (Chenou et al., 2021); these are just the most relevant effects among them.

References

Araújo, B., & Prior, H. (2020). Framing political populism: The role of media in framing the election of Jair Bolsonaro. *Journalism Practice, 15*(5), 1–17.

Arnaudo, D. (2017). *Computational propaganda in Brazil: Social bots during elections* (Working paper no. 2017.8). University of Oxford. Available at: http://www.philosophyofinformation.net/wp-content/uploads/sites/89/2017/06/Brazil-Ready.pdf

Baker, A., Ames, B., & Rennó, L. (2020). *Persuasive peers. Social communication and voting in Latin America*. Princeton University Press.

Barredo Ibáñez, D. (2021). *Medios digitales, participación y opinión pública*. Tirant Lo Blanch.

Barredo Ibáñez, D., Arcila, C., Arroyave, J., & Silva, R. (2015). Influence of social networks in the decision to vote: An exploratory survey on the Ecuadorian electorate. *International Journal of E-Politics, 6*(4), 15–34. https://doi.org/10.4018/IJEP.2015100102

Becerra, M. (2014). Medios de comunicación: América Latina a contramano. *Nueva sociedad, 249*, 61–74.

Boas, T. C. (2005). Television and neopopulism in Latin America: Media effects in Brazil and Peru. *Latin American Research Review, 40*(2), 27–49.

Boas, T. (2013). Mass media and politics in Latin America. In J. Domínguez & M. Shifter (Eds.), *Constructing democratic governance in Latin America* (pp. 48–77). Johns Hopkins University Press.

Bradshaw, S., & Howard, P. N. (2017). *Troops, trolls and troublemakers: A global inventory of organized social media manipulation* (Working paper no. 2017.12). University of Oxford. Available at: https://comprop.oii.ox.ac.uk/wp-content/uploads/sites/89/2017/07/Troops-Trolls-and-Troublemakers.pdf

Calvo, E., & Aruguete, N. (2018). #Tarifazo. Medios tradicionales y fusión de agenda en redes sociales. *InMediaciones de la comunicación, 13*(1), 189–213.

Cañizález, A., & Lugo, J. (2007). Telesur: Estrategia geopolítica con fines integracionistas. *Confines de relaciones internacionales y ciencia política, 3*(6), 53–64.

Chenou, J. M., Cabarcas, D., & Sepulveda, M. N. (2021). Social media and political polarization in Latin America. Analyzing online discussions during the 2018 presidential campaign in Colombia. In D. Ramírez, B. Carvalho, & A. Plaw (Eds.), *The politics of technology in Latin America* (Vol. 2, pp. 129–146). Routledge.

De la Garza, D. J., LaRosa, A., Barredo Ibáñez, D., & Freundt, Ú. (2019). Medios sociales, capital social y sentimiento de eficacia política: Un estudio comparativo entre las juventudes de México y Perú. In M. Ezequiel Badillo, C. Pérez, N. Jessenia Medranda, & M. Isabel Cortés (Eds.), *Ciudadanías digitales. Perspectivas desde los medios, el periodismo y la educomunicación* (pp. 133–154). Politécnico Grancolombiano.

Garrido, A. P. (2015). El poder blando en la globalización: algunos aspectos de la comunicación en el sistema internacional. *Revista Panorama, 8*(15), 102–115.

Gordon, S. (2017). The political power of social media revisited. In Twenty-third Americas Conference on Information Systems. Proceedings of AMCIS "*Social Technical and Social Inclusion Issues (SIGSI)*".

Gronemeyer, M. E., & Porath, W. (2017). Framing political news in the Chilean press: The persistence of the conflict frame. *International Journal of Communication, 11*, 24.

Groshek, J. (2008). Homogenous agendas, disparate frames: CNN and CNN International coverage online. *Journal of Broadcasting & Electronic Media, 52*(1), 52–68.

Hyun, K. D., & Moon, S. J. (2016). Agenda setting in the partisan TV news context: Attribute agenda setting and polarized evaluation of presidential candidates among viewers of NBC, CNN, and Fox News. *Journalism & Mass Communication Quarterly, 93*(3), 509–529.

Jaráiz Gulías, E., Pereira López, M., & Rivera Otero, J. M. (2021). Análisis de emociones originadas por las publicaciones Twitter de los candidatos en las elecciones generales de Bolivia y España en 2019. *Journal of Iberian and Latin American Research.* "Digital Communication, Social Networks and Online Processes: Studies".

Lego Muñoz, C. L., & Towner, T. L. (2017). The image is the message: Instagram marketing and the 2016 presidential primary season. *Journal of Political Marketing, 16*(3–4), 290–318.

Lippmann, W. (1929). *Public opinion.* Macmillan Company.

López-López, P. C., & Oñate, P. (2019). De la videopolítica a la ciberpolítica: debate entre candidatos y televisiones en cinco elecciones presidenciales. *El profesional de la información (EPI), 28*(5).

López-López, P. C., & Vásquez-González, J. (2018). Agenda temática y Twitter: elecciones presidenciales en América Latina durante el período 2015–2017. *Profesional de la Información, 27*(6), 1204–1214.

López-López, P. C., Oñate, P., & Chavero Ramírez, P. (2018). El horse-race campaign frente al issue-campaign en la agenda digital: elecciones presidenciales en América Latina en el período 2015–2017. *Revista ibérica de sistemas e tecnologias de informação, E16*, 270–282.

López-López, P. C., Oñate, P., & Rocha, Á. (2020). Social media mining, debate and feelings: Digital public Opinion's reaction in five presidential elections in Latin America. *Cluster Computing, 23*, 1875–1886.

López-Rabadán, P., López-Meri, A., & Doménech-Fabregat, H. (2016). La imagen política en Twitter. Usos y estrategias de los partidos políticos españoles. *Index Comunicación, 6*(1), 165–195.

Lupu, N., Ramírez, M. V., & Zechmeister, E. J. (2020). Social media disruption: Messaging mistrust in Latin America. *Journal of Democracy, 31*(3), 160–171. https://muse.jhu.edu/article/760080/summary

Martínez-Pandiani, G. (2006). El impacto de la televisión en la comunicación política moderna. *Signos universitarios, 25*(1), 69–88.

Morgus, R., Fonseca, B., Green, K., & Crowther, A. (2019). Are China and Russia on the cyber offensive in Latin America and the Caribbean? *New America, 26*, 1–50. Available at: https://gordoninstitute.fiu.edu/policy-innovation/publications/are-china-and-russia-on-the-cyber-offensive-in-latin-america-and-the-caribbean.pdf

Moyo, L. (2011). The CNN defect: Representations of race and historical justice in the Zimbabwean election. *Journal of International Communication, 17*(2), 121–138.

Muñiz, C., Saldierna, A. R., & Marañón, F. D. J. (2018). Framing of electoral processes: The stages of the campaign as a moderator of the presence of political frames in the news. *Palabra clave, 21*(3), 740–771.

Parker, C. (2016). Religious pluralism and new political identities in Latin America. *Latin American Perspectives, 43*(3), 15–30.

Puyosa, I. (2017). Bots políticos en Twitter en la campaña presidencial #Ecuador2017. *Contratexto, 27*, 39–60. https://doi.org/10.26439/contratexto.2017.027.002

Ramonet, I. (1998). *La tiranía de la comunicación.* Temas de debate.

Robinson, P. (2011). The CNN effect reconsidered: Mapping a research agenda for the future. *Media, War and Conflict, 4*(1), 3–11.

Rubio Ferreres, J. M. (2009). Opinión pública y medios de comunicación. Teoría de la 'agenda setting'. *Gazeta de Antropología, 25*(1), 1–17.

Santana, L. E., & Huerta, G. (2019). ¿Son bots? Automatización en redes sociales durante las elecciones presidenciales de Chile 2017. *Cuadernos.info, 44*, 61–77. https://doi.org/10.7764/cdi.44.1629

Schill, D. (2012). The visual image and the political image: A review of visual communication research in the field of political communication. *Review of Communication, 12*(2), 118–142.

Shaw, D. L., McCombs, M., Weaver, D. H., & Hamm, B. J. (1999). Individuals, groups, and agenda melding: A theory of social dissonance. *International Journal of Public Opinion Research, 11*(1), 2–24.

Shirky, C. (2011). The political power of social media. *Foreign Affairs, 90*(1), 28–41.

Strobel, W. P. (1996). The CNN effect. *American Journalism Review, 18*(4), 32–38.

Stromer-Galley, J., & Bryant, L. (2011). Agenda control in the 2008 CNN/YouTube debates. *Communication Quarterly, 59*(5), 529–546.

Toxtle, A., & González, R. A. (2020). Facebook, una extensión de marketing y no un espacio deliberativo: Caso de Andrés Manuel López Obrador en elecciones presidenciales de México en 2018. *Global Media Journal México, 17*(33), 72–95. https://doi.org/10.29105/gmjmx17.33-4

Vaquerizo Domínguez, E. V. (2020). Medios de comunicación y flujos culturales internacionales: la vigencia actual del informe McBride. *Revista de Comunicación de la SEECI, 51*, 43–62.

Vu, H. T., Guo, L., & McCombs, M. E. (2014). Exploring "the world outside and the pictures in our heads". A network agenda-setting study. *Journalism & Mass Communication Quarterly, 91*(4), 669–686.

Woolley, S. C., & Guilbeault, D. R. (2017). *Computational propaganda in the United States of America: Manufacturing consensus online* (Working paper no. 2017.5). University of Oxford. Available at: http://silicon-valley-mobsters.com/Comprop-USA.pdf

Yagade, A., & Dozier, D. M. (1990). The media agenda-setting effect of concrete versus abstract issues. *Journalism Quarterly, 67*(1), 3–10.

Conclusions

This edited compendium gathers in a single volume the latest trends in digital political communication as analysed by authors who have dealt with the topic from different fields of knowledge for more than 20 years. Though 25 years have elapsed since the inception of digital political communication, a multidisciplinary and holistic approach is needed to go beyond the old reductionist perspectives which dealt with the typically unidirectional and asymmetrical communication among the three traditional actors: political parties, the media, and citizens. The boundaries between them have blurred as new actors have arisen who need to be considered. This book tackles this new reality by reflecting on the role of digital platforms as political actors, the role of lobbies, the importance of citizen co-production of political messages and election campaigns, or the role of fiction as a shaper of political scenarios.

These dynamics are examined from a multidisciplinary perspective that compiles research results from historiographic hermeneutics, audio-visual communication, journalism, and political science fields which are too often dealt with in isolated silos.

Thirty authors from different universities broadly reflect on politics, going beyond the quantitative and technological analyses normally employed to address political communication. As indicated in the first chapter, scientific research, like political communication, has undergone a

B. García-Orosa (ed.), *Digital Political Communication Strategies*, The Palgrave Macmillan Series in International Political Communication, https://doi.org/10.1007/978-3-030-81568-4

process of platformisation and has uncritically followed the patterns set by the innovations and interests of technology companies. Thus, communication researchers have often studied the implementation of a particular technological tool, mainly social networks, by a particular actor or group of actors in the same sector at a given time. As such, several studies deal with the use of social networks, mainly Twitter and Facebook, by political parties or during electoral campaigns. Not to undermine the relevance of such in-depth analyses of precise moments in time, we thought it necessary to offer the reader a holistic view of the implications of technological innovation not only in the political system but also in society and culture, as well as a comprehensive analysis of communication as a source of power.

Throughout these pages we have identified the cross-cutting axes, phases, and milestones of the last 25 years of digital communication which have brought us to this fourth wave, referred to in Chap. 1 as it highlights the central role of artificial intelligence and astroturfing along with a reconfiguration of the public sphere and the concept of citizenship (McNair, 2017).

The 12 chapters that make up Manuel Castells's book and preface will afford students of political science, communication sciences, sociology, history, and natural language processing a panorama of the fundamental aspects of political communication in several countries since its inception at the end of the last century.

For researchers, this work will prove useful as it offers them a compendium of methods, perspectives, and approaches to the most relevant milestones, as well as an analysis of important strategies in today's context.

In the professional world, we are confident that this book will be a valuable resource for communication directors and policy advisors interested in the latest trends in online political communication, which are usually scattered amongst countless articles in scientific journals or monographs. We analyse the influence of platforms, the use of social networks, citizen engagement and the evolution of election campaigns vis à vis the image of the candidate, the use of emotion or 360° video. Leveraging examples from different countries and contexts, communication directors will have new ways of designing policy.

Finally, the book is designed for the citizenry, who need to familiarise themselves with the backroom of political communication and the great influence on public opinion which old and new actors exert mainly by using big data at all stages of information production. We believe that this book will help all those who read it to participate more frequently and more meaningfully in public life.

Main Topics

The book has been conceived in two parts with complementary but distinct goals. In the first part, the authors reflect upon the evolution of the main actors in political communication over the last 25 years (parliaments, political parties, media) but also on those more hidden actors, the research into which has been less visible: lobbies, citizens, and minorities.

The first part addresses three phenomena: (1) The confluence in evolution through a transformation marked fundamentally by the technological innovations which, during this fourth wave, have led us to the consideration of a new paradigm, the common thread of this book. All political actors have seen their communication strategies (and political actions) determined by the innovations offered by large technology companies: websites and blogs marked the first wave, but every social network which has since come to market has been adopted uncritically by traditional and alternative actors' communication directors. Political parties and social movements have carried out a significant part of their political action on Facebook, Twitter, Instagram, YouTube, and, most recently, TikTok. This frequent use of technology has not been neutral; rather it has conditioned and sometimes directed political actions. At present, the intensive use of artificial intelligence has taken a step forward and is taken as a driving force throughout this compendium. (2) Next is greater efforts to increase the presence of the recipients (mainly citizens) through processes of co-creation, debate, or simply the appearance of participation. The opening of communication to previously marginalised actors, mainly through social networks, has triggered different reactions in traditional and new actors, but in all chapters their presence is felt. (3) The last is the paradigm shift and implementation of hermeneutics, observed and demanded by some authors, which we will surely witness in the coming years (Mancini, 2020; Mare et al., 2020; Tianru, 2020).

Within these sea changes, two traditional political actors have maintained their positions, albeit with blurred boundaries and their roles thrown into question. This book allows for a general reflection on parliaments and political parties with a broad, longitudinal perspective. It sheds light on the bipolar situation of parliament which, on the one hand, has witnessed how digital transformation, over recent decades, has helped to improve both parliamentary procedures and public access to parliamentary information. At the same time, the public demands for greater transparency, accountability, and participation have led to more interactive parliamentary initiatives taking place in increasingly uncertain and fragmented democratic contexts.

Political parties have faced this two-pronged trend in many countries: on the one hand, the intensive use of technology with innovations that could increase engagement and conversation with citizens and other political actors, and on the other the disaffection and distance vis-à-vis the citizenry and the emergence of new games that change the rules of engagement and force new actions.

Historically, research has placed the media in the middle of these dynamics, but media organisations have begun redefining their political roles. This book discusses the recent breakdown of the borders which once divided professionals, citizens, and activists. In addition to the incorporation of technological innovations by each of the previous three actors, in this case, the authors point out the trends towards co-creation and, above all, the renewed importance of local and hyperlocal scenarios in shaping political reality.

In recent years, lobbies have been one of the least transparent and most influential political actors. Nonetheless, given the hidden nature of their activities and, until 2008, the near total lack of EU legislation regulating them, they have also been one of the least analysed. This book approaches lobbies as a political actor which influences not only the political reality of national and supranational spaces but also shapes the public space for debate—or perhaps reality itself—through its discursive strategies. Without knowledge of lobbies' presence and actions, it would be difficult to understand politics today.

The citizenry is a cross-cutting concept with presence in all chapters of the first section of the book, above all as a recipient or target of strategies and messages designed by other actors. Given that the citizenry's presence as an independent actor is increasingly salient, we thought it necessary to observe how the citizenry have empowered themselves through social movements when the time was right during the Arab Spring, Me Too, or Spain's M-15 movement. Nonetheless, it is also worth noting that other phenomena, such as femicide, have received scant attention from traditional political actors such as the media and political parties, even in countries where this problem is salient.

This context of new actors, the hybridisation of actors, actions and speeches, the rebirth of the 1980s' and 1990s' concept of *glocalisation*, citizen co-creation and the intensive use of artificial intelligence has promoted changes which will be discussed in the second part of the book. Taking the main points of the evolution of digital political communication as a starting point, the second part of this book aims to delve into those fundamental trends which tend to be present in every actor that is analysed in the first part. As such, the authors discuss new narrative techniques, the use of social networks, the instrumentalisation of emotion, the social audience, and its combination with traditional media such as television, as well as the importance of digital platforms in the shaping of public spaces. By way of conclusion, a case study on elections in Latin America is also offered.

In the second part of this book, we see that several characteristics of the current (fourth) wave of digital political communication are cross-cutting: (a) the intensive use of artificial intelligence and big data in all phases, especially during election campaigns; (b) the validation of falsehoods as a political strategy (among other fake news and post-truth phenomena); (c) the combination of hyperlocal and supranational elements; and (d) promotion of audience engagement and co-production processes. Thus, each chapter deals with the three trends mentioned at the beginning of the book which pose threats to democracy: the polarisation of opinions, echo chambers, and bubble filters.

Among advances in narrative techniques, immersive storytelling stands out not only because it has changed the way viewers produce, distribute, and even consume information but also because of the ethical issues and manipulation of reality it entails. The failed attempts at parallel reality discussed years ago in *Second Life* could arise once again with the creation of false presence through virtual reality, that is, an environment in which the political actor may come to believe, but which is, nevertheless, naught but a political communication strategy. Recent international examples highlight immersive storytelling's significance, its potential to influence political communication and, above all, the ethical questions it will soon pose.

Most of the strategies analysed in this compendium focus on the citizenry's political participation and commitment. The book addresses engagement as a concept which still needs redefining (Ballesteros & Díez, 2018; Ballesteros Herencia, 2019), even though it has been studied for over 30 years in the field of communication (Dhanesh, 2017; Shen & Jiang, 2019) and some authors already call this the age of engagement

(Morehouse & Saffer, 2019). Definitions come from different areas and range from engagement as a form of interactivity or consumption, to more complex concepts linked to psychological engagement (Taylor & Kent, 2014; Devin & Lane, 2014; Motion et al., 2012; Men & Tsai, 2013; Travaglino et al., 2020), to a behavioural manifestation of motivation or productive participation in a learning activity or more abstract dimensions (Wenzel & Nelson, 2020). The terms "public engagement", "engaging with the public", and "engaging the public" have recently gained relevance in this context (Carvalho et al., 2017).

In this sense, political engagement may be linked to public participation or effects of a cognitive or attitudinal nature or a psychological one. In general, it is an action with an individual or dialogic goal, is usually supported by cognitive and/or motivational processes, and is linked to interaction or participation as discussed in this book. The studies given herein analyse the role of emotions in such participation and demonstrate the importance of emotional framing, especially when negative, as a generator of political engagement. Secondly, engagement is analysed through those traditional media with greater weight in political communication: television as a strategic element in the management of information companies. The behaviour of the social audience can even determine the content of debates before they take place. What happens on social media, especially on Twitter, is as important as what happens on television.

Finally, different social media platforms are dealt with as creators of political reality in a case study and an overview of more than a dozen electoral contests which took place in Latin America between 2015 and 2020. Among the most important conclusions, we find, with some major regional differences, that people assign negative attributes to political candidates and that digital social networks, with their filter bubbles and echo chambers, are flourishing.

These reflections and analyses allow us to observe the already distant beginnings of digital communication, when it was common to publish on the Internet information which was conceived and produced for an offline world. Former US President Barack Obama's 2008 presidential campaign marked a milestone in political communication (Bimber, 2014; Lilleker et al., 2015; Stromer-Galley, 2014). Since then, political actors have moved from producing content for traditional media to seeking multichannel, polysynthetic, and integrative language and experimenting with new narratives (Gander, 1999; Jenkins et al., 2015; Shin & Biocca, 2017), already commonplace in other areas of online communication. Throughout the pages of this book, we can see how, in the last 25 years, political actors have come to rely heavily on social networks (Popa et al., 2020), big data, the automation of the production and dissemination of information (Keller & Klinger, 2019) and the emergence of new spaces for communication.

Open Questions

Upon reaching the end of the book, the reader will have enjoyed an overview of the latest trends in political communication, manifested in the various actors therein, but most importantly, he or she should have many questions. During this liquid (Bauman, 2015) and hybrid era (Chadwick, 2013; Hamilton, 2016) threatened, moreover, by a pandemic, we need to reflect on what we have lived so far so that we may face head on our uncertain future with new hermeneutical tools which may bring us closer to a complex and sometimes bipolar reality. At times, online political communication has resembled one-way propaganda, to the detriment of civic deliberation and democratic debate. Cambridge Analytica's role in Brexit, Facebook's and Twitter's actions in relation to Trump's messages about SARS-CoV-2, and warnings from different international bodies about bots' interference in politics are just a few examples illustrating the importance of this phenomenon. But, at the same time, technology has given a voice to previously marginalised citizens, been present in social movements and boosted the emergence of new actors.

Moreover, emerging trends such as artificial intelligence and the use of algorithmic big data pose a great opportunity and, at the same time, a great challenge in adapting to these new times and a big question for democracies. The co-creations and the reappearance of local citizens have emerged in a global world and breathed new life into *glocalization*.

The citizenry's digital literacy has become essential for digital democracy, for understanding *algorithmised* public opinion and for using big data.

This book has allowed us to observe the converging lines in the evolution of digital political communication and the main trends and characteristics of various political actors. Moreover, it has allowed us to pose new questions, made more poignant by the SARS-CoV-2 pandemic in which most countries are still mired upon the finalisation of this project.

References

Ballesteros Herencia, C. A. (2019). La representación digital del engagement: hacia una percepción del compromiso a través de acciones simbólicas. *Revista de comunicación, 18*(1), 215–233. https://doi.org/10.26441/RC18.1-2019-A11

Ballesteros-Herencia, C., & Díez-Garrido, M. (2018). Tenemos que hablar. El Compromiso 2.0 en Facebook durante la cibercampaña española del 20D de 2015. *Communication & Society, 31*(1), 169–193. https://doi.org/10.15581/003.31.1.169-193

Bauman, Z. (2015). *Modernidad líquida*. México: Fondo de cultura económica.

Bimber, B. (2014). Digital media in the Obama campaigns of 2008 and 2012: Adaptation to the personalized political communication environment. *Journal of Information Technology & Politics, 11*(2), 130–150. https://goo.gl/YSfc7v. https://doi.org/10.1080/19331681.2014.895691

Carvalho, A., Van Wessel, M., & Maeseele, P. (2017). Communication practices and political engagement with climate change: A research agenda. *Environmental Communication, 11*(1), 122–135. https://doi.org/10.1080/17524032.2016.1241815

Chadwick, A. (2013). *The hybrid media system: Politics and power*. Oxford: Oxford University Press.

Devin, B. L., & Lane, A. B. (2014). Communicating engagement in corporate social responsibility: A meta-level construal of engagement. *Journal of Public Relations Research, 26*(5), 436–454. https://doi.org/10.1080/1062726X.2014.956104

Dhanesh, G. (2017). Putting engagement in its proper place: State of the field, definition and model of engagement. *Public Relations Review, 43*(5), 925–933. https://doi.org/10.1016/j.pubrev.2017.04.0

Gander, P. (1999). *Two myths about immersion in new storytelling media*. Lund University Cognitive Studies. Retrieved from https://www.researchgate.net/publication/228957892_Two_myths_about_immersion_in_new_storytelling_media

Hamilton, J. F. (2016). Hybrid news practices. In T. Witschge, C. W. Anderson, D. Domingo, & A. Hermida (Eds.), *The SAGE handbook of digital journalism* (pp. 164–178). SAGE.

Jenkins, H., Ford, S., & Green, J. (2015). *Cultura transmedia: la creación de contenido y valor en una cultura en red*. Barcelona: Gedisa.

Keller, T., & Klinger, U. (2019). Social bots in election campaigns: Theoretical, empirical, and methodological implications. *Political Communication, 36*(1), 171–189. https://doi.org/10.1080/10584609.2018.1526238

Lilleker, D. G., Tenscher, J., & Štětka, V. (2015). Towards hypermedia campaigning? Perceptions of new media's importance for campaigning by party strategists in comparative perspective. *Information, Communication & Society, 18*(7), 747–765. https://goo.gl/FXo49G. https://doi.org/10.1080/1369118X.2014.993679

Mancini, P. (2020). Comparing media systems and the digital age. *International Journal of Communication, 14*, 5761–5774.

Mare, A., Mabweazara, H. M., & Moyo, D. (2020). "Fake news" and cyber-propaganda in sub-Saharan Africa: Recentering the research agenda. *Africa Journalism Studies, 40*, 1–2. https://doi.org/10.1080/23743670.2020.1788295

McNair, B. (2017). *An introduction to political communication*. UK: Routledge.

Men, L. R., & Tsai, W. H. S. (2013). Beyond liking or following: Understanding public engagement on social networking sites in China. *Public Relations Review, 39*(1), 13–22. https://doi.org/10.1016/j.pubrev.2012.09.013

Morehouse, J., & Saffer, A. (2019). Illuminating the invisible college: An analysis of foundational and prominent publications of engagement research in public relations. *Public Relations Review, 45*(5). https://doi.org/10.1016/j.pubrev.2019.1018

Motion, J., Haar, J., & Leitch, S. (2012). A public relations framework for indigenous engagement. In Sriramesh, K, Verčič, D. *Culture and Public Relations: Links and Implications*, 54–67.

Popa, S. A., Fazekas, Z., Braun, D., & Leidecker-Sandmann, M.-M. (2020). Informing the public: How party communication builds opportunity structures. *Political Communication, 37*(3), 329–349. https://doi.org/10.1080/10584609.2019.1666942

Shen, H., & Jiang, H. (2019). Engaged at work? An employee engagement model in public relations. *Journal of Public Relations Research, 31*(1–2), 32–49. https://doi.org/10.1080/1062726X.2019.1585855

Shin, D., & Biocca, F. (2017). Exploring immersive experience in journalism. *New Media & Society, 19*(11), 1–24. https://doi.org/10.1177/1461444817733133

Stromer-Galley, J. (2014). *Presidential campaigning in the internet age*. UK: Oxford University Press.

Taylor, M., & Kent, M. L. (2014). Dialogic engagement: Clarifying foundational concepts. *Journal of Public Relations Research, 26*(5), 384–398. https://doi.org/10.1080/1062726X.2014.956106

Tianru, G. (2020). Comparative political communication research in the digital epoch: A typology of national communication spaces. *The Information Society, 36*(2), 59–70. https://doi.org/10.1080/01972243.2019.1703866

Travaglino, G. A., Li, Z., Zhang, X., Lu, X., & Choi, H. S. (2020). We are all in this together: The role of individuals' social identities in problematic engagement with video games and the internet. *British Journal of Social Psychology, 59*(2), 522–548. https://doi.org/10.1111/bjso.12365

Wenzel, A., & Nelson, J. L. (2020). Introduction "engaged" journalism: Studying the news industry's changing relationship with the public. *Journalism Practice, 14*, 515–517. https://doi.org/10.1080/17512786.2020.1759126

Index[1]

A

B

C

[1] Note: Page numbers followed by 'n' refer to notes.

B. García-Orosa (ed.), *Digital Political Communication Strategies*, The Palgrave Macmillan Series in International Political Communication, https://doi.org/10.1007/978-3-030-81568-4

The manufacturer's authorised representative in the EU is Springer Nature Customer Service Centre GmbH, Europaplatz 3, 69115 Heidelberg, Germany. If you have any concerns regarding our products, please contact ProductSafety@springernature.com

Printed and bound by CPI Group (UK) Ltd, Croydon, CR0 4YY
22/09/2026
02221054-0005